"YOU SAY YOU WANT A REVOLUTION?"

"YOU SAY YOU WANT A REVOLUTION?"

1968–2018 in Theological Perspective

Susie Paulik Babka
Elena Procario-Foley
and Sandra Yocum
Editors

**THE ANNUAL PUBLICATION
OF THE COLLEGE THEOLOGY SOCIETY
2018
VOLUME 64**

ORBIS BOOKS
Maryknoll, New York 10545

ORBIS BOOKS
Maryknoll, New York 10545

Fathers and Brothers
MARYKNOLL™

Founded in 1970, Orbis Books endeavors to publish works that enlighten the mind, nourish the spirit, and challenge the conscience. The publishing arm of the Maryknoll Fathers and Brothers, Orbis seeks to explore the global dimensions of the Christian faith and mission, to invite dialogue with diverse cultures and religious traditions, and to serve the cause of reconciliation and peace. The books published reflect the views of their authors and do not represent the official position of the Maryknoll Society. To learn more about Maryknoll and Orbis Books, please visit our website at www.maryknollsociety.org.

Library of Congress Cataloging-in-Publication Data

Names: Babka, Susie Paulik, editor.
Title: You say you want a revolution? : 1968-2018 in theological perspective / Susie Paulik Babka, Elena Procario-Foley, and Sandra Yocum, editors.
Description: Maryknoll : Orbis Books, 2019. | Series: The annual publication of the College Theology Society ; VOLUME 64 | Includes bibliographical references.
Identifiers: LCCN 2018055475 | ISBN 9781626983205 (pbk.)
Subjects: LCSH: Government, Resistance to—Religious aspects—Catholic Church—Congresses. | Revolutions—Religious aspects—Catholic Church—Congresses. | Church and social problems—Catholic Church—Congresses. | Christianity and politics—Congresses. | United States—Church history—Congresses.
Classification: LCC BT738.3 .Y68 2019 | DDC 230.09/045—dc23 LC record available at https://lccn.loc.gov/2018055475

#1057305387

Contents

Part III
Contemplation, Action, and Revolution

Introduction

Susie Paulik Babka, Elena Procario-Foley,
and Sandra Yocum

"We all want to change the world," sang the Beatles in August 1968. When they recorded *The White Album* (*The Beatles*), one of the most extraordinary years in American history still had far to go—revolutions of all kinds, some violent, such as the Tet Offensive in January, and some peaceful, such as Thomas Merton's participation in interreligious dialogue with the Dalai Lama in the month of his death, were causing seismic shifts in the political, cultural, and religious landscape. Technology also changed the cultural landscape, bringing the world closer together, while also introducing unfamiliar ways of life and diverse religious beliefs into America's living rooms. The photo of Earthrise taken by Apollo 8 on December 24, the first of its kind, ended 1968 with a new perspective on our relationship with, as Buckminster Fuller termed it, "Spaceship Earth."

1968 might be called the year when the universal longing for inclusion and recognition, for mutual sharing of resources, for equality and respect, clashed with deeply entrenched power structures that resorted to all forms of violence to remain in power. While those oppressed throughout the world acted courageously on behalf of human rights, the world's standard bearers do not give up societal, cultural, and religious advantages easily. Police killed college students protesting a whites-only bowling alley in Orangeburg, South Carolina; Bobby Kennedy met with Cesar

Chavez during his hunger strike on behalf of United Farmworkers. Seventeen days after US troops ravaged the village of My Lai, Martin Luther King Jr. was assassinated in Memphis while in town to support black public works employees. Seventeen days after the Berrigans were arrested protesting the Vietnam War, Robert Kennedy was assassinated. *Humanae Vitae*, Medellín, the American Indian Movement, the Black Power salute at the Olympics, and more—a year of challenging, a year of protesting, a year of mourning, a year of hope.

Has the revolutionary spirit of 1968 been crushed by entrenched attitudes, wealth, and power such that we might never witness the fulfillment of what the activists sought? Revolution's etymology, from the Latin *revolvere*, to turn or roll back, suggests the ambiguities in the endeavor. Revolution connotes a shifting of attitudes, structure, values, and norms—some subtle, some immediate, some cataclysmic—but what has been the trajectory of these shifts? To what extent has the trajectory been a turn toward a more inclusive justice and to what extent a rolling back to an ever increasing privilege for the few? How do we assess the power of these events when, fifty years later, Native Americans are disenfranchised of voting rights in North Dakota, when persons of color are targets of white fear for studying late in a Yale common room, or barbecuing in a park, or waiting for a friend at a Starbucks? Was a year of such tumult, such loss of life, and yet such promise all for nothing when, fifty years later, the Catholic Church and US democracy are facing some of the deepest divisions and existential crises we have ever seen?

What does it mean theologically to frame enormous cultural change? Can theology shape societal directions? Or does it merely respond from the midst of the tumult? How can Christians follow Jesus Christ's example of protesting oppressive power? What is the theological meaning of protest? What are the limits of Christian and religious identification with political and social movements? How can we maintain solidarity with other persons, cultures, and our planet until the work of inclusion and equality is complete? How can we continue to read "the signs of the times" in theological reflection and teaching to articulate for today the interruption of privilege and coercive power in a way authentic to discipleship?

This volume of essays presents personal, pastoral, and theological reflections on the meaning of revolution, the future of revolutions, and the effort to assess where we are now. For Catholic theologians, such assessment proceeds, implicitly or explicitly, within the horizon of the Second Vatican Council, for some a particularly Catholic revolution. Though concluded three years before 1968, many teachings of the council inspired Catholics to act on the mandate of their baptism and informed their actions and reactions in 1968 and since. Within this fifty-year arc, Catholic actions, as readers of this volume know, mean not only Sunday church attendance (or not) but also engagement for the common good in all dimensions of social, religious, and political life. Catholic action or activism thus issues, for example, in teaching and protesting, in direct action, advocacy, and solidarity for and with the materially poor, in lay movements for justice within the church and the world, and in dialogue with the religious other. Many Catholics engaged the revolutionary spirit of 1968 as they were inspired to new forms of discipleship after the council.

The prophetic hopes of so many peoples as expressed in world events in 1968 and subsequent responses to them cannot be adequately represented in one volume. It is painfully clear to the editors of this volume that structures of sinful oppression remain as intransigent as ever as record numbers of people are displaced around the globe due to the violence of war, poverty, and catastrophic climate change. Yet people of faith look for signs of hope. New twenty-first-century prophetic and revolutionary protests against vile and unprovoked violence such as the #BlackLivesMatter and #MeToo movements or the Voice of the Faithful, raised against the horror of clerical sexual abuse, and the Catholic Climate Covenant demonstrate that the revolutionary hopes for justice and peace are not yet lost but not yet actualized.

The authors gathered in this volume map the trajectories of continuity and discontinuity between 1968 and 2018, retrieve models of faithful action for our consideration, and critically and honestly analyze the failures of the Catholic Christian community to incarnate the prophetic, moral, and spiritual wisdom of Jesus Christ. The volume is divided into three parts: "Race, Hope, and Revolution"; "Sex, Families, and Revolution"; and "Contemplation, Action, and Revolution." In a short study, the subdivision of parts as well as the chapters within each section can only be representative of the issues at stake. Neither the volume nor individual essays claim a comprehensive overview of the topics raised by considering the theological responses to revolution and protest.

In the first part, "Race, Hope, and Revolution," Rev. Dr. Willie James Jennings delivers a powerful reflection on how his boyhood memories of King's assassination frame his understanding of the racial imagination today, the meaning of whiteness in Western society, and the hope that holds us and "sets us toward revolution." Erin Kidd articulates in her essay how the colonial legacy of whiteness contributes to the "designer societies" that shape our identities and experience, "scaffolding" prereflexive ways of being in the world. She articulates the role such scaffolding plays in our cognition "to expand the scope of our moral responsibility." Stephanie Edwards skillfully weaves the poetry of Audre Lorde into an exploration of insights from the neuroscientific field of epigenetics in the interest of healing the vestiges of intergenerational trauma from racism. "To move forward in the work of justice, it is essential to understand how the past shapes us, how we inherit the past, how the past is inscribed on us, and a corresponding theological vision," she writes. Oswald John Nira contributes the story of Mexican American students in San Antonio, formed in the principles of Catholic social teaching, who founded La Raza Unida in 1968 to stand against oppressive social and political structures, including the Catholic Church, which they saw as demanding "obedience to *gringo* masters." They were concerned about their Westside neighborhood but were inspired by the larger revolutionary movements of 1968. Tracy Sayuki Tiemeier's essay on pedagogy after the August 2017 events in Charlottesville, Virginia, describes using fantasy and science fiction literature to expand the imaginations of her students toward racial equity and justice.

"Sex, Families, and Revolution," Part II, explores the tensions between changing social paradigms surrounding sexuality, its effect on notions of family and gender, and the response of Catholics, both lay and magisterial. The contributors offer studies that both name our theological failings and provide trajectories of creativity and hope from within the tradition. Julie Hanlon

Rubio provides an unflinching overview of Catholic responses to the so-called sexual revolution of the late 1960s. She provides us with an important challenge to retrieve the wisdom of the Catholic revolution regarding sex, gender, and families while recognizing that it was not "all [it] should have been." Daniel Rober examines trends toward disaffiliation and trenchantly applies cognitive dissonance theory to the dilemmas Catholics can face around issues of sexuality as they navigate the intersections of living in both the dominant culture and the church. He suggests the need for a more robust theological anthropology of wholeness, faithfulness, and community. Doris Kieser's essay homes in on *Humanae Vitae* with a specific focus on the physical reality of women's menstruating bodies. She analyzes how the magisterial teaching and the teaching of the faithful revisionists left out the physical experience of real women as well as the experience of unmarried women, causing, she suggests, an unintended revolution. "Leaping" from the insights of the gender revolution, David von Schlichten's essay deftly uses Joan Didion's work to assist our "diagnosing" of the alienations and self-delusions that come from the "loss of center" in 2018. Searching for an embodied hope, he applies a particular feminist eschatology so that "the center can hold" and injustice can be addressed in the present. Part II concludes with a study that provides an example of how Catholics have created diverse family lives as a faithful response to elements of the tradition. William Collinge explores the Catholic agrarianism of Eugene and Abigail McCarthy and how their initial intentions to live as a family from the land inspired by the Benedictine balance of prayer, manual work, and intellectual labor led to a career in politics. Eugene McCarthy's "refusal to separate politics from morality" might be a model for how Catholics respond to the crises of 2018.

On December 24, 1968, the Apollo 8 mission took the photograph that has come to be known as "Earthrise." The photo could be used simply as proof of human technological achievement, of an "I-it" or "subject-object" relationship between humans and the universe, but its mystic beauty more powerfully evinces a sense of spiritual awareness that connects human beings to a reality beyond: that is, to each other and to God. Appropriately, the book's final part, "Contemplation, Action, and Revolution," opens to revolutions of the spirit that intersect with and accompany the revolutions surrounding race and gender plumbed in the first two parts. In a richly textured plenary address, Christopher Pramuk seeks to "examine systems and structures of power that exclude and marginalize." He does so through the use of his own spiritual journey in addition to those of writers and artists across religious traditions. Pramuk offers a meditation on grace, providing "notes for a pedagogy of racial justice and reconciliation" and preserving a place for Christians to account for the hope that is in them.

Donna Teevan explores Bernard Lonergan's series of essays that argued that a sea change in Catholic theology was occurring in the late 1960s. In fact, the four theological shifts that Lonergan identified provide the foundation for the type of engagement in social and cultural situations that Pramuk addresses in the first part of his essay. Teevan's analysis of Lonergan reminds theologians that sometimes revolutions in theology are necessary to respond authentically to the needs of the church and world. B. Kevin Brown offers readers a chance to consider the prophetic ecclesial spirituality of Sandra Schneiders. He combines the prophetic dimensions of scripture with spirituality in an ecclesial setting. The more abstract discussions of Lonergan considered in the preceding chapter come into focus in feminist theology and its prophetic challenge to contemporary Christians with Brown's evaluation of Schneiders as one of the most significant American Catholic theologians of the past fifty years. Glenn Young introduces readers to Néstor Paz, a Bolivian religious educator who joined a resistance movement that took up arms against the government. Deeply spiritual, Paz found God in political engagement. Young suggests that "political engagement itself may be a means by which mystical consciousness develops." Part III concludes with John Sniegocki's application of the themes of the Latin American bishops' meeting in Medellín, Colombia, to the present moment. He does so by focusing on Pope Francis's discussion of social movements within his ecclesial vision.

It is entirely fitting that a work of the College Theology Society concludes with an essay from a former president, William Portier. It is also appropriate that the essay considers the state of Catholic theology within Catholic higher education some fifty years after the Land O'Lakes Statement. Portier's honest and sobering appraisal of the marginalization of "Catholic theologians in both church and academy" due to a "politicization of knowledge" should give all CTS members pause. He recommends a more pastoral emphasis for academic theology in the key of Pope Francis, making "theology more ecclesial."

The revolutions and hopes of 1968 contained many contradictions, and not everyone will agree that the common good is equally well served by particular revolutions. Christians, however, bring the virtues of faith, hope, and selfless love in a self-reflective way to the social and political concerns that they share with other people of good will. There is much work that remains before we realize a kin-dom of God on earth, an era of peace and wholeness for all peoples. The editors hope that these essays edify and inspire the readers toward the work that awaits.

Acknowledgments

The editors thank the board of directors of the College Theology Society for supporting and accepting the proposal to devote the 2018 CTS convention to the theme of revolution and 1968. Particular gratitude is owed to William Collinge, executive director of publications for the College Theology Society, who went above and beyond the call of duty in assisting the editors, to Dr. Jill O'Brien of Orbis Books for her guidance in bringing this book to fruition, and to the editorial staff for their good work. Finally, the editors thank their families for their support and patience as they gave us the time and space to complete the project.

Acknowledgments

PART I

RACE, HOPE, AND REVOLUTION

Teaching and Living
toward a Revolutionary Intimacy

Willie James Jennings

I remember 1968. I was only seven years old, but I remember 1968. I remember when Martin Luther King Jr. died. All the events of 1968 (and there were many) are defined for me and for many others by and through the event of King's death. His death is what "1968" means. I remember vividly because the day after his assassination, on April 5, 1968, two of my magnificent older sisters came to get their baby brother out of his classroom and take him home *before all hell broke loose*. "Hell breaking loose" in Grand Rapids, Michigan, was a relative thing, however. Grand Rapids was not Detroit or Los Angeles. Grand Rapids was a sea of mostly white people, mostly Dutch people, and we were part of a small black community. But we were angry, and now that anger reached all the way down deep into the entire black community and deep into my elementary school.

Class was dismissed that day not by choice but by anguish. I remember both my small hands in my big sisters' hands and them pulling me as fast as they could, through the school and through flying paper and pencils and books, and navigating in between yelling and screaming and crying kids. There were no cell phones or text messages with which to communicate, but my sisters instinctively knew what my parents demanded of them: watch out for your little brother and bring him home if there is trouble. My sisters were doing what they knew my parents were thinking.

I remember my parents' prescient clarity that King's death was inevitable, and as the years after his assassination unfolded, I saw with their clarity as well. His death, they said, was inevitable not because he pressed for our civil rights, but because my parents knew that King was struggling against something much grander than rights, more fundamental than even the struggle for justice. Those black folks knew that King was struggling against a form of life that had taken hold in this country and around the world, a form of life revolving around white supremacy and bone-deep racial segregation.

How do you struggle against something that so many people, that so many Christians, had promoted as natural, as a signature of the created order, as a signature of the divine order, but that you knew was not natural, and not divine? How do you struggle against whiteness, against white privilege—the privilege of never having to be concerned about race—against behavior, yes, but also something much more, something that you knew your faith as a child of Africa was formed against? There is one word that captures what my parents understood about the struggle and what my faith was formed to anticipate: *revolution.*

Revolution is a good word; revolution is a *holy* word.

Being black and being Christian in this racialized world taught me to love that word: *revolution.* All of us should love that word because it is close to the heart of our reality as Christians and especially meaningful to those of us who inhabit the academy.

This country, however, has taught us to fear that word. That word falls from the lips of all the villains in our movies and in the fabricated histories of a "cold war." *Revolution* is a safe word only if it has *American* in front of it. *Revolution* is a safe word if it is hidden from us in the many revolutions this country has helped to start and sustain around the world, in the name of "America." But we Christians serve a God of Revolution, a God of overturning. In the words of the late, great Samuel DeWitt Proctor, we serve a God who has turned this upside-down world, this death-bound world, right side up, turned it toward life.[1] To be a Christian is to be convinced that you are in the midst of a revolution. To be a Christian, to serve the God of Revolution, is having eyes to see that *what is*—socially, economically, geographically, in the actual shape of our lives and our living—*should not be* and that what should be has in fact already been shown to us through Jesus Christ.

It is precisely this sight, this holy vision of revolution that must be used to address the contemporary racial condition. We have been in a centuries-long struggle against the racial condition. It is a struggle not against flesh and blood, but against that which has always sought to *define* flesh and blood. It has been a struggle against powers and principalities, but especially against the principality of whiteness. We are watching right now this country submit to its deep addiction to whiteness. We must become revolutionaries against whiteness and understand together what that revolutionary life means at this moment.

We have finally reached a moment in our history as Christians when we can grasp what whiteness actually *is*. Whiteness was never a person or a people, whiteness was never an aspect of creation, and whiteness has certainly never been a state of grace. Whiteness was and is a way of being in the world and a way of perceiving the world at the same time. Whiteness was and is a way of imagining oneself as the central facilitating reality of the world, the reality that makes sense of the world; whiteness is a frame of reference that interprets, organizes, and narrates the world, and whiteness is having the power to realize and sustain that imagination. Whiteness was and is a form of life built upon imperial possibilities, possibilities that so many people have sought and yet still seek to realize.[2]

"White people" was never meant to be a designation for a particular people, or a particular nation. Although we have made whiteness a placeholder for the multiple peoples of European descent, the designation "white people" has rather been formed as an invitation, a hoped-for becoming, a transformation from vagabond immigrants set adrift and vulnerable in this world, into an accomplished people, a people who control the land, and who are masters of their worlds. We Christians have failed to understand just how deeply modern colonialism has set us all on the trajectory toward becoming white people, making mastery justifiable, such that people are defined as those who either control their world, geographically, economically, and socially, or people who are commodities controlled by others. This was the dream and the nightmare, born of Euro-colonial Christian settler life, where women and men sought control of their land and its resources, sought mastery over native inhabitants, and sought a freedom built on the bodies of nonwhite peoples, a freedom built on the control and mastery of dark bodies. Remember the famous words of that great, patriotic, eighteenth-century British anthem "Rule, Britannia!":

> When Britain first, at Heaven's command
> Arose from out the azure main;
> This was the charter of the land,
> And guardian angels sang this strain:
> "Rule, Britannia!" rule the waves:
> "Britons never will be slaves."[3]

In the song, these words are declared from heaven to Britons, from the mouths of angels, speaking the word of God. *Either rule or be slaves*. Verse 5 continues this dream, this fantasy:

> To thee belongs the rural reign;
> Thy cities shall with commerce shine:
> All thine shall be the subject main,
> And every shore it circles thine.
> "Rule, Britannia!" rule the waves:
> "Britons never will be slaves."[4]

Either rule or be slaves. It is precisely this fear that the current occupant of the White House plays with daily, delivering promises of control ("law and order") and exhortations toward mastery. The civil rights movement and the black church's parental role in both its founding and its life constituted from the very beginning a struggle against whiteness, against a demonic power daily seducing peoples to claim an identity that promised them *the power to control their worlds*.

We lose much historical precision and theological clarity when we narrate the civil rights movement as something other than this struggle against the power of domination. The civil rights movement was narrated to many of us children of the sixties as an extended argument about fairness and justice rooted in an American idea that was actually a white fiction: that America was the new Israel, a place of opportunity, where people could by their own merit and hard work move forward in life, that people should be judged by their own merit, by what they have "earned," and not by any other factor. To be sure, the power of the civil rights movement was found in part in the ability of its greatest voices to do wonderful things with words: to employ words such as *fairness, equality, justice*, and *freedom*, with a new spiritual depth that those words had lacked when they had been used in relation to the construction of a country that depended on the exploitation and mistreatment of black flesh. Black folks have always done more to reveal the authentic meaning of those words—*fairness, equality, justice, freedom*—than those words have done for us. But the civil rights movement (as have all movements in this country and in the West) has still left in place the power of whiteness and its horrific work of building and forming a vision of life and a people aimed at becoming white.

It is the *becoming white*, the formation in and toward whiteness, that must be overturned. In order to understand what I am saying, you must forget about whiteness as phenotype, as bodily characteristics, even as a European heritage, and see it for what it is: a sick vision of a so-called maturity, a vision of reaching toward and arriving at a maturity that can judge the whole world by how well it has achieved mastery of its world, control of its land and resources, and a "freedom" to live unencumbered by other peoples. This work of becoming white has been bequeathed to the world through a Christian vision turned sickeningly against itself. We were the potters at the wheel ruining the clay. This vision grew from Christian colonial settlers who arrived in the new world convinced that God had given the new world to them and that their fundamental task was to bring the new world and its inhabitants to "civilization," to maturity of mind, body, and Christian spirit, of land and living, of behavior, and of architecture. This is the essence of whiteness: to form the new world to look and act just like them. From this impulse to transform the world into their image grew the work of becoming white, work that continues today.

Whiteness is a theological and spiritual disease, an invasion of Christianity, and to overcome it we need a spiritual practice that helps us renounce the ways of whiteness—renouncing the way whiteness thinks, the way whiteness feels, and the way whiteness hides. That spiritual practice must embody the revolutionary vision of life together born of the life of Jesus. It must embody what I call a revolutionary intimacy.

Renouncing the Way Whiteness Thinks

The way whiteness thinks, or to be more precise, the way being white has framed thinking, has operated inside an imperial masculinist position. We are the inheritors of what I have called a pedagogical imperialism born of a distorted vision of the Christian mission. That distorted vision has imagined a world locked in ignorance—ignorance of the true God and ignorance of the true nature of the world itself—that white thinking assumes it must save, that white thinking assumes it must master. Hence this is a pedagogical imperialism, within which Christians entered the new world imagining themselves as the teachers of the world, as the bringers of civilization and sophistication, and the world as perpetual learners, as infants always in need of arriving at the truth.

We Christians presented a God who knows everything and needs to learn nothing; we thereby performed and still perform a Christianity that knows everything and needs to learn nothing. We have turned the educational life of a Christian on its head. God delights in learning of God's own creation, and in and through Jesus, God learns. God has entered the time and the places of God's creatures, moving in and enjoying each moment of the creature's existence. Jesus learned and then he taught. His teaching, however, was embedded in his learning. It is precisely this deeper reality of incarnation, of God living and moving in relation to making disciples, that we Christians have lost. We have preferred to impose our mature, superior theological knowledge, to denigrate indigenous knowledge, and to present a God who cannot be found in the learning, but only in the teaching. Imperial Christianity gave birth to this pedagogical imperialism, which turned the entire world outside the colonial West into perpetual students and those in the West into eternal teachers. *Whiteness thinks always as a teacher and never as a learner.*

To be a learner is to enter the world of another's ecology of knowing, to be willing and eager to listen and to perceive the world through the senses and sensibilities of another people. The colonialist legacy we inherited, however, has fundamentally denied other ways of knowing and turned knowledge itself into a commodity. Because the goal of knowledge for the colonialists was never reciprocity, the goal of entering the new world was not based in relationship, and so the colonialists never envisioned an abiding communion and life together with the peoples they encountered or with the land. Knowledge for the colonialists was a matter of acquisition always aimed at possession, control, and mastery for the sake of more acquisition. Within this colonialist framework, within the construction of whiteness, to know a thing is to own a thing. In this framework, the work of gaining knowledge, the work of securing knowledge, was and is always a work of contention.

Whiteness thinks always inside of white masculinist form. Most of us have been mis-formed or de-formed to imagine serious intellectual engagement in only one modality—through confrontation. Through such *disputatio*—through the European mode of disputation, which is rooted in European chivalric culture based on organizing for war, only through intense and heated exchange, do we arrive at the truth, rigorous thinking, and strong and sure thought.[5] Organization for war as the basis for encounter has meant we are locked in a continuous position of confrontation.

Beginning with the colonial period, this European cultural form of chivalric intellectual engagement combined with capitalist forms of economic exchange and resulted in the fragmentation of knowledge. Together, capitalism and chivalric intellectualism became the foundation of the sick ecologies of knowledge that characterized so much of Western intellectual exchange—where our skirmishes and arguments are over increasingly smaller and smaller bits of knowledge, extracted from their life-worlds, from their own contexts and their own communities, and turned into commodities.

We must renounce the way whiteness thinks by entering freshly into the life of Jesus *as a learner.* He learns from both the creation and the creatures, and in and through his learning, he creates a life of humility and communion. Humility and communion should mark the character of our intellectual life, where we are called by Jesus to show a deep desire to learn from those whose ways of knowing have been excluded and marginalized. We are called to aim all our knowing toward a life lived in mutuality, *together.* This means we all need to critically interrogate our doctoral and doctrinal formations. We need to do a whiteness inventory. We have all been formed inside the cognitive structures of whiteness; even our subjectivities have been subject to the infection of whiteness. Whiteness is inescapable. No one becomes a professor, especially in theological or religious studies, unless they have been mastered by, and become masters of, intellectual obedience. All intellectual obedience is geared toward performing in the white masculine form. It does not matter how radical we think we are—we are first and foremost intellectually obedient to the notion of truth as within our possession, as something we own. This is a much wider reality than being trapped in Eurocentrism, although that is a continuing signature of this wider reality. Intellectual obedience has to do with the evaluative frameworks we live within both explicitly and implicitly, and the ways we promote ourselves as pedagogical colonialists, as masters of worlds.

Renouncing the Way Whiteness Feels

We must also renounce the way whiteness feels. Whiteness feels. It has an affective structure. Like extremely comfortable clothing that moves with the body, whiteness becomes what Anne Anlin Cheng calls a second skin.[6] Whiteness feels because whiteness never needs to make a distinction between *being* and being *white*. Whiteness thus presents itself as skin and not as clothing. Many of the obstacles to overturning whiteness are based on the success of that powerful affective structure. Whiteness feels normal and natural because it is woven into how we imagine we are moving toward maturity. Whiteness feels normal and natural and therefore is always something positive, *unless* it is being questioned. So to question whiteness feels terrible, because it feels as if we are tearing at the fabric of people's lives, at their very skin, and questioning the right of their form of life to exist. To question whiteness feels like throwing people into chaos and fragmentation. It feels like hate speech.[7]

In this sense, anyone who questions whiteness is seen as being obsessed with matters of identity, being swallowed by "identity politics," and having lost a sense of common purpose. But the issue with whiteness has never been in having a common purpose. The issue has always referred to the matter of who gets to define the common purpose, the myth of merit and success, and what energies and instruments have been used to force people into a hegemony of common purpose, a metanarrative that destroys the varieties of life. So from the beginning of the workings of whiteness, from the beginnings of colonialism and imperialism, people have used the only weapon consistently at their disposal to challenge that common purpose—their bodies, their stories, their memories and hopes, all found in their identities.[8]

Questioning whiteness brings people into a forest of feeling, a thicket from which they would prefer to escape. Such is rife with feelings of fear, of guilt, and of feeling overwhelmed by the sheer expansiveness, the insidious ubiquity of whiteness's roots and reach into our lives. The deepest anxiety of so many people is not that whiteness is inescapable, but that the feelings of whiteness are inescapable, its disease and discomfort, its guilt and its addictive and seductive power. Whiteness feels good as long as no one tries to make it feel bad.

We renounce the way whiteness feels first by recognizing that whiteness feels. Whiteness feels as it thinks and thinks as it feels. The first mistake we make is to fail to recognize how much racial reasoning and racial discourse is driven by deeply entangled thought and feeling. But to renounce the way whiteness feels is not to renounce feeling. It is to question the structure of feeling that has taught people to so deeply identify with whiteness that they cannot imagine a life freed from its vision and shaped inside a whole new affective structure of joy and peace. They cannot imagine what so many people of color imagine every day: a life freed from the derogatory racial visions of their existence and shaped inside a new affective structure of joy and peace.

Intellectual after intellectual, from one generation to the next, has struggled to articulate a path between their realization of dignity and the world constructed against it, between a life lived in integrity, in wholeness, in a psychic space between who they are and a racialized world's vision of blackness or Asian-ness or Indigenous-ness. It is that struggle that holds the key to renouncing the way whiteness feels. All of us must join together in the shared work of cutting and carving psychic space between our lives and racialized vision, but that work must be fully engaged in by those who have been formed to see their whiteness as their *skin*. This has always been a work of soteriology, of imagining and enacting a saved life, a life freed from bondage through the name of Jesus and by the Holy Spirit.

Renouncing the Way Whiteness Hides

Whiteness always aims at invisibility and ignorance. It wants invisibility not through concealment but through looking. Whiteness wants to make itself a way of regarding the world without ever announcing itself as a way of regarding the world. Whiteness wants to be the eyes looking through the camera, before it becomes the eyes being seen by the camera. Whiteness wants to become the eyes being seen by the camera, the eyes of humanity, the eyes of everyone, and of anyone wishing to be seen. This is the wish born of whiteness. Whiteness aims at being the norming norm, the baseline upon which we can imagine the true, the good, and the beautiful. But to ensure this kind of invisibility, this kind of *visible invisibility*, if you will, whiteness needs to control space. Race has always been a matter of geography, and whiteness always aims to structure itself geographically, on the ground: in the shape of communities, cities, towns, rural and urban areas, neighborhood by neighborhood, always creating geographic whiteness.

Whiteness comes to rest in space. The maturity at which whiteness aims always forms segregated spaces. It forms lives lived in parallel, whether separated by miles or inches. Whiteness constructs bordered lives, in which life is lived in separate endeavors of wish fulfillment. I continue to be amazed by people who have been raised in all-white communities. All-white communities are those in which the presence of people of color is highly monitored and controlled, but such constructed habitation is accepted as a naturally occurring phenomenon, like a waterfall or a rock formation. Such places breed a profound ignorance that conceals its deformity, denying to those so formed within those places the truth that their worlds are highly structured segregationist spaces enabled by the vestiges of genocide, the continuation of forced and slave labor for the sake of cheap goods, of market manipulations, "city planning," the wishes and whims of developers, the actions of real estate brokers who redline neighborhoods, the police, and the unrelenting will of whiteness to exist unencumbered by nonwhite peoples.

We all wear our places on our bodies soft or hard. Some wear the unease of being in places and spaces no longer governed by a geographic whiteness. I know students and colleagues in the academy, and so do many of you, who have never in their entire lives faced an authority figure who was other than white or so assimilated as to never show a difference from whiteness that would shock anyone into a sense of a shared world. I see their unease at being outside that white geographic space and in a world that they cannot control and their desperate (often secret) desire to return to that place or turn the world itself into that geographic whiteness. Some wear the resentment of being raised in, and perhaps still living in, places and spaces not governed by a geographic whiteness, and having to live in places that suffer the outside: outside excellent public schools, outside community resources at your fingertips, outside police only present in *good behavior*, outside safely walking, talking, strolling in the evening breeze like Almighty God looking for Adam and Eve in the Garden. I know those students and colleagues in the academy, and so do you, who cannot see the forest for the trees, who cannot see that they are driven by an (often) tacit desire to create a geographic whiteness, aiming at a suburbia of the mind if not of place, especially in urban places that they see as filled with despair and violence. They work sometimes unwittingly, sometimes knowingly, toward a habitation that performs even more refined, nuanced forms of segregation.

We renounce the way whiteness hides by overturning segregated spaces. Segregated spaces must be turned toward living places where people construct together an everyday that turns life in health-giving directions. Overcoming whiteness begins by reconfiguring life geographically so that all the flows work differently, the flows of money and education, support and attention, move across spaces where people have been separated by the processes that have formed us racially, economically, and nationally. We resist the sealed bubbles of our campuses that recapitulate the white world. We start with the communities that have been left behind in the movement of white myths of progress and maturity, those communities no longer imagined through the goals of whiteness: goals of possession, of control and mastery. There is nothing to master in abandoned communities, nothing to possess with people in need and with no money. But for Christians, this is where we go: we join such places and such people, we move to them, or we stay in them, or we form them, or we advocate for them, or we protect them. The "we" here, the Christians of the revolution, are all those willing to live toward a different formation of places and against the formation of geographic whiteness. We fight against the segregation that shapes our worlds, and we work to weave lives together. We become what Gerhard Lohfink many years ago called a "contrast society" by forming contrast communities. But that contrast must be formed on the actual ground, in neighborhoods and living places.

So a spiritual practice of renunciation of the ways of whiteness, of the ways it thinks, feels, and hides must be a shared work of the people of God aiming at an intentionality of intimacy of life together. But I want to be clear. I am not naïve and neither are you. There are great advantages to being white and aiming your life at becoming white. As with all spiritual practices, renunciation is a choice, but it is a choice that I am convinced that all of us have to make today.

As the years unfolded for me after 1968, I remember that I never saw my parents give up hope. Because they knew that hope was never something you *have*. Hope is something that holds you, something that sets you toward the revolution. These days I remind myself that I must be disciplined by hope because my hope is built on the revolutionary life of God in the flesh who calls us to a life together, to a life that aims to overturn this world, especially a world formed in whiteness.

Notes

[1]Samuel Proctor, *My Moral Odyssey* (Valley Forge, PA: Judson Press, 1989), 92–127.

[2]Willie James Jennings, "Can White People Be Saved? Reflections on the Relationship of Missions and Whiteness," in *Can "White" People Be Saved? Triangulating Race, Theology, and Mission*, ed. Love L. Sechrest, Johnny Ramírez-Johnson, and Amos Yong (Downers Grove, IL: IVP Academic, 2018).

[3]www.historic-uk.com.

[4]Ibid.

[5]Nigel Saul, *Chivalry in Medieval England* (Cambridge, MA: Harvard University Press, 2011); Maurice Keen, *Chivalry* (Yale Nota Bene) (New Haven, CT: Yale University Press, 2005); Tison Pugh, *Queer Chivalry: Medievalism*

and the Myth of White Masculinity in Southern Literature (Baton Rouge: Louisiana State University Press, 2013).

[6]Anne Anlin Cheng, Second Skin: Josephine Baker and the Modern Surface (New York: Oxford University Press, 2013).

[7]Robin DiAngelo, White Fragility: Why It's So Hard for White People to Talk about Racism (Boston: Beacon Press, 2018).

[8]Jennings, "Can White People Be Saved?"

The Scaffolding of Whiteness

Race and Place in the Christian Imagination

Erin Kidd

One hundred years after the emancipation of slaves, the civil rights movement sought to finally secure rights for black Americans—what Langston Hughes had already referred to in 1951 as "a dream deferred." We stand now fifty years after the assassination of the Rev. Dr. Martin Luther King Jr. on April 4, 1968. The dream is still deferred. The material effects of slavery continue to manifest in significant disparities between black and white Americans in health, education, homeownership, economic stability, and incarceration.[1] As I argue in this essay, this deferral is due in part to the way that whiteness has structured our world and, therefore, continues to structure our cognition.

The Theo-Logic of Whiteness

"Whiteness" emerges in the colonial era as part of a racial ideology designed to justify the violence of colonialism.[2] As sociologist Joe Feagin writes, "After developing an extensive colonial system involving land and labor theft across the Atlantic basin, the colonizers worked hard to rationalize, explain, and structure in their minds and writings how it was that they, as 'good and virtuous' Christians, could create such a violent and bloody system of human exploitation and subordination."[3] In *The Christian Imagination: Theology and the Origins of Race*, Willie James Jennings identifies the particular theo-logic of this new colonial identity.[4] He writes, "Europeans enacted racial agency as a theologically articulated way of understanding their bodies in relation to new spaces and new peoples and to their new power over those spaces and peoples."[5] European colonizers who came to the Americas displaced indigenous and African peoples, reordering black and brown bodies into a racialized caste system without reference to kinship or place. This system marked both one's rights and one's capacity for conversion to Christianity based on one's proximity to whiteness.[6] Thus the colonial creation of race entailed a revolution in the conception of the relationship between identity and place: "With the emergence of whiteness, identity was calibrated through possession of, not possession by, specific land."[7]

As Jennings argues, European colonizers were enabled not by an allegedly secular spirit of conquest, but by a theological perversion in which they saw themselves as the agents of God in the New World.[8] This belief was characterized by a "Gentile hubris" in which Europeans forgot both the Jewishness of Jesus and their own status as Gentiles grafted into the people of God.[9] This cultural amnesia cut them off from resources in the Christian tradition for thinking about how to respect the identity of the other and allowed them to read the scriptures as a license for domination.[10] The colonial theo-logic that has contributed to the understanding and function of race in the modern world thus has at its roots a pernicious supersessionism. Before European Christians displaced indigenous and African peoples, they imagined that they had replaced Israel as the people of God. At the foundation of our current racial order is therefore a theological distortion of the relationship between identity and place, founded on a misunderstanding of God's love of creation, the election of Israel, and of the incarnation in Jesus of Nazareth.

"White," therefore, does not refer to anything natural, ontological, or biological, but rather, as Bryan Massingale writes, "The term 'white' refers to the dominant cultural group in our country."[11] "Whiteness" refers not to a phenotype marker, but to an ideology of racial domination that has segregated our society and shaped the foundation of our religious, legal, and educational institutions, as well as the fundamental way we imagine and navigate our world. After all, who has been considered "white" in the United States has changed over time, with various ethnic communities attaining "whiteness" as they gain greater cultural and political recognition.[12] In Jennings's words, whiteness is not a category of people but "a means of seeing all peoples."[13]

How is this white colonial theo-logic perpetuated today? At his plenary address to the 2018 Convention of the College Theology Society, Jennings spoke of the "cognitive structures of whiteness." To unpack the meaning of such structures, scholars such as Joe Feagin have relied on frame analysis. In the cognitive and social sciences, a "frame" refers to an interpretive model that structures one's understanding of the world.[14] According to Feagin, the dominant racial frame in the United States is "an overarching white worldview that encompasses a *broad and persisting set of racial stereotypes, prejudices, ideologies, images, interpretations and narratives, emotions, and reactions to language accents as well as racialized inclinations to discriminate.*"[15]

Recent work in philosophy of mind and the cognitive sciences allows us to better understand the mechanism by which the ideology of whiteness is perpetuated.[16] This mechanism, or frame, has persisted despite the fact that it is less socially acceptable for whites to be openly racist. Indeed, as Feagin and Eduardo Bonilla-Silva argue, part of the operation of the white racial frame today is the pretense of "colorblindness."[17] Whites who believe that they are beyond racism may claim that they "don't see color" when encountering a person. Racism, however, persists in the deliberate attempt to ignore the history of color in America. In particular, the concept of "the extended mind" can show us how whiteness is socially reproduced, even in the absence of conscious and explicit racism.

The Extended Mind

Andy Clark and David Chalmers first developed the idea of the "extended mind" in an essay[18] asserting that the "mind" extends beyond the "boundaries of skin and skull."[19] For example, we often solve math problems by jotting numbers on a piece of paper, performing an activity in the world that is simulated in the mind.[20] Clark and Chalmers consider not just the latter activity "thinking," but the former activity, acting in the world, as "thinking" also.[21] While the activities are functionally equivalent with respect to their role in cognition, they vary greatly in efficiency. There is a reason, after all, that people do math on paper more often than in the head. As the math becomes more complicated, the activity with a pen and paper will not only outpace the activity without, but will very quickly ascend in complexity. So it is not only that our thinking *can* extend outside our skull, but that much of our thinking *must*.

In an example from *Being There: Putting Brain, Body and World Together Again*, Clark considers what happens when a fielder attempts to catch a fly ball. It is easy to fall into the trap of imagining the centerfielder performing some sort of calculation—even a visual tracing of the parabolic trajectory of the ball—to decide where to run to get underneath it. But if the centerfielder were to spend too much time thinking through this process, the runner will already have made it home. Instead, most of the time, the centerfielder will use a simple trick called linear optical trajectory (LOT). The outfielder will run so that the ball appears to move in a straight line rather than the curve—effectively, she will be under the ball as it decelerates and perceive the downward motion as a continuation of the initial ascent.[22] Learning to catch a ball has little to do with the calculus of parabolas, and everything to do with accustoming oneself to the feeling of seizing a ball dropped from the sky.

In this example, the activity of intelligence is not about perceiving information, performing calculation, and executing commands. Rather, it is about the ballplayer exploiting tricks in the relationship between her and her environment in real time. In other words, thinking is not something the outfielder does in between seeing the ball and running—thinking *is* the running. Nor is intellectual activity something that merely happens *inside* her skull, but is performed through her bodily actions on the field. The "extended mind" hypothesis extends the human mind both in time and space, weaving together the loops between organism and environment as a constitutive part of cognition.

Much of human intelligence, Clark argues, "is based on similar environment-specific tricks and strategies."[23] Human cognition extends beyond the limits of the human body, supported by external scaffolding which, as Clark defines it, "denotes a broad class of physical, cognitive, and social augmentations—augmentations that allow us to achieve some goal that would otherwise be beyond us."[24]

One of the ways that human intelligence is "scaffolded" is through the development of what Clark calls "designer environments."[25] To illustrate, Clark mentions the painting of white lines on mountain roads, which provide a helpful visual cue for those driving to be able to manage dangerous curves.[26] Humans make and explore designer environments in order to offload their cognition onto the world. This happens at an individual level (such as when I leave the books I need to read in a separate pile on my desk) and a cultural level (such as when linguistic signifiers are passed down from generation to generation). At this broader cultural and biological level, designer environments function as living memories—passing on the knowledge of previous generations (to learn to use a tool like a sextant is to inherit the practical knowledge gained through a long process of discovery)[27] actively contributing to brain development in early childhood so that we both make and are made by tools,[28] and, in the present, constituting part of the loop between organism and environment that is the basis of our cognition.

Colonial Scaffolding

Designer environments may hold a clue to how colonial theo-logic is passed down and perpetuated. Indeed, I want to argue that our intelligence is both augmented and constrained by *white* designer environments that scaffold racist ways of being in the world. Consider the legacy of colonial theo-logic. Jennings notes that American culture constructs space into units of private property,[29] with the concomitant imagining of land in terms of ownership grids rather than geographical features,[30] and the strengthening of racial identities over and above geographic or ethnic-based identities.[31] Each of these phenomena contributes to the economic and racial segregation experienced in our society today. Jennings writes that the "spatial dimension [of segregation] must be seen not primarily as a product of behavior (that is, peoples isolate themselves along cultural difference), but as the dual operation of the way the world is imagined and the way social worlds constitute the imagination."[32]

Let us attend closely to this dual operation. The existence of all-white neighborhoods in the United States has a pernicious history, in which practices such as redlining kept postwar black middle-class families from benefiting from the economic boom of the 1950s. Historic black neighborhoods were often razed in the name of highway construction, displacing many urban black communities—highways that were built precisely so that white families could flee urban cores. Current maps of segregation, such as all-white neighborhoods and gated communities, are therefore the result of a long process that disenfranchised people of color and kept homeownership and its subsequent wealth consolidated in the white middle and upper classes.[33] Through these maps of segregation, which thereby influence those with whom whites grow up, develop friendships, and attend school, we see the effects of a white colonial imagination, a white *frame*, on our world.

In addition to perpetuating various forms of structural injustice, such as disparities in education, this segregated social world in turn shapes the formation of our imaginations. For example, white people who grow up not knowing many people of color are prone to believing stereotypes reinforced through the media. In this frame of reference, whites may find themselves uncomfortable around people of color in ways that contribute to how whites perceive those who belong in positions of authority, or how whites manage access to job opportunities for people of color. The extended mind hypothesis allows us to add another level of analysis: the existence of segregated environments plays a constitutive role in cognition, in how both whites and people of color think about and navigate the world. In other words, both our construction of the world around us and our formation by it—whether social or somatic, embedded or embodied—are brought together in one loop of cognition.

Consider the gated community where George Zimmerman killed Trayvon Martin.[34] Zimmerman reports that he was initially suspicious of Martin because "it's raining, and he's just walking around looking about."[35] In his interview with police, he claims to be suspicious because he had never seen him before.[36] Both his 911 dispatch call and early interviews with police demonstrate Zimmerman's concern that the men he spots walking through his neighborhood, men who he is convinced are responsible for recent burglaries, always "get away."[37]

In her analysis of the Trayvon Martin shooting, Kelly Brown

Douglas argues that Zimmerman's actions, as well as his acquittal, are manifestations of a current instantiation of white
colonial theo-logic: what she calls "stand-your-ground culture"
in which protecting white property is valued more than black
and brown lives.[38] Concern with protecting white spaces leads
to an imagination that constructs people of color as criminals.[39]
Gated communities and other enclosed suburban neighborhoods
are examples of Clark's designer environments that scaffold such
belief. How might Zimmerman have imagined the space around
his home if there was no wall around it, no clear division between
neighborhoods, where anyone might walk? Instead, the gated,
defined borders of Zimmerman's space also mark bodies as licit
or illicit. A stranger seen against this polarity becomes an *intruder*,
therefore viewed as a threat. Additionally, Zimmerman views the
space within the boundary as "his" to defend. As Zimmerman
glimpses a young man walking with his sweatshirt hood up, he
does not in his head carefully measure crime statistics to calculate
the risk Martin poses. Like the outfielder, Zimmerman quickly
exploits environment-specific tricks, offloading his cognition
onto his surroundings, springing into action. The structure of
the neighborhood itself offers the conceptual logic for Zimmerman's actions.

Thus we need not presume that George Zimmerman intentionally or consciously valued white property over black and brown
bodies in order to argue that the shooting of Trayvon Martin was
an effect of white colonial theo-logics, distorting our conception
of identity and place. Rather, the gated community becomes an
artifact of a cultural value, whiteness, much like the sextant is
an artifact that encodes navigational knowledge. Such artifacts
shape our imagination and activity in the world. Thus as long as
our society is organized according to the value of white property,
within a racialized imagination and according to a white frame,
violence will be done to people of color.

The organization of American culture around whiteness is not
just inherited from the legacy of a colonial logic that prioritizes
white property ownership over black and brown bodies (though
it is), nor is whiteness only a structure that makes it difficult for
people of color to navigate this world (though it is), but in light
of the notion of extended mind, whiteness is also an ongoing

constitutive part of human meaning-making. The well-worn ruts of our colonial history continue to direct the wheels of our thought, so that awareness of and resistance to racism require not just engaging with our past, or our embodied habits, or our entrenched social structures, but also with the environment's role on our cognition.

What are the benefits of analyzing such scaffolding of whiteness in the wider problem of whiteness? First, it complicates the distinction between the personal and the structural so that a white person like me is tempted neither to (a) confine my analysis to a false individualism nor to (b) shore up my own goodness by always locating racism outside myself in external structures, as though racism occurs and is perpetuated outside my actions. The dynamic interplay between brain, body, and world means that I must take responsibility for the ways in which I am constituted by my environment and direct my moral responsibility toward reconfiguring it. Just as Christian understandings of concupiscence have highlighted the need to refashion one's impulses into a life of holiness, so discipleship demands that we must also take up the material of our broader world, reconfiguring it in light of the gospel of Jesus Christ.

Second, such analysis demonstrates why racism is so intractable. The extended mind hypothesis allows us to better understand the feedback loop between personal and structural sin: these support each other and materialize through the loop of cognition. Understanding in greater detail the relationship between the personal and the structural better enables us to dismantle white colonial theo-logics by highlighting the urgency of tearing down the scaffolding that supports their construction of our world.[40] If we attempt to build new worlds while standing on old scaffolding, we will only rebuild the same racial order with a new facade. New worlds require new scaffolding.

In highlighting the active role the environment plays in our cognition, I wish not to diminish human freedom but to expand the scope of our moral responsibility. The interwoven connection between identity and place means that we cannot hope to overturn the racial order without attending to how it has reconfigured both the construction of space and our imagination of it. Jennings writes, "We must narrate not simply the alteration of bodies but of space itself."[41] To reimagine and reconfigure frames of whiteness is to proclaim that the world is created and possessed only by God, and that our identities are founded in Jesus of Nazareth.

Notes

[1] For overviews of these racial disparities, see, for example, Michelle Alexander, *The New Jim Crow: Mass Incarceration in the Age of Colorblindness* (New York: New Press, 2010); Eduardo Bonilla-Silva, *Racism without Racists: Color-Blind Racism and the Persistence of Racial Inequality in America*, 4th ed. (Lanham, MD: Rowman & Littlefield, 2014), particularly Chapter 2, "The New Racism: The US Racial Structures Since the 1960s," 25–72; Jeannine Hill Fletcher, *The Sin of White Supremacy: Christianity, Racism, and Religious Diversity in America* (Maryknoll, NY: Orbis Books, 2017), 63–70, 84–93.

[2] For support of this claim outside the discipline of theology see Eduardo Bonilla-Silva, *Racism without Racists*, 8–11; Joe R. Feagin, *The White Racial Frame: Centuries of Racial Framing and Counter-Framing*, 2nd ed. (New York: Routledge, 2013), particularly Chapter 2, "Building the Racist Foundation," 23–38, and Chapter 3, "Creating a White Racial Frame," 39–57.

[3] Feagin, *White Racial Frame*, 39.

[4] Willie James Jennings, *The Christian Imagination: Theology and the Origins of Race* (New Haven, CT: Yale University Press, 2010). Whereas Feagin argues that early understandings of whiteness were only "dressed up in religious language," or "religiously sanctioned" (*White Racial Frame*, 26), Jennings is among many theologians who have argued that the origins of race lay in Christian theologies of the sixteenth century designed to justify European colonial expansion. See J. Kameron Carter, *Race: A Theological Account* (Oxford: Oxford University Press, 2008); M. Shawn Copeland, "White Supremacy and Anti-Black Logics in the Making of US Catholicism," in *Anti-Blackness and Christian Ethics*, ed. Vincent W. Lloyd and Andrew Prevot (Maryknoll, NY: Orbis Books, 2017), 61–74; Kelly Brown Douglas, *Stand Your Ground: Black Bodies and the Justice of God* (Maryknoll, NY: Orbis Books, 2015), particularly Chapter 1, "America's Exceptionalism," 3–47, and Chapter 2, "The Black Body: A Guilty Body," 48–89; Jeannine Hill Fletcher, *The Sin of White Supremacy*, particularly Chapter 1, "How Christian Supremacy Gave Birth to White Supremacy," 1–44; Santiago Slabodsky, "It's the Theology, Stupid! Coloniality, Anti-Blackness, and the Bounds of 'Humanity,'" in *Anti-Blackness and Christian Ethics*, 19–40; and Rima Vesely-Flad, *Racial Purity and Dangerous Bodies: Moral Pollution, Black Lives, and the Struggle for Justice* (Minneapolis: Fortress Press, 2017), particularly Chapter 1, "A Socio-Historical Review of Race and Morality," 3–29.

[5] Jennings, *Christian Imagination*, 58.

[6] Ibid., 25–26, 29–30, 35, 58–59, 138.

[7] Ibid., 59.

[8] Ibid., 60–61.

[9]Ibid., 167.

[10]Ibid., 248.

[11]Bryan Massingale, *Racial Justice and the Catholic Church* (Maryknoll, NY: Orbis Books, 2010), 2.

[12]Ibid., 3; Fletcher, *Sin of White Supremacy*, 1–3, 22–23.

[13]Jennings, *Christian Imagination*, 58.

[14]Feagin, *White Racial Frame*, 9. For more on how frame analysis is useful for theology reflection, see *Putting God on the Map: Theology and Conceptual Mapping*, ed. Erin Kidd and Jakob Rinderknecht (Lanham, MD: Lexington Press/Fortress Academic, 2018).

[15]Feagin, *White Racial Frame*, 3 (emphasis in original).

[16]I have written more broadly about how contemporary cognitive science ought to inform theological anthropology and white supremacy; see Erin Kidd, "The Subject of Conceptual Mapping: Theological Anthropology across Brain, Body, and World," *Open Theology* 4, no. 1 (2018): 117–35.

[17]Feagin, *White Racial Frame*, particularly Chapter 5, "The Contemporary White Racial Frame," 89–121; and Bonilla-Silva, *Racism without Racists*, particularly the first three chapters.

[18]Andy Clark and David Chalmers, "The Extended Mind," *Analysis* 58, no. 1 (January 1998): 7–19. Clark and Chalmers circulated the article informally beginning in 1995, but it was not published until 1998. By then Clark had already published *Being There: Putting Brain, Body, and World Together Again* (Cambridge: Cambridge University Press, 1997), which deals with the topic in greater detail. For an overview of this history, see Larissa Mac-Farquhar, "The Mind-Expanding Ideas of Andy Clark," *New Yorker*, April 2, 2018, available at www.newyorker.com, and David Chalmers, foreword to Andy Clark, *Supersizing the Mind: Embodiment, Action, and Cognitive Extension* (Oxford: Oxford University Press, 2008), ix–xvi.

[19]Clark and Chalmers, "Extended Mind," 7.

[20]Ibid., 8.

[21]Ibid., 10. Clark and Chalmers admit that one could model this behavior in terms of a series of thoughts and actions, but that such a model should be rejected for being needlessly complicated.

[22]Clark, *Being There*, 27–29. See also Andrew D. Wilson and Sabrina Golanka, "Embodied Cognition Is Not What You Think It Is," *Frontiers in Psychology* 4, no. 58 (February 2013): 5–6. I have simplified both the process and the debate around it—specific situations, like a ball approaching head-on, may require different approaches. Some studies suggest that outfielders use the LOT method sparingly, stopping occasionally to re-correct. What is clear is that the outfielder exploits tricks to navigate the relationship between her body and the environment. Outfielders tend not to run in straight lines, which would be the case if they were running to a particular spot they had calculated.

[23]Ibid., 13.

[24]Ibid., 194–95.

[25]Ibid., 191.

[26]Andy Clark, *Surfing Uncertainty: Prediction, Action, and the Embodied Mind* (Oxford: Oxford University Press, 2016), 279–81.

[27]Clark, *Being There*, 191–92.

[28]Clark, *Supersizing the Mind*, 67.

[29]Jennings, *Christian Imagination*, 247.

[30]Ibid., 225–56, 235–36.

[31]Ibid., 247.

[32]Ibid., 248.

[33]Fletcher, *Sin of White Supremacy*, 63–70, 79–80, 85–93.

[34]*Mother Jones* hosts one of the most comprehensive collections of material on the shooting at "The Trayvon Martin Killing, Explained," www.motherjones.com. Many of the primary sources are available at "George Zimmerman Trial," the University of Missouri's *Famous Trials* website operated by Douglas Linder, www.famous-trials.com.

[35]"Trayvon Martin Killing, Explained."

[36]"George Zimmerman Trial."

[37]"Trayvon Martin Killing, Explained," and "George Zimmerman Trial."

[38]Douglas, *Stand Your Ground*, 44. Douglas notes that the "Stand Your Ground" law itself was not used in Zimmerman's defense, but it is indicative of the broader cultural background behind Zimmerman's actions and his acquittal, 47.

[39]Ibid., 69, 76.

[40]For more on how tools in embodied cognition can help us understand the relationship between personal and structural sin in regard to white supremacy, see Kidd, "The Subject of Conceptual Mapping," 131–34.

[41]Jennings, *Christian Imagination*, 63.

"In the Bone"

Race, Theological Anthropology, and Intergenerational Trauma

Stephanie C. Edwards

In 1968, Audre Lorde (1934–1992) published her first volume of poetry, *The First Cities*. In his review of the volume, Dudley Randall asserted that she "does not wave a black flag, but her blackness is there, implicit, in the bone."[1] How might we understand what in us lives so deep that it is "in our bones"? Neuroscience, specifically the subfield of epigenetics, provides a new way to understand what is "in our bones," as it explores the inheritance of experiences, particularly traumatic experiences, from those in our familial lineage. Using Lorde's work as insight into the race and gender politics of the late sixties, this essay rereads her volume[2] in tandem with emerging scientific research focused on traumatic inheritance as well as with the theological insights of Mayra Rivera's *Poetics of the Flesh* and Shelly Rambo's *Resurrecting Wounds*.

From this interdisciplinary reflection, it is clear that flesh and bone are marked by trauma in a way that theology still largely ignores. The lack of attention to the realities of the flesh, including its inherited aspects, means that our vision of ourselves and "the other" is circumscribed. Understanding persons as holding "in the bone" much more than we present to the world—or even more than we consciously know about ourselves—influences how we see, speak about, and care for others and ourselves in Christian community. The richer understanding of the person provided by epigenetic research is especially necessary in considerations of structural racism and the ongoing violence against black and brown people in the United States. By asserting the intricate connections and complexities of inherited experience, I seek to affirm M. Shawn Copeland's call for theological anthropology to grasp "the sacramentality of the body in the concrete as an expression of the freedom of the human subject" that resists society's tendency to cover over and "forget" oppression. Instead, I here engage in what she names as the "Christian exercise of memory that purports to be radically different: We pledge to remember, we are obliged to do so."[3] We must remember the past trauma caused by systemic racism in the United States, not least signified by Lorde's poetry published in the same year as the assassination of Martin Luther King Jr. and the 125 city riots that followed. We must also remember our ongoing societal and theological failure to recognize and address the level of trauma under which communities of color continue to suffer.

Toward this goal, I first briefly introduce the scientific field of epigenetics, which seeks to uncover how the behavioral and experiential changes we experience in our lifetimes may be passed biologically to our offspring. Although this will by no means be a full treatment of the research, it is necessary for theology that seeks to do interdisciplinary work to provide clear parameters for the discussion. Second, I turn to theologians Mayra Rivera and Shelly Rambo to read their meditations on aspects of the flesh that seek to expand the dualistic, Enlightenment-based thinking still entrenched in much theological as well as scientific work. Taking up Rivera's and Rambo's tasks of categorical expansion of the Christian concepts of "flesh" and "wound," respectively, is necessary to understand what an epigenetic inheritance of trauma might mean theologically. Finally, I conclude with a brief discussion of what I call an "enfleshed counter-memory" that can potentially respond in Christian community to complex biological inheritances, such as those stemming from systemic racism.

What Is Epigenetics?

"From then / I can only distinguish / One thread within running hours / You . . . flowing through selves / toward you," writes Lorde.[4] As selves flow through selves, epigenetics is the study of potentially heritable changes in gene expression—active versus inactive genes—that do not involve changes to the underlying DNA sequence (a change in phenotype without a change in genotype). Epigenetic changes affect how cells read our genes, and these changes can affect the expression of human appearance and behavior.[5] This can be thought of as a change in "software" versus "hardware": the change is still heritable, but it is highly malleable and subject to variation across the lifetime. Phenotypic changes are not constant—our "software" transforms in response to environmental changes and the physiological and morphological changes associated with aging. However, the things known to alter our "software" most dramatically are our environment and our experiences, particularly those that are severe in nature, such as lack of nourishment or intense trauma.

With emerging scientific research, it is imperative not to leap too quickly to deterministic conclusions. A deterministic reading of epigenetic research comes very close to the fallacy that phenotypic changes give rise to genotypic modifications (for example, the blacksmith's children do not necessarily inherit strong forearms; and a person with a severely traumatized parent will not necessarily develop posttraumatic stress disorder, PTSD). However, the inheritance thesis—that *something* is inherited from our parents' experiences, particularly those experiences with sizable effects—is quite popular within both neuroscience and psychology. Both fields are currently attempting to disentangle biological, genetic change ("nature") and environmental change ("nurture") relative to how the parents' experiences are passed to the child. As of this date, there is no consistently proven, direct causal link between parental trauma (an environmental factor that changes the parents' gene behavior and is potentially heritable) and a child's predisposition to the development of chronic stress or PTSD, whether in the wake of the child's own trauma or tied to family or group history. Some studies show higher stress levels in children of traumatized persons; others show higher levels of resilience.[6] What we do know is that the individual who suffered trauma *directly* changes epigenetically. That person's body is now marked and changed through the experience. It will never return to the biological "before": the body's physical state before the event cannot be re-created. Of course, healing and restoration for the individual are still possible, through methods such as physical treatment, talk therapy, pharmaceutical treatment, and communal practices; but the point of employing epigenetic research is to emphasize that each and every experience in our lives is, in a way, coded into our bodies. This means that the likelihood is quite high that *something* related to a parent's trauma is inherited by the child; ongoing research attempts to separate and identify positive, adaptive changes from negative, maladaptive ones in a person's genetic code.[7] Rachel Yehuda, one of the leading researchers in epigenetics, observes: "People say, when something cataclysmic happens to them, 'I'm not the same person. I've been changed. I am not the same person that I was.' And epigenetics gives us the language and the science to be able to start unpacking that."[8]

Trauma and Fleshly Experience

"I have a child / Whose feet are blind / on every road / But silence," Lorde writes.[9] Children of trauma survivors often name silence and a sense of loss as central to their understanding of self. In her memoir and research history, *Survivor Café,* Elizabeth Rosner explores her parents' survival of the Shoah: at age sixteen, her father spent the year before liberation in the Buchenwald labor camp; her mother lived first in the Vilna ghetto, then was hidden by a rural Polish family. Rosner then traces the way her family's history intersects with both historic and contemporary accounts of mass suffering. Rosner struggles with the particularity of her family's tragic past as well as its almost mundane repetition throughout the world, in events such as Hiroshima, the Armenian genocide, Rwanda, and so on. She finds children of trauma survivors, including children of the perpetrators of trauma, haunted with "ghosts of experience that both did and did not seem to belong to us."[10] She patterns her work like a quilt: small patches of knowledge uncovered throughout a lifetime of near-obsession with her identity as a "2G" (or "second generation," what she calls those persons born to direct trauma survivors). She explains: "Amid the disordered fragments of my childhood recollections, I cannot remember first hearing my parents' war stories. It seems to me that I always knew. Shards of their past lodged themselves inside me at birth, if not before."[11] Theologian

Monica Coleman similarly ponders her own layered inheritances in her book *Bipolar Faith:*

> No one diagnosed my great-grandfather with depression. No one diagnosed Grandma. Who's to know or care about the mental and emotional state of poor sharecroppers from South Carolina? And who can stop to think of a clinical illness when the children need to be fed? What's the difference between depression, war, being black in the Jim Crow South, and plain old hard living? Who would know to alert children or grandchildren to the slippery slope of despair?[12]

Although too intricate to fully parse here, Mayra Rivera's postmodern theo-poetic work can offer us some insights into these still mysterious but deeply embodied connections. Rivera strives to reclaim the term "flesh" explicitly, particularly within Christian theology. She argues that the term "body" has been co-opted to do the work of dominating—to relegate individuals into parts, and to dissect, separate, and even amputate parts considered undesirable. Flesh, in contrast, "accents the complex textures of those [material and religious] relations—their inherent multiplicity; the sedimentation of past events; the constant flow of elements in and out of bodies."[13] Flesh, for Rivera, encapsulates the vulnerability of persons that is often socially determined and maintained, as well as inherited through the family.

Socially, flesh is the "connective and co-constitutive *tissue* between body and things."[14] Flesh is itself a physicality, as it has physical impacts and individual iterations. Reading Maurice Merleau-Ponty and Frantz Fanon together, Rivera draws a vision of the positive disruption of the flesh, as an entity that undoes rational discourse, but disrupts to reveal the only thing that can potentially bind us—our common enfleshment. Rivera explores how Fanon's narratives attempt to place himself, a Martinique-born, Afro-Caribbean psychiatrist and philosopher, within the wider world. The only site upon which he lands is his body itself. Whereas Fanon deconstructed this location, specifically for the ways society, culture, and religion acted upon it, Merleau-Ponty attempted to vocalize affirmations of fleshly experience.[15]

With Fanon and Merleau-Ponty, Rivera holds the two strands,

deconstructive and constructive, in tension, yet always together—an essential task when considering an enfleshed identity, particularly in light of epigenetic trauma. Even as Fanon struggles, he asks that his body continue to *make* him, and "to keep him open toward the world."[16] Rivera recognizes the temptation to turn away from our bodies, and all that bodies carry, and turn instead toward the spirit (as if through escaping materiality one would alleviate suffering), but she argues that "rejection of carnality is just the other side of the [dualistic] system."[17] She thus refuses to accept the traditional Western dualism between body and spirit, turning instead toward hope in dynamism and the "messiness" of flesh. Rivera orients this understanding of the person within Christ's incarnation, stating that by "focusing on the circuitous paths of flesh—connecting past and present, spirit and earthly elements—the incarnation brings to mind and may help us reevaluate carnal/earthly bonds as grounds for a commitment to a shared life."[18] Our flesh is inescapable, yes, but not without hope. In fact, for Rivera, the way out of pain, including inherited trauma, must be found in the malleable complexities of flesh itself. Orientation toward flesh in this sense allows for more nuance in theology's consideration of epigenetics and trauma in general. In this project, "flesh" allows for the recognition of the body's multidimensional reality as divinely created "flesh," as well as the power of the biological and the social to shape embodied personal identity in both negative and positive ways.

Wounds on the Body of Christ

"For we purchased bridges with our mothers' bloody gold / We are more than kin who come to share / Not blood, but the bloodiness of failure," writes Lorde.[19] Christ's body, the literal bloody flesh as well as the mystical bond of the people of faith, must be examined in light of epigenetic trauma. In *Resurrecting Wounds,* Shelly Rambo examines the gospel of John's account of the risen Christ's return to his disciples bearing the wounds of his crucifixion, and his encounter with the disciple Thomas. Taking to task her Calvinist inheritance, Rambo argues that, for reasons of polemics as well as belief, Calvin mollified or downright ignored the visceral, deeply upsetting, imagery of Thomas's probing of

Christ's wounded flesh. Although Calvin may want to turn his followers' gaze from bodies, even or especially from the wounded divine body, and onto the "Word," Rambo argues that John's description of Thomas's and Christ's interaction speaks directly to the experience of life in the aftermath of trauma—namely, through "bodily markings, an awareness of multiple witnesses present, and the status of death within this precarious sphere of life."[20] Specifically, Rambo is concerned with the pressure we may feel to erase wounds, as in the Christian narrative: "Life, if it is to triumph over death, must not retain the marks of death. Wounds must be erased."[21] Such erasure is particularly complex in the aftermath of trauma, when one does not necessarily fully heal from the experience and will forever carry the markings of the event, even passing it on to children. Instead of the antiseptic triumphalism too often represented in Christ's resurrection, Rambo focuses on how the Holy Spirit is "engrafted" into Christ's wounds, which as such display a potential entry point for resurrection within ordinary human life. Although she by no means glorifies Christ's wounds, she seeks to recognize and attend to the enduring wounds, reminding us not only that they remain on Christ's risen body, but also that the wounds are the site of life-giving intimacy between Thomas and Christ.

Rambo searches the gospel for what she calls *"ways of resurrecting"* by inviting ghosts into the Upper Room: not just the Holy Ghost, but specters that are tied to events we would rather forget.[22] She argues that there is something fundamental that can be reclaimed through the sense of haunting that pervades John's account: "Ghosts signal unsettling memories coming forward. . . . [But] ghosts [also] do important work of resurrecting pasts in order to heal them."[23] Being haunted in this way empowers the faithful with a task: with the Holy Spirit comes the power to transform—not erase—even the most horrific, wounding experience. The Holy Spirit within the wounds of Christ attests a something-to-be-done, from within and without. In relation to inherited trauma, Rambo argues: "As the wounds of history return, reappearing in the present, Christian theology might offer a vision of resurrection that addresses these wounds, precisely because the wounds return."[24]

"The Old Bones Rose"

Lorde writes: "Like an ocean of straws the old bones rose / Fearing the lightning's second death."[25] In reimagining the theologically important terms "flesh" and "wound" in conversation with emerging epigenetic research, a broader understanding of the human person, and what is "in their bones," is revealed. The vestiges of trauma that remain in the body may not be one's own, but are nonetheless integral to the consideration of self as they can indeed "rise." Rosner recalls the Israelites wandering in the desert, "the generation of slaves whose memories of Egypt had to be lost so that a new generation would be allowed to enter the Promised Land." She then asks, "Do I possess choices about what I carry forward, about what I am able to taste of my own life? How many generations beyond slavery does inherited memory last?"[26] Although epigenetics may someday offer the scientific answers to such inquiries, the Christian response to inherited trauma, and indeed all suffering, must not wait. The task of theology, as Rambo states, "demands a language of life that can account for the ruptures of experience and history without succumbing to despair."[27]

A partial response may be found in what I call a Christian "enfleshed counter-memory."[28] The wording is purposeful: "enfleshed," in relation to complex and incarnational embodiment; "counter," as trauma often confronts structures of power; and "memory," as the essential category that unites epigenetics and inherited trauma with Christian theology. An ethic of enfleshed counter-memory is practiced through the pursuit of justice in three primary realms: (1) empowerment of individual agency and integrity as self; (2) community support and participation in re/ integration of persons; and (3) global solidarity and preferential option for the poor.[29] Although Christian communities cannot provide all facets of care, they should be mindfully allied with medical, psychiatric, and social work providers to attend to the existential dimensions of trauma, an area to which they are particularly equipped to respond with the language of enfleshed counter-memory. Here I follow Phillis Sheppard's work on trauma healing. She writes, "Theologically, we are speaking of (1) being *in* and recognized by a community that affirms our relationship to the *imago dei;* and (2) being in relationship to a community that is deeply related to the Idealized One."[30]

However, practices of enfleshed counter-memory do not urge a "rush to redemption," to borrow Rambo's phrase. Rambo argues that by too quickly becoming an "Easter people," Christianity loses its distinctive, liminal space that can honor experiences of direct or inherited trauma. Rather, Rambo encourages the much more difficult work of Holy Saturday, embodying a community that does not move *to* a prescribed goal but moves *through* pain together.[31] Such a view of trauma healing, particularly in light of emerging knowledge of inherited traumas, is a unique contribution of theological anthropology, which creates and holds a space for relationship, fruitful tension, and "unknowing" that medical and psychological models do not and cannot offer. Creating this space is a necessary move in the struggle for racial justice, where, from this exploration, it is clear that our individual and collective inheritances of structural racism are not only sociological but are embedded in our very bones: the bones of both the perpetrators and the victims. To move forward in the work of justice, it is essential to understand how the past shapes us, how we inherit the past, how the past is inscribed on us, and a corresponding theological vision. Although it may be years before we understand our epigenetic inheritances and trauma's marking of our flesh, inherited social and individual wounding must be interpreted theologically to account for the fullness of the created person. As Rosner reflects on the Japanese art of *kintsugi,* or pottery repair, she asks: Will we fill our cracks with dust, or with gold?[32]

Notes

[1] Beverly Threatt Kulii, Ann E. Reuman, and Ann Trapasso, "Audre Lorde's Life and Career," *Modern American Poetry* online, www.english.illinois.edu.

[2] Reprint permissions prevent a full presentation of Lorde's poetry in this volume. For full poems please refer to Audre Lorde, *The Collected Poems of Audre Lorde* (New York: W. W. Norton, 1997).

[3] M. Shawn Copeland, *Enfleshing Freedom: Body, Race, and Being* (Minneapolis: Fortress Press, 2010), 130; and M. Shawn Copeland, "Memory, #BlackLivesMatter, and Theologians," *Political Theology* 17, no. 1 (January 2016): 1.

[4]Audre Lorde, "Now That I Am Forever with Child," in *The Collected Poems of Audre Lorde*, 8. Used with permission.

[5]See Rachel Yehuda et al., "Influences of Maternal and Paternal PTSD on Epigenetic Regulation of the Glucocorticoid Receptor Gene in Holocaust Survivor Offspring," *American Journal of Psychiatry* 171, no. 8 (2014): 872–80; and National Institutes of Health, "NIH Study of WWII Evacuees Suggests Mental Illness May Be Passed to Offspring," *Science Daily*, November 29, 2017, https://www.sciencedaily.com/. There is also ongoing research identifying the exact genes involved in PTSD; see Kumaraswamy Naidu Chitrala, Prakash Nagarkatti, and Mitzi Nagarkatti, "Prediction of Possible Biomarkers and Novel Pathways Conferring Risk to Post-Traumatic Stress Disorder," *PLoS ONE* 11, no. 12 (2016): e0168404; and Rachel Yehuda et al., "The Role of Genes in Defining a Molecular Biology of PTSD," *Disease Markers* 30 (2011): 67–76.

[6]S. Yeshurun and A. J. Hannan, "Transgenerational Epigenetic Influences of Paternal Environmental Exposures on Brain Function and Predisposition to Psychiatric Disorders," *Molecular Psychiatry* (2018): https://doi.org/10.1038/s41380-018-0039-z. See also Elizabeth Rosner, *Survivor Café: The Legacy of Trauma and the Labyrinth of Memory* (Berkeley, CA: Counterpoint, 2017), 7.

[7]A. S. Zannas, N. Provençal, and E. B. Binder, "Epigenetics of Posttraumatic Stress Disorder: Current Evidence, Challenges and Future Directions," *Biological Psychiatry* 78 (2015): 327–35.

[8]Krista Tippett, "Rachel Yehuda: How Trauma and Resilience Cross Generations," *On Being* (July 30, 2015): onbeing.org. For further information on *how* people change, see, for example: T. Y. Kim et al., "Epigenetic Alterations of the *BDNF* Gene in Combat-Related Post-Traumatic Stress Disorder," *Acta Psychiatrica Scandinavica* 135 (2017): 170–79.

[9]Audre Lorde, "A Child Shall Lead," in *The Collected Poems of Audre Lorde*, 23. Used with permission.

[10]Rosner, *Survivor Café*, 4.

[11]Ibid.

[12]Monica Coleman, *Bipolar Faith: A Black Woman's Journey with Depression and Faith* (Minneapolis: Fortress Press, 2016), xviii.

[13]Mayra Rivera, *Poetics of the Flesh* (Durham, NC: Duke University Press, 2015), 12.

[14]Ibid., 121.

[15]Ibid., 119.

[16]Ibid., 130.

[17]Ibid., 154.

[18]Ibid., 155.

[19]Audre Lorde, "Generation," in *The Collected Poems of Audre Lorde*, 17. Used with permission.

[20]Shelly Rambo, *Resurrecting Wounds: Living in the Afterlife of Trauma* (Waco, TX: Baylor University Press, 2017), 10.

[21]Ibid., 36.

[22]Ibid., 8–9.

[23]Ibid., 37.

[24]Ibid., 14.

[25]Audre Lorde, "To a Girl Who Knew What Side Her Bread Was Buttered On," in *The Collected Poems of Audre Lorde*, 13. Used with permission.

[26]Rosner, *Survivor Café*, 9.

[27]Rambo, *Resurrecting Wounds*, 5.

[28]This proposal forms the conclusion to my dissertation and is more fully developed there.

[29]The poor and marginalized are much more likely to experience preventable death and disease, including trauma—see J. S. Seng et al., "Marginalized Identities, Discrimination Burden, and Mental Health: Empirical Exploration of an Interpersonal-Level Approach to Modeling Intersectionality," *Social Science and Medicine* 75, no. 12 (2012): 2437–45.

[30]Phillis I. Sheppard, "Mourning the Loss of Cultural Selfobjects: Black Embodiment and Religious Experience after Trauma," *Practical Theology* 1, no. 2 (2008): 251.

[31]Shelly Rambo, *Sprit and Trauma: A Theology of Remaining* (Louisville, KY: Westminster John Knox Press, 2010), 35.

[32]Rosner, *Survivor Café*, 257.

Sources of Revolution in San Antonio's Westside

Women's Voices and Youth Power

Oswald John Nira

On April 6, 1968, San Antonio, Texas, celebrated its 250th anniversary.[1] Only two days earlier, Martin Luther King Jr. was assassinated in Memphis, Tennessee. The United States was rocked by his assassination; urban unrest and riots raged for days in over 100 cities throughout the country. In San Antonio, however, a 250th-anniversary celebration—HemisFair '68—was about to commence. Years in planning, with a cost of over $150 million, this officially recognized International Exposition was titled "Confluence of Civilizations in the Americas" and marked the initial effort of city leaders to establish San Antonio as a cultural and commercial hub, particularly between North America and South America. So while much of the United States fumed with anger and revolution,[2] San Antonio continued its plans for celebration. Newspapers and other media outlets did not record any civil unrest or riots in San Antonio.[3]

Yet San Antonio was ripe for revolution. A few weeks after the opening of HemisFair '68, a documentary aired on CBS television titled "Hunger in America."[4] This documentary examined San Antonio as one of three communities across the United States that grappled with health and food security issues. It reported that 100,000 of San Antonio's Mexican American citizens—one-quarter of all its Mexican American residents—experienced daily hunger. Most of these citizens resided in Westside San Antonio; Fr. Richard Ruiz, pastor of the Westside Our Lady of Guadalupe

Church, was interviewed.[5] These three 1968 events—the reaction to the assassination of Martin Luther King Jr., the opening of HemisFair '68, and the documentation of abject hunger in Westside San Antonio—shaped San Antonio fifty years ago.[6]

This essay briefly examines the ways the Missionary Catechists of Divine Providence and the Westside San Antonio Youth began to articulate protest and how this protest developed the two communities. Additionally, this essay initiates a theological discussion on the sources of revolution and its relation to theological reflection today, fifty years after calls for change were heard throughout the United States of America.

Missionary Catechists of Divine Providence

In the summer of 1969, the Missionary Catechists of Divine Providence (MCDP) began consideration of a biblical text that encapsulated the spirit and vision of their religious community.[7] The text was Matthew 7:13–14: "Enter through the narrow gate, for the gate is wide and the road is broad, that leads to destruction, and those who enter through it are many. How narrow the gate and constricted the road that leads to life. And those that find it are few." It was suggested by a Sister of Divine Providence (CDP), Sr. Benitia Vermeersch, who first began organizing young Mexican American women in Houston in 1930.[8] At that time, Sr. Benitia's rationale was that such a biblical passage would elicit a positive response from parents and students as to the necessity of biblical and catechetical instruction, instruction for which the MCDPs were trained and zealous to give.

Matthew 7:13–14 elicited strong discussion by the group tasked with initial considerations of the biblical text, the Spirit of the Institute committee. Some referred to the passage as too harsh, too restrictive, and too "gloomy." The committee voted to delete it from consideration. Yet the next day, some committee members took the issue up again, arguing that the passage selected by Sr. Benitia had historical and spiritual value, as it was identified by the first organizing sister as reflecting the spirit and purpose of the first community. A new vote was called for, this time ending in a tie. Through subsequent discussions and votes, at day's end, voting on this issue remained deadlocked. Sr. Elizabeth McCullough, Mother Superior of the Congregation of Divine

Providence, learned of the discussions and deadlocked votes. She attended the MCDP General Assembly held later during Chapter proceedings, expressed her disappointment that she had not been part of previous discussions, and expressed her reluctance to use the text identified by Sr. Benitia almost forty years earlier. According to Sr. McCullough, the biblical text did not carry substantial weight considering the present post–Vatican II times, as these times called for new processes and new methods.[9]

These tensions, and the subsequent actions by the community—to reject Matthew 7:13–14 as their founding and inspirational scriptural passage, and to identify their patroness as Our Lady of Guadalupe—demonstrate CDP leadership, and MCDP acceptance, of a ministry practiced within a specific time and culture. Their rejection of a scriptural passage considered to be too constrictive, especially a passage selected and developed by their founder, Sr. Benitia, reveals an openness to contemporary movements and inspirations. Although research for a selected passage by the 1969 Chapter did not yield a conclusive result, the MCDP current website lists Luke 4:16 as articulating their vision—to take up Jesus' mission to heal, proclaim and liberate.[10] This scripture has a different emphasis from Matthew 7:13–14; whereas the "narrow," "constricted," and "life" terms in Matthew were interpreted as descriptions of catechetical formation and adherence to sacramental and liturgical practice, Luke's passage is driven by mission, directed toward the needs and desires of the people in their midst.

These considerations in the summer of 1969 were discussed one year after the MCDPs initiated a difficult transition toward self-governance as an affiliate order of the CDPs. Transition toward their own leadership was met with dissatisfaction, however, as three members of the MCDP "spoke out" against the superior of the "experimental administration" on New Year's Day 1968, initiating a series of planned reflections and deliberations that extended into the summer. Governance and leadership were the primary contested issues; members expressed their perspectives at the General Assembly in the summer of 1968. These perspectives were sometimes met with silence, sometimes acceptance. Some members left the community after their perspectives elicited no response. Most stayed. Ultimately, the MCDPs solidified establishment of their missionary order, elected new leaders, and developed new guidelines and rules. This experience of self-governance and administration was made possible through the serious reception of the catechists who initially revolted—"spoke out"—as well as the deliberate consideration of structure and mission of the MCDPs.[11]

Following this establishment, the MCDPs were liberated to engage with families and communities of their own culture through their own cultural values and practices. As the MCDPs developed their religious community, they emphasized a formation process drawing from their own experience of growing up in Mexican American families and culture, inclusive of Mexican and Mexican American religious practices and symbols. These developments in their formation and community life relied on their love for and close relationship with the Westside Mexican American communities and their religious practices.[12]

Such developments did not come easily. CDP leaders, who maintained oversight on this filial community, reviewed the new MCDP formation and community rules, and tension arose. For example, just as close familial relations were practiced among Westside Mexican American families, so too did women in MCDP formation develop a rule wherein regular family visits and communication were permitted, and even expected. This rule developed in stark contrast to the formation process of the Congregation of Divine Providence, wherein young women were definitively removed from their family homes and relations; many CDP women recall the stress that occurred during such times of transition.[13] The MCDPs, however, developed their formation process sensitive to the cultural place of family, established among family members throughout the course of these members' lives; religious vocation and vows were not understood as a rejection of family—where the experience of faith had taken root and grown—but as a complement to a continuing process of growth and celebration of faith.[14]

Westside San Antonio Youth

On January 6, 1968, at Kennedy High School on the Westside of San Antonio, La Raza Unida (The United Race) Party was born. Gestated by Mexican Americans living in communities where neighborhood gang warfare and police brutality were common, and public education institutions tended to be underfunded and inattentive, La Raza Unida had founders who structured this political party to develop effective political responses to these problems, utilizing techniques derived from Saul Alinsky's *Rules for Radicals*, Paulo Freire's *Pedagogy of the Oppressed*, and works by similar theorists.[15] Many of the young leaders of La Raza Unida were introduced to these thinkers through Catholic education. From Catholic primary school systems to Catholic higher education, particularly St. Mary's University and Our Lady of the Lake University—both located on the Westside of San Antonio—all were sources of young Mexican American leaders.[16]

The formation of La Raza Unida in San Antonio had a ripple effect across the country. In 1968, students attending East Los Angeles high schools walked out to protest substandard school facilities, inattentive school administrators, and underperforming academic programs. A concerted group of 200 students walked out in March 1968; the number of protesting students grew to approximately 5,000 students across East Los Angeles,[17] inspiring Mexican American families and students across the United States. Public schools in South Texas had similar walkouts, particularly in San Antonio, Crystal City, and Hondo, the school system I attended beginning in 1968. These protests, difficult and confusing as they were at the time, nevertheless had positive effects, especially as school academic programs developed curriculum reflecting underrepresented experiences and histories, and administrators restructured school organizations to be more inclusive of Mexican American individuals. The protests at Our Lady of the Lake University (OLLU) developed into others. On January 8, 1968, OLLU students protested against the Texas Rangers, a law enforcement agency with an established history and practice of vigilantism during the late nineteenth and early twentieth centuries, as Texas property owners endeavored to establish their residency in a land heretofore controlled by Mexican residents and imbued with their civic, religious, and cultural practices.[18]

The Mexican American Catholic Church in San Antonio was also affected by the development of Westside San Antonio Youth leaders. In substantial ways, the Catholic Church of South Texas was taken aback by the Chicano[19] voices calling out the injustices in their lives. Fr. Virgilio Elizondo, a young priest from the Archdiocese of San Antonio, was initially surprised by the frustration expressed by Chicano leaders, sometimes directly accusatory toward the Catholic Church. The protest meetings were volatile. Young leaders proclaimed the church, and indeed all of religion, as oppressive, racist, and sexist—not a community that valued the humanity of all individuals—much less the humanity of Mexican Americans. Fr. Elizondo writes:

> At protest meetings I was told in no uncertain terms, "If you want to be of help, get out of the way. Your church only kept us down by preaching obedience to the *gringo* masters. How do you want to control us now?" It was not easy to take but there was much truth in what they were saying. The serious accusations forced me and many others to take a much deeper and more critical look at the inner functioning of our church and, even deeper yet, of religion itself. . . . For the first time I started to realize that religion, even my own Christian-Catholic religion, could function as a powerful tool of oppression. I was frightened! So many of the things we had dared to say and do "in God's name" all of a sudden appeared scandalous. I started to ask deeper questions about my church, my religion, and about the gospel itself.[20]

Fr. Elizondo's openness to this criticism led to his own self-reflection and constructive reception of many other criticisms. Tensions continued between these young Mexican American leaders and the church, but lines of communication were initiated, signifying the potential for understanding and collaboration.

Bishop Patrick (Patricio) Flores, the "Mariachi Bishop," who invigorated the entire South Texas Catholic community through his priestly and episcopal ordination, is another example of Westside San Antonio Youth leadership's interaction with Catholic ecclesial authority. He also felt the brunt of Chicano leaders calling for change. His installation as bishop in 1970 was cause for great joy; numerous celebrations were held in San Antonio and Houston, with thousands attending. Among the participants proclaiming the readings at the liturgies were Cesar Chavez, leader of the United Farm Workers Union, and José Ángel Gutiérrez, a young leader from San Antonio's Westside and La Raza Unida party.[21] Bishop Flores affirmed the inclusion of young Mexican American revolutionary voices when he was interviewed by local media. He emphasized that these voices gave hope to many

Mexican Americans, instilling within them dignity and a love for their culture. Bishop Flores added that La Raza Unida and other Chicano activist groups were saying "what I should have been saying twenty years ago."[22]

Bishop Patricio Flores traced his faith and leadership roots to Sr. Benitia Vermeersch. When Patricio turned seventeen years old, he announced his desire to become a priest to his local parish priest in Pearland, Texas, a small town outside of Houston; he was met with indifference.[23] The priest asserted that Hispanics were too close to their families to succeed in the solitary life of priesthood; furthermore, the rigors of education were daunting, and other Hispanic individuals interested in the priesthood were not successful. After this disheartening discussion with his local priest, Patricio traveled to the seminary in the Houston-Galveston Archdiocese, only to be told directly that he would not be admitted into the seminary. Two primary reasons were given: the director of the seminary claimed that Patricio did not meet his standards and that the costs were prohibitive for his financial means.

Enter Sr. Benitia, who was in the area conducting catechetical classes to migrant youth. She asked the youth about their interest in the religious life, and young Patricio declared, "Yes, I want to be a priest, but you all don't want me." He told Sr. Benitia of his past interactions with church leaders. She responded, "In the church, you don't start at the bottom, you go straight to the top." Borrowing a Model-A Ford the next day, Sr. Benitia and Patricio traveled to the Diocese of Galveston-Houston and met with Bishop Christopher Byrne to present Patricio's desire to become a priest. They worked out details for Patricio to follow his vocation, as well as a plan for Patricio to return to his studies, since he had dropped out of high school.[24] Sr. Benitia's direct challenge to and affirmation of the young Patricio and the affirmation of Patricio's vocational call by the Bishop of Galveston-Houston shaped Bishop Flores's developing religious vocation and leadership.

Theological Reflection on Revolution

In his illuminative survey of Christian thought, Justo Gonzalez sketches out three models of theology developed by early Christian theologians. These models developed interpretations of the typical theological categories, such as Christ, salvation, and sin. Gonzalez suggests that the model most reflective of marginalized communities is that articulated by Irenaeus of Lyon, wherein God is experienced as a shepherd, rather than as a judge or as abstract truth. The shepherd journeys with people, continually deepens intimacy, and fulfills God's promise of realized love within community. In this model, the burden of the Christian community is in maintaining the freedom to grow and develop communal relationships, rather than adhering to laws set forth by a judgmental God, or contemplating eternal truths revealed by saints, prophets, or mystics.[25] The community members discover themselves, shepherded by a God intimately aware of and concerned for their continued growth in a community of love, justice, and beauty.

The MCDP community and Westside San Antonio Youth image this model developed by Irenaeus. Rather than experiencing the community as one held to a specific set of laws or held to contemplate a set of eternal truths, individuals within this community are bound to one another, to continually discover themselves as individuals and in relation to one another. This continuing discovery calls for responses that further the creation of a community developing in love. On the Westside of San Antonio, revolution found its source and power in the MCDPs, who discovered their voice in expressing their mission and their culture, and in the Westside San Antonio Youth, who discovered their value, gift, and power as they met their community in relation to its challenges.

Theologians, as they develop their theological projects fifty years past the 1968 revolutions in US society and culture, would do well to consider the relevance to their own work of the sources of these revolutions. Jon Sobrino, in his essay "Extra Pauperes Nulla Salus," considers whether Jesus was evangelized by the people he encountered.[26] In Matthew 11:25 and Luke 10:21, Sobrino finds Jesus praising God for bestowing the reception of revelation upon the "childlike." Sobrino then notes several occasions where Jesus underscores the great faith of the poor, found in the hemorrhaging woman, the blind man, the poor widow, and the Canaanite woman. Sobrino ends with a reference to Archbishop—now Saint—Óscar Romero, who noted the ease in pastoring his flock in El Salvador; in Sobrino's words, he felt "blessed by their faith."[27] Although those who call for revolution may not be poor in the same way as those encountered by Jesus and pastored by Archbishop Romero, they speak for the poor and marginalized, reflecting the prophetic tradition and the proclamation of the good news.

Several more recent theologians have structured their work through the revolutionary struggle of the oppressed. María Pilar Aquino's essay on intercultural theology maintains that recognition of rational forms is the key to developing the ecclesial and global community. For her, every community is "loaded with context and culture."[28] The narrative of contemporary experience—received as graced and promised—is to seek other communities, as "they are also voices of reason, manifestations of intellectual autonomy or autochthony. They affirm their right to 'see' things from within their context and culture."[29] In the context of this brief theological reflection, the call for change and revolution in the voices and actions of the MCDPs and Westside San Antonio Youth are graced, and call out for response. What Aquino terms "interdiscursive communication" is a model of historical process, revolutionary at its core and continually open to new life and community.[30]

In his theological reflection on "traditioning," Orlando Espín outlines a framework wherein the voices and experiences of the poor and marginalized are a necessary part of Christian teaching, teaching rooted in the "demonstrated compassion" of individuals and communities that find their example in the rejected, "crucified peasant Jesus."[31] Demonstrated compassion is the sine qua non of the Christian life, which in turn necessarily leads to the building of community, developing a tradition of instruction that does not become "doctrinified" as long as it resists universal applications insensitive to particular contexts.[32] The voices of the Westside San Antonio Youth and the MCDPs exemplify responses to encounters with the rejected and marginalized.

These reflections lead to an understanding that challenges to established norms of institutions and life are critical to the continuing renewal of relationships and community. The revolutionary fervor on the Westside of San Antonio reached a fever pitch in the late 1960s. Years of inattention to the poor and marginalized developed an environment ripe for revolution. The current, broken US immigration policy, wherein many of the forcibly separated families may never be reunified, similarly calls for voices of the migrant and immigrant to be heard, since their experience reveals the will of God through Jesus: compassion toward all. The leaders in the Westside San Antonio communities then, and refugee populations around the world now, lift their voices and provide steps toward the revolutionary change that will strengthen community and continue the Christian tradition of faith, hope, and love.

Notes

[1] "HemisFair '68" at https://tshaonline.org/handbook.

[2] Over 100 US cities rioted or engaged in civil unrest from April 4–8, 1968. See Peter Levy, *The Great Uprising: Race Riots in Urban America in the 1960s* (Cambridge: Cambridge University Press, 2018), 153–88; Clay Risen, *A Nation on Fire: America in the Wake of the King Assassination* (Hoboken, NJ: John Wiley & Sons, 2009).

[3] Over 6 million individuals visited HemisFair, yet the event lost $7 million. *Handbook of Texas Online*, Frank Duane, "HemisFair '68," accessed March 9, 2018, www.tshaonline.org.

[4] "Hunger in America," CBS Documentary, 1968, www.youtube.com.

[5] Fr. Ruiz's interview begins at 4:30 in the documentary "Hunger in America."

[6] San Antonio's history is filled with revolution and conflict. Along with the Battle of the Alamo (1836), the Battle of Medina (the largest battle on Texas soil, wherein approximately 1,500 individuals lost their lives in 1813 to a militia loyal to the Spanish crown; battle leaders engaged twenty miles south of San Antonio so that the city itself would incur as little damage as possible) characterizes San Antonio as a locality saturated with conflict. For an outline and introductory references to military conflicts in San Antonio, see the Texas Historical Association Handbook Online at www.tshaonline.org.

[7] The order of the MCDPs began through the efforts of Sr. Benitia Vermeersch in 1930s Houston. Sr. Benitia herself was a member of the Congregation of Divine Providence, a French Catholic order that settled in Texas in the last half of the nineteenth century at the behest of Bishop Claude Dubuis.

[8] Read Sr. Benitia Vermeersch's biography in Sr. Mary Paul Valdez, *History of the Missionary Catechists of Divine Providence* (San Antonio: Missionary Catechists of Divine Providence, 1978), 173–89. Sr. Benitia, as a member of the Congregation of Divine Providence (CDP), sponsored and nurtured the MCDPs consisting of Mexican American women in Houston and San Antonio; she reflects concern for and openness toward women and communities from different cultures. Her example would positively affect her religious community, the CDPs, in relation to service toward and integration with the Mexican American community. See Sr. Christine Morkovsky, *Living in God's Providence: History of the Congregation of Divine Providence of San Anto-*

nio, Texas, 1943–2000 (Bloomington, IN: Xlibris, 2009), Chapters 1–3, 5.

⁹Valdez, *History of the Missionary Catechists of Divine Providence*, 56.

¹⁰Luke 4:16 begins the passage wherein Jesus reads from prophet Isaiah in the synagogue, only to be driven out of town.

¹¹Valdez, *History of the Missionary Catechists of Divine Providence*, 82–85.

¹²Stephen Privett, SJ, *The US Catholic Church and Its Hispanic Members: The Pastoral Vision of Robert E. Lucey* (San Antonio: Trinity University Press, 1988), 132.

¹³Morkovsky, *Living in God's Providence*, 23.

¹⁴Valdez, *History of the Missionary Catechists of Divine Providence*, 124–30.

¹⁵David Montejano, *Quixote's Soldiers: A Local History of the Chicano Movement, 1966–1981* (Austin: University of Texas Press, 2010), 60–61.

¹⁶Ibid., 24.

¹⁷"Walkout: The True Story of the Historic 1968 Chicano Student Walkout in East L.A.," retrieved May 2, 2018, democracynow.org.

¹⁸Montejano, *Quixote's Soldiers*, 82.

¹⁹The meaning of the words Chicano, Mexican American, Latino/a/x has been widely discussed. I use "Chicano" to refer to a specific time of USA history referred to as *El Movimiento*, wherein Mexican American leaders reclaimed a cultural and historical awareness of their origins and purpose, and enacted political power. See Luis D. León, *The Political Spirituality of Cesar Chavez: Crossing Religious Borders* (Oakland: University of California Press, 2014).

²⁰Virgilio Elizondo, *The Future Is Mestizo: Life Where Cultures Meet* (Boulder: University Press of Colorado, 2000), 38.

²¹Martin McMurtrey, *Mariachi Bishop: The Life Story of Patrick Flores* (San Antonio: Corona, 1988), 71–76.

²²Ibid., 81.

²³Ibid., 31.

²⁴Ibid., 36–38.

²⁵Justo Gonzalez, *Christian Thought Revisited: Three Types of Theology* (Maryknoll, NY: Orbis Books, 1999), 59, 143–45.

²⁶Jon Sobrino, SJ, *No Salvation Outside the Poor: Prophetic-Utopian Essays* (Maryknoll, NY: Orbis Books, 2008), 54–55.

²⁷Ibid.

²⁸María Pilar Aquino, "Theological Method in U.S. Latino/a Theology: Toward an Intercultural Theology for the Third Millennium," in *From the Heart of Our People: Latino/a Explorations in Catholic Systematic Theology* (Maryknoll, NY: Orbis Books, 1999), 10. Here Aquino is quoting Raúl Fornet-Betancourt, *Hacia una filosofía intercultural latinoamericana* (San José, Costa Rica: Departamento Ecuménico de Investigaciones, 1999), 20.

²⁹Ibid.

³⁰Ibid., 11.

³¹Orlando Espín, *Idol & Grace: On Traditioning and Subversive Hope* (Maryknoll, NY: Orbis Books, 2014), 130–32.

³²Ibid.

Teaching Comparative Theology
after Charlottesville

Tracy Sayuki Tiemeier

The United States has made great strides in appreciating diversity in religion since the Immigration and Nationality Act of 1965 ended a discriminatory quota system that limited immigration by national origin. However, religiously, racially, and/or ethnically motivated violence is growing.[1] Comparative theology, in its particular attention to encounter with religious others, has revolutionary possibilities for building interreligious understanding and social justice. Such possibilities necessitate more careful attention in the field of comparative theology to the relationship between religion and race.

This became clear in a public way with the convergence of religious intolerance and racism at the Unite the Right rally in Charlottesville, Virginia, on August 12, 2017. The rally, ostensibly held to oppose the removal of a statue of Robert E. Lee, brought white nationalism and white supremacists to the national stage. During the rally, protesters chanted racist and anti-Jewish slogans, such as "Jews will not replace us." Indeed, racism and religious intolerance have been entangled throughout Christian history. As a result, a revolutionary comparative theology must contend with racism and religious intolerance, especially in the classroom, even as many students signing up for a course in comparative theology generally see themselves as open-minded people who are appalled by Unite the Right. However, students rarely understand the extent to which they may have problematic assumptions about race and religion. When instructors attempt to deconstruct those assumptions, students can become defensive. We therefore need deliberate strategies for targeting deeply held assumptions in productive ways. In this essay, I focus on the ways in which the imaginary worlds of speculative fiction can be an effective strategy for approaching the very real, very volatile intersection of race and religion comparatively. By shifting imaginations, and by offering possibilities for students to develop multireligious, multiracial theological imaginations, the comparative theological classroom can become a revolutionary space to educate for religious and social justice.

Anti-Judaism, Racism, and Comparative Theology

J. Kameron Carter, in *Race: A Theological Account*, argues convincingly that "modernity's racial imagination has its genesis in the theological problem of Christianity's quest to sever itself from its Jewish roots."[2] The Christian supersessionist articulation of a "new" covenant, through the person of Jesus, which supplants the "old" covenant with the Jewish people, creates a theological framework that has been used to justify the othering and oppression of entire peoples. Although the dynamic of anti-Jewish oppression and violence is seen throughout Christian history, a new racialized form emerges in the development of Western modernity.

Indeed, the project of modernity is a complex, interdependent convergence of scholarship, politics, and race.[3] Early modern European philosophy, theology, and anthropology portrayed Jews as a racial group separate from Western Christians. In this portrayal, Jews became the paradigmatic "other" against which the Christian West was understood.[4] This racialized definition and exclusion became "the condition of possibility for the expulsion of all others."[5] Thus, the entanglement of racism and anti-Judaism was fundamental to the West and Western Christian identity. It became the justification for the colonization of "new" worlds as well as the domination of anyone conceived of as "other."[6] Carter argues that the foundation of the racial imagination is found in downplaying or denying the Jewishness of Jesus and constructing a Christianity separate from and triumphant over Judaism. Christianity then becomes racist when racialized prejudice becomes embedded in a system of oppression. As a result, racial justice requires more than anti-racist language and work; it also requires "a new theological imagination . . . that sutures the gap between Christianity and its Jewish roots and thereby reimagines Christian . . . identity."[7]

Since the racist imagination emerges through, is entangled with, and is justified by a theological mind-set, theology cannot be dismissed from contemporary debates about racism and racial justice. A revolutionary Christian theology that seeks racial justice must tackle both religious and racial injustice, embracing a Christology of "Jewish covenantal flesh" rather than that of "Jewish racial flesh."[8] However, it is not enough to challenge the notion of the Jewish people as racialized "other." A Jewish, covenantal Jesus could still enable a problematic supersessionism whereby Christianity *replaces* Judaism. Christians must consistently affirm that the divine covenant with the Jewish people remains intact; it is ongoing, dynamic, and distinct from Christianity, and from Christianity's regard for Jesus.

In the process of rooting out anti-Judaism, dialogue between Jews and Christians is essential. Since the Western roots of racism lie in Christian supersessionism, Willie James Jennings asserts that Jewish and Christian dialogue cannot lose sight of racism.[9] Dialogue between Jews and Christians must be accompanied by attention to racialization and the intertwining of racism and anti-Judaism in the Western imagination.[10] Racism and anti-Judaism have been tied together, and they must be addressed together.

Interreligious work more broadly is also entangled in a structure of racialization and white Christian domination. Concepts of religion, activities of comparison, and forms of dialogue developed in a Western Christian framework based on an imaginary racialized Jewish "other." Thus, the approaches taken and questions asked in interreligious dialogue and comparative theology are not immune to this totalizing framework simply because they seek to encounter religious others in a deep way. A revolutionary comparative theological imagination must be both interreligious and critically conscious;[11] it must employ anti-racist and anti-supersessionist strategies that self-consciously decenter the white Western Christian body and deconstruct religious categories that privilege Christian ideas of religion, belief, and practice—such as, for example, a definition of "religion" that requires a deity, a savior, or a book.

The problem of Christian dominance in comparative theology has not been consistently ignored in scholarship and practice. It is a constant anxiety, even obsession, for those of us engaged in comparative and interreligious work.[12] But the extent to which that work is entangled in an implicit Christian supersessionism and an underlying racial imagination must be taken more seriously. Even if it is not visibly apparent, Christian domination and racism are intertwined and embedded deep within the comparative theological project. Without constant and explicit attention to the insidious hold of racism and anti-Judaism, comparative theology cannot be a revolutionary force for justice and will simply reinforce white Western Christianity.

Developing a New Theological Imagination through the Comparative Theology Classroom

How might a college course in comparative theology attend to the interlocking realities of race and Christian domination, as well as promote a revolutionary theological imagination that can help build a racially and religiously just world? My early approaches to the comparative theology classroom had been intersectional, emphasizing how the interaction between traditions and persons has been complex across time, cultures, and religions. An intersectional framework allowed me to discuss the ways in which borders are fluid, power dynamics are multifaceted, and religions themselves are not singular or self-contained.[13] However, I struggled with the extent to which students clung to problematic notions of religion. Religious texts and practices were evaluated uncritically and through white Western Christian assumptions. Even students of color, Jewish students, female students, multireligious students, and "nones" often demonstrated worldviews dominated by white Western Christian perspectives. J. Kameron Carter and Willie James Jennings help diagnose the problem: students should first *deconstruct* the entangled racial and anti-Jewish assumptions often operating within them and embedded at the core of Western culture.

Brian Bantum's notion of Jesus Christ as mulatto, or racially mixed, provides space to explore the problem of examining anti-Judaism and racism together in the classroom. Bantum argues that the hybridity of Jesus as human and divine is like the hybridity of the multiracial person: "Christ's existence is the mulattic assertion of utter difference inhered within one person. In Christ this inherence, this hybridity, is not tragic, but rather the tragic is overcome."[14] Bantum does not specifically address Jesus's Jewishness or anti-Judaism. But his image is instructive, for it is a theological affirmation of multiplicity that also attends to the realities of racism. Supersessionism and the racist imagination can be frustrated by the insistence that Jesus was himself a divine-human "mulatto." To imagine a mulatto Jesus is not to say that there is a "melting pot" or "mixture" that dilutes divinity and humanity, body and spirit, Jew and Gentile, black and white. Instead, "It is the fullness of each bound to one another, but without division or confusion or dilution."[15] In the theological affirmation of multiplicity, the mulatto Jesus disrupts both racism and supersessionism. If Jesus is multiple, then multiplicity itself—racial, religious, and otherwise—is rendered holy; this offers a foundation for a renewed Christian theological imagination.

I developed a comparative theology course in light of this multiracial image called "Sacred, Sinister, Strange," which emphasizes the disruptive realities and revolutionary possibilities of multireligious, multiracial "monstrosities." This upper division course examines the ways in which the alien, monstrous, and divine "Other" often functions to map, define, control, engage, host, and/or construct religious, racial, and gendered others. The course discusses the implications of those portrayals for an ethics of encounter and the subversive power between and among religions. The course intends to help students, whether or not they belong to a confessional religion, develop a revolutionary comparative theological imagination equipped to build a more just world.

In order to engage students in questions of theology and race, I must help them avoid becoming defensive or shutting down. Creating a space for inclusion and a revolutionary imagination for comparative work is enabled by speculative source material, such as science fiction, fantasy and horror novels, comic books, and films from around the world, authored primarily by women artists and artists of color. Most assigned sources feature multiracial or multireligious characters or persons; some, like Helen Oyeyemi's

The Icarus Girl[16] are both multiracial and multireligious. Many sources tackle the violence that may occur in encounter, such as Nnedi Okorafor's Afro-futurist novella *Binti*,[17] in which the main character, of the Himba people indigenous to northern Namibia, is taken without her consent and made into an alien-human hybrid.

A number of these speculative sources feature fictional religions. Marjorie Liu and Sana Takeda's groundbreaking comic *Monstress*,[18] for example, features an elaborate world of religions practiced by humans, animals, monsters, and hybrids. Even sources that are rooted in one culture or one religious tradition, such as G. Willow Wilson's Islamic cyber fantasy *Alif the Unseen*,[19] examine the sacred in fluid and multiple ways, disrupting notions of culture, religion, and race through surreal characters, settings, and narratives while refusing to neglect the brutal realities of racial and religious domination.

Two key sources allow the class to address the relationship between anti-Judaism and racism: Mary Doria Russell's "Jesuits in space" novel, *The Sparrow,* and Octavia Butler's Afro-futurist dystopian novel *Parable of the Sower*. Because of the fantastical settings, students can explore serious issues without feeling attacked and defensive, without falling into media sound bites or stereotypes, or devolving into political partisanship. Speculative worlds shift students' imaginations and allow them to analyze race and religion from an altered perspective.

The Sparrow follows the character of the brilliant mestizo Puerto Rican Jesuit linguist Emilio Sandoz, a group of Jesuits and lay people, and a Jewish woman, Sofia Mendes, as they make first contact with two groups of aliens on the planet Rakhat. Their mission is noble in its intention—the Society of Jesus and the rest of the group simply hope to meet these alien "children of God"—but the story ends in tragedy. Over the course of the novel, characters contend with the brutal history of Christian missionaries. The character Sofia Mendes is herself a survivor of sexual violence, trafficking, and indentured servitude; she wrestles with whether she is willing to work with the Jesuits in their mission to Rakhat. The Jesuits, eager to avoid the evangelizing sins of their past, have no intention to proselytize in this setting; rather, they attempt to atone for their violent history of missions in an attempt to "do it right" this time, with alien worlds. But, once again, a Christian mission leads to mass destruction, death, and near extinction.

As the class works through *The Sparrow*, students are tempted to focus only on the violence done to Emilio Sandoz and his struggle with faith. But the character of Sofia Mendes challenges Sandoz, his faith, and Christianity. Indeed, Mary Doria Russell's own religious story is complicated. She grew up Catholic in a mixed Congregationalist and Catholic home. Although she became an atheist, she was moved to convert to Judaism as she wrote *The Sparrow*.[20] The author's own growing engagement with Judaism can be seen in her construction of Mendes's character, as well as with her positioning of Sandoz and Mendes in parallel journeys of violence and faith. This becomes even clearer in the book's sequel, *Children of God*.

Problems of suffering and divine inaction in the face of suffering are left unresolved in these novels. But the end of *The Sparrow* employs a comparative example that provides the class with a way to consider the meaning of suffering, the possibility of divine work in the world, and the relationship between Judaism and Christianity. In the novel, Felipe Reyes, a disabled Puerto Rican Jesuit, is introduced to debrief Sandoz the lone survivor of the failed mission. He reflects with the character of the Jesuit Father General, Vincenzo Giuliani, and with John Candotti, Emilio Sandoz's appointed Jesuit confessor. Reyes says,

> "There's an old Jewish story that says in the beginning God was everywhere and everything, a totality. But to make creation, God had to remove Himself from some part of the universe, so something besides Himself could exist. So He breathed in, and in the places where God withdrew, there creation exists." "So God just leaves?" John asked, angry where Emilio had been desolate. "Abandons creation? You're on your own, apes. Good luck!" "No. He watches. He rejoices. He weeps. He observes the moral drama of human life and gives meaning to it by caring passionately about us, and remembering." "Matthew ten, verse twenty-nine," Vincenzo Giuliani said quietly. "'Not one sparrow can fall to the ground without your Father knowing it.'" "But the sparrow still falls," Felipe said.[21]

The Jewish commandment to remember (*zakhor*) becomes a hermeneutical key for *The Sparrow*. Prior to our examination of this novel, the class had analyzed Jewish "monster narratives" to glean their religious and social significance. These narratives are prevalent throughout Jewish history, in stories about the golem of Prague, an animated clay being created to protect Prague Jews from anti-Jewish attacks. Students had also studied the anti-Jewish narratives constructed by Christians, in order to understand how they sanction Christian violence against Jews, such as *The Life and Miracles of St. William of Norwich*. Examining these stories highlights how narrative interacts with reality; examining the history of these stories prepared the class to understand more deeply what *zakhor* means for the Jewish people. *Zakhor* is used in the commandment to keep Shabbat; it is also now used in articulating the importance of remembering the Shoah (Holocaust). *Zakhor* is sacred, participative, and collective: at once the practice of both ritual and ethics.

The emphasis on Judaism and *zakhor* in *The Sparrow* is poignant, with the subtext Christianity's history of anti-Judaism and violent mission. Russell's developing conversion to Judaism makes the use of *zakhor* a powerful indictment of Jesuit overoptimism and Christian theologies of glorified suffering, salvation, and divinely directed missions. There is no easy resolution offered in the novel, which is deeply unsettling for many of my Christian students. Rather than try to defuse the discomfort, I encourage students to stay with it, so that it may haunt their own spiritual quest in a way that can combat creeping presumptions of Christian supremacy.

The Sparrow is a unique way for the class to learn about Jewish faith and practice as well as Christian racializing through underlying issues raised in the novel's treatment of Sandoz's mestizo identity and Mendes's Sephardic Jewish identity. Octavia Butler's *Parable of the Sower*, however, examines more explicitly the relationships among religion, power, and race. The main character, Lauren Olamina, is a black teenager living in a near-future dystopia caused by a collapse of American society in the wake of climate change. She struggles with hyperempathy syndrome and so is debilitated by the pleasure and pain of those around her. She senses herself in a vast nondual web of life and death and develops a new religion called "Earthseed." Rejecting the religion of her father, a Baptist minister, as well as problematic concepts of an external savior or of vertical, unilateral power, Lauren writes her own scriptural text, "Earthseed: The Books of the Living": "All that you touch you Change. All that you Change Changes you. The only lasting truth is Change. God is Change."[22] Later, the character writes, "We do not worship God. We perceive and attend God. We learn from God. With forethought and work, We shape God. In the end, we yield to God. We adapt and endure, For we are Earthseed and God is Change."[23] The religion of Earthseed privileges empathy, resilience, community, and strength of the vulnerable through cooperation. As a pioneer in Afro-futurism, Octavia Butler retrieves African ways of being in a cosmic web of life and challenges many white, as well as black, Christian assumptions about religion, spirituality, and liberation.

In the novel, the Earthseed community is resilient and inclusive, full of people others would see as a liability: people of color, women, the elderly, children, disabled people, and escaped slaves. Together, they form a community that survives and thrives. Lauren Olamina condemns Christian passivity and naïveté. Any external savior is portrayed as problematic, a relinquishing of one's freedom, agency, and inner divinity to another. Instead, power is conceived as radically horizontal, an interconnected matrix of life, death, change, and resilience. Although Lauren herself rejects Christianity, there are many symbols and elements from the Hebrew Bible that remain. For example, the group's journey from a gated community in Southern California to a farm in Northern California and then to their destination in space reads like the people of Israel's journey to the Promised Land. Though Lauren Olamina is no savior, she is very much a prophet. As with much of Black Christian religious thought and practice, the Hebrew Bible is central to the story of Earthseed. But there is no Christ in the novel, no singular savior. This decentering of Christ or saviorism allows our class to decenter Christianity, and then to bring together Jewish history and experience with black history and experience. The novel thus alludes to the parallel journeys of Jewish and black peoples, which allows the class to imagine racial liberation and religious liberation together, but without reducing one to the other.

At this point in the course, I introduce videos and images from the August 2017 Charlottesville protests as well as other recent white nationalist statements on immigration, Judaism, and people of color. Contemporary media and rhetorical analyses concretize the ways in which racism and anti-Judaism often converge, and how deliberate deconstruction of both is necessary for social justice. After reading *The Parable of the Sower*, students are more receptive to these contemporary analyses, even when students realize they may have internalized deeply problematic assumptions of race and religion.

At the end of the unit, I ask students whether they think Octavia Butler actually rejects Christianity or whether she rejects *white* Western Christianity. Most students conclude that Butler does not reject Christianity, even though they are aware that Butler herself grew up in a Baptist home but left Christianity at a young age, as Lauren Olamina does in the novel.[24] For these students, Butler promotes a just, multiracial, and inclusive vision of Christianity. The students interpret the book's title, *Parable of the Sower*, as indicating some interest in retrieving Christianity because it refers to Matthew 13. Earthseed also seems to incorporate Christian elements: it even has a familiar missional impulse. But despite the novel's title and the title of its sequel, *Parable of the Talents*, Butler's intention is to reveal that there are fundamental and structural problems with Christianity. In Butler's work, any kind of retrieval of Christianity is a Christianity radically deconstructed and re-visioned. Butler's imagination provides a horizontal Christianity of divine immanence without a singular universal savior or Christ. If there is any kind of Christ figure for Butler, it is less as an external savior for a privileged few and more as a prophet who emerges from within the oppressed and marginalized. This prophet, Jesus, is more in line with the Jewish prophetic tradition, a tradition that Lauren Olamina herself embodies in the novels, calling for justice without saviorism.

Mary Doria Russell and Octavia Butler both work to decenter the place Christianity holds in Western history through their narratives. Their own theological visions shifted and developed through their process of creating novels, and they used science fiction to imagine themselves and the world anew. These works, as well as the other speculative fiction we read, are invitations for students to develop their own theological imagination, whether they are committed to a particular faith tradition or not. Developing an expansive, multiracial, and multireligious imagination is necessary if they hope to build a truly just world.

We live in a time in which xenophobia, intolerance, and violence against black and brown bodies are everyday occurrences, and many think that these are compatible with Christian faith. Transforming these realities requires targeting the foundational thinking that allowed Charlottesville to happen. Anti-racist activism is important, but it is not enough; interreligious dialogue and comparative theology are important, but they are not enough. Rooting out anti-Judaism must be the task of all Christian theologians, not just the ones working in Jewish and Christian dialogue. Rooting out racism must be taken up by all Christian theologians, not just the ones working on race theory. Supersessionism and the racist theological imagination must be dismantled systematically in favor of a new multireligious and multiracial imagination. Using science and fantasy fiction is one of many possible approaches to reforming the theological imagination. If we hope for comparative theology to be revolutionary as well as relevant in the future, we must rethink our pedagogical approaches and find new ways to practice and teach comparative theology in the future.

Notes

[1]See Katayoun Kishi, "Assaults against Muslims in US Surpass 2001 Level," Fact Tank (Pew Research Center), November 15, 2017, www.pewresearch.org; Jenny J. Chen, "First-Ever Tracker of Hate Crimes against Asian-Americans Launched," Code Switch (NPR), February 17, 2017, www.npr.org.

[2]J. Kameron Carter, *Race: A Theological Account* (Oxford: Oxford University Press, 2008), 4.

[3]See Theodore Vial, *Modern Religion, Modern Race* (New York: Oxford University Press, 2016).

[4]Carter, *Race: A Theological Account*, 4.

[5]Ibid.

[6]Ibid., 200.

[7]Ibid., 4.

[8]Ibid., 8.

[9]Willie James Jennings, *The Christian Imagination: Theology and the Origins of Race* (New Haven, CT: Yale University Press, 2010), 275.

[10]Ibid., 285–86.

[11]For an explanation of critical consciousness, see Paulo Freire, *Pedagogy of the Oppressed*, 30th anniversary ed., trans. Myra Bergman Ramos (New York: Continuum, 2000).

[12]See Francis X. Clooney, SJ, ed., *The New Comparative Theology: Interreligious Insights from the Next Generation* (New York: T&T Clark, 2010); Hugh Nicholson, *Comparative Theology and the Problem of Religious Rivalry* (New York: Oxford University Press, 2011).

[13]Tracy Sayuki Tiemeier, "Comparative Theology at the Intersections of (Multi)Racial and (Multi)Religious Boundaries," in *Comparative Theology in the Millennial Classroom: Hybrid Identities, Negotiated Boundaries*, ed. Mara Brecht and Reid Locklin (New York: Routledge, 2016), 75–84.

[14]Brian Bantum, *Redeeming Mulatto: A Theology of Race and Christian Hybridity* (Waco, TX: Baylor University Press, 2010), 108–9.

[15]Ibid., 108.

[16]Helen Oyeyemi, *The Icarus Girl* (New York: Anchor Books, 2006).

[17]Nnedi Okorafor, *Binti* (New York: Tor.com, 2015).

[18]Marjorie Liu and Sana Takeda, *Monstress*, vol. 1 (Berkeley, CA: Image Comics, 2016).

[19]G. Willow Wilson, *Alif the Unseen* (New York: Grove Press, 2012).

[20]Mary Doria Russell, "The Novelist as God," interview by Krista Tippett, The On Being Project, August 20, 2009, audio, 52:08, https://onbeing.org.

[21]Mary Doria Russell, *The Sparrow*, 20th anniversary ed. (New York: Ballantine, 2016), 478–79.

[22]Octavia E. Butler, *Parable of the Sower* (New York: Grand Central Publishing, 1993), 3.

[23]Ibid., 17.

[24]Christian Coleman, "Our Eyes Weren't Watching God: The Empathetic Secular Vision of Octavia Butler," Beacon Broadside (Beacon Press), June 22, 2017, www.beaconbroadside.com.

PART II

SEX, FAMILIES, AND REVOLUTION

Sex, Gender, and Revolution

Where Was Theology?

Julie Hanlon Rubio

We have been called together to think about 1968–2018 "in theological perspective." When I was invited to deliver one of the plenaries for the College Theology Society's annual convention, my first question was, "Do I have to talk about *Humanae Vitae*?" As an ethicist who specializes in family, sex, and gender, I assumed this would be my charge. "Well," our fearless organizers assured me, "you don't have to focus on it, but you will say something about it, right?" Of course I will. Because we cannot gather as Catholic theologians at a conference focusing on 1968 and *not* talk about it, even when there is so much more to talk about. So I will leave aside, for the most part, war and peace, race and the civil rights movement, the Yippies and social protest, in order to do what moral theologians do best: talk about sex.

Some may wonder, "Why are we doing this? Why focus on 'pelvic issues' instead of social ethics and politics?" But by the end of my remarks today, I hope I will have made a compelling case that paying attention to Catholic conversations about sex in 1968 is important because these conversations are revelatory of Catholic thinking not only about sex, but about family, gender, and social justice. By attending to the larger context of developments in sexual ethics in the 1960s, we can better appreciate and perhaps recover the distinctively Catholic revolution of those times. In this moment, when we as a culture struggle to respond to the #MeToo movement that includes not only the Harvey Weinsteins but the pervasiveness of "bad sex," we may need wisdom from elsewhere.[1] Clearly, we as a culture, we as a church, do not have sex or justice figured out. Perhaps theology from the 1968 revolution has something to tell us.

One caveat: I started out thinking about this topic by asking the question, "Where was theology in 1968?" I quickly realized that I could not tell the story I wanted to tell without a broad definition of theology. I did not want to speak only of the major theological players, almost all of whom happen to be white, celibate men. Instead, I will ask what feminist theologians Mary Daly, Elizabeth Farians, and Rosemary Radford Ruether were saying. I will consider female Catholic activists and intellectuals who were not trained as theologians but nonetheless contributed to the theological conversation about sex, family, and gender. With this broad definition of theology in hand, I will begin with sex and the infamous encyclical of 1968, before moving to gender and family, with the aim of recovering the wisdom of the Catholic revolutions of 1968.

Sexual Revolution

Prior to the Second Vatican Council, some prominent Catholic theologians, including Bernhard Häring, Edward Schillebeeckx, and Louis Janssens, had begun questioning the official teaching against contraception, while others, notably Cardinal Suenens, Josef Fuchs, and John Ford, upheld the traditional view, filling the pages of academic journals of the time.[2] Catholic physician John Rock had developed the birth control pill, and this seemed to open up new possibilities as the suppression of ovulation might be viewed differently from the physical interruption of the procreative potential of what was then called "the sexual act" or even "the marital act," as if there were only one.[3] Rosemary Ruether "created a sensation when the *Saturday Evening Post* published her article "Speaking Out: A Catholic Mother Tells Why I Believe in Birth Control.' "[4] Catholic married couples were also discussing the issue in parish basements, kitchens, and the pages of *Commonweal* and the *National Catholic Reporter*.

Looking back, it seems that this multilayered conversation about sex is the most significant legacy of *Humanae Vitae*. The papal birth control commission was convened to study the possibility of a change in Catholic teaching on contraception. It started as a group of six men, most of them scientists, and eventually expanded to include over sixty members, including four women, which is significant even in comparison to the most recent synod on the family.

In *Turning Point: The Inside Story of the Papal Birth Control Commission*, Robert McClory details the crucial roles played by Pat and Patty Crowley, a Catholic couple from Chicago, whose testimony was influential in pushing the majority of the commission toward acceptance of artificial birth control. Initially, the Crowleys did an informal survey of the membership of the group they created and led: the Christian Family Movement (CFM—a network of small groups of couples who met twice monthly in their homes to apply the "See, Judge, Act" method of ethical discernment to their communities). Previously, CFM had taken an anti–birth control position. The Crowleys were staggered to find that "even the most dedicated, committed Catholics are deeply troubled by this problem."[5] Frustrated users of the rhythm method testified in their letters that the method "seriously endangered [their] chastity," "[made them] obsessed with sex throughout the month," and allowed them to show only "guarded affection" in fertile times.[6] The Crowleys urged the commission to allow married couples to decide for themselves when sex was appropriate, taking account of all relevant dimensions of their sexual relationship and their married life.[7] According to Patty Crowley, at the end of the commission's third meeting in 1964, Pope Paul VI urged the group to "continue its deliberations, listen to the anxiety of so many souls, and work diligently without worrying about criticism or difficulties."[8]

The Crowleys returned to the next meeting of the commission with a more systematic survey of over three thousand couples in eighteen countries that was to have an even greater effect. Though most couples said the rhythm method worked well enough, and 64 percent said it helped them grow in self-sacrificial love, 78 percent believed that it was harmful to their marriage.[9] The Crowleys' surveys, which were complemented by similar studies from Europe and Australia, significantly influenced members of the commission.[10] When a straw vote was taken among the nineteen theologians of the group at the commission's final meeting, fifteen agreed that contraception was not intrinsically evil.[11]

Commission members then asked the women to speak of their experience, and they did. Imagine this moment. Theologians used to arguing in all-male lecture halls, seminar rooms, conference venues, and academic journals, allowed another potential source of wisdom into the room at the invitation of a pope in order to consider whether a long-held Catholic moral teaching needed to change. Patty Crowley testified to the negative psychological effects of rhythm, to the testimony of married couples that it did not foster married love or unity, to their belief that it felt unnatural.[12] She and others on the commission hoped their testimony would lead to change.

Around the same time, Sally Cunneen, a founding editor of *Cross Currents*, published a book called *Sex: Female; Religion: Catholic*, which corroborated the findings of the Crowleys. Cunneen surveyed over 1,500 Catholic women about their hopes and concerns. Although only a minority of priests and women religious told Cunneen they thought the teaching on birth control should change (they were more likely to counsel "sacrifice or self-control"), most single and married women and men argued for change, because they believed sex was important for a loving marriage, and because they had seen and experienced suffering, marital breakdown, and the difficulties of caring for very large families.[13]

Even though Paul VI did not respond to the growing consensus among Catholics by offering the faithful the change they sought, the conversation that started well before 1968 was not stopped by his encyclical. It continued in the pages of academic journals, among male theologians, concentrating on natural law arguments, the authority of the documents, and pastoral adaptations, including the recently revived "gradualism."[14] Catholic University professor Charles Curran authored a dissenting letter that was signed by over six hundred Catholic scholars within a few weeks.[15] Many moral theologians wrote articles developing the idea of totality[16] or showing the legitimacy of dissent from non-authoritative specific magisterial moral teachings.[17] This is all widely known.

But the theological conversation also continued among the laity, with a focus on the experience of married couples and the absolute seriousness of resolving the issue for the sake of their marriages. *National Catholic Reporter* played a key role in continuing that conversation. In 1967, *NCR* was already in the thick of the controversy, taking heat from the local bishop for "causing confusion," but holding firm because, according to the editors, "resolution of the birth control issue is the single most important problem of the church, and readers have a legitimate interest in developments relating to this question."[18] Documents from the papal birth control commission were leaked to two news organizations, *Le Monde* and *NCR*. They were sent in unmarked packets lacking a return address. Both papers started to translate the documents and agreed to a release date, but *Le Monde* waited an extra day, so *NCR* ended up breaking the story to the world. In 1967 and 1968, *NCR* continued to report on the story, despite criticism. For covering the birth control debate, along with other sex and gender issues, the local bishop condemned the newspaper in October of 1968.[19] Editor Bob Hoyt responded in a lengthy editorial, claiming that though cut off from above, *NCR* "intend[s] to go on being a Catholic paper, concerned with Catholic activities, values and ideas, trying also to be present to the world."[20] Their reporting about the birth control commission contributed to the ongoing conversation about sexual ethics among lay Catholics.

Meanwhile, the Crowleys, along with the other US lay members of the commission, publicly urged couples to follow their consciences.[21] Lay people who had been in conversation at the Vatican at the center of things were now speaking directly to their fellow lay Catholics and expressing their hopes for "a more positive pedagogy on marriage" to replace what they saw as negative and harmful counsel.[22] Sally Cunneen's research showed that in the mid-1960s, the majority of Catholics were using rhythm and would go on doing so while hoping for the teaching to change, often seeking confession in the meantime, but gradually, attitudes began to shift.[23] The majority of American Catholics stopped using the rhythm method, and most came to believe they should be permitted to make their own decisions about family planning.[24]

Lay Catholics were not necessarily swayed by theologians as much as by popular books on sexuality, literature, art, and their own experience. In Cunneen's study, Catholic respondents were presented with a question asking for their thoughts on the attempts of a "famous theologian" (Bernhard Häring) to provide subtle natural law argumentation for contraception.[25] They were not impressed. For most respondents, the issue was far less complicated: contraception was necessary to marital love and parental responsibility.[26] Catholic lay people continued to talk in the pages of Catholic magazines, parish halls, and living rooms, but they were less convinced that official ecclesial spaces were available for the kind of discussion they needed to have.[27]

Did Catholics embrace the sexual revolution in conversation about *Humanae Vitae* in 1968? Not exactly. There is little evidence of interest among theologians or ordinary Catholics in the sort of sexual freedom championed in the famous "summer of love" of 1967 San Francisco. Mary Daly saw calls for sexual freedom as thinly veiled assertions of male privilege. Even in *Beyond God the Father*, she writes, "Female becoming is *not* the so-called sexual revolution. The latter has in fact been one more extension of the politics of rape, a New Morality of false liberation foisted upon women, who have been told to be free to be what women have always been, sex objects."[28] Most were not quite this extreme but the majority of Catholic theologians and lay people were focused on sexual liberation within marriage rather than outside it. Even the most radical were more interested in claiming freedom for intimacy rather than in trying to disentangle sex from commitment.[29] Though married people were convinced of the seriousness of the contraception issue, they claimed the right to modify Catholic sexual teaching, not completely overturn it. Prominent Catholic progressives of the time included several long-time married couples (e.g., the Callahans, the Cunneens, the Crowleys, and Sheed and Ward), as well as singles like Thomas Merton, Dorothy Day, the Berrigans, and Flannery O'Connor, who were, for the most part, celibate.[30] Catholic heroes from this era were not your typical sexual revolutionaries.

Yet the changes these Catholic revolutionaries sought were real. Historian Leslie Tentler connects evolving views on contraception with the rise in communion and decline in confession that began in the 1960s.[31] After decades of obedience and trust in the church's teaching, most married Catholics were no longer convinced that their loving sexual practice was sinful, and fewer believed priests in the confessional could help them. They did not feel unworthy to join the Eucharistic table or compelled to confess birth control as a sin. But they were not, for the most part, joining the radicals who sought to free sex from all constraints. Even more remarkably, Catholic revolutionaries saw a deepening of marriage and family commitments as part of the revolution.

Family Revolution

In a retrospective essay in *America: The Jesuit Review* magazine in 2013, Sidney Callahan looked back at Betty Friedan's second-wave feminist blockbuster of 1963, *The Feminine Mystique*:

> Was it really that bad? the young may ask. Yes, it was. In the 1950s my father, who told me I was intelligent enough to be a doctor, also warned, "Don't be too smart or no one will marry you." Women were not welcome in graduate and professional schools, and the glass ceiling was universally in place. Married women could hardly aspire to combine work and family. Women were considered too different from men to expect fulfillment in anything other than marriage, children and the domestic arts.[32]

Yet despite her agreement with Friedan's critique of the cult of domesticity and limitations on women's professional advancement, Callahan pushed back against Friedan's disdain for religion and marriage on the lecture circuit and with her own books *The Illusion of Eve: Modern Woman's Search for Identity* (1965) and *Beyond Birth Control: The Christian Experience of Sex* (1968). Callahan's disagreement with second-wave feminism on marriage and religion was typical of Catholic feminists of the era.[33] She recalls that Friedan called her "an Aunt Tom" for supporting "motherhood, marriage, religious vocations and love's free gift of service." She was also critical of Friedan's seeming unwillingness to balance children's needs with women's quest for identity.[34] Callahan insisted that her faith in a Christian God who could be addressed as "Mother," Christ in whom "there is no male or female," and a tradition alive with saints who "transcend their gender differences" in pursuit of discipleship grounded her feminism. For her, the connections between

Christianity, egalitarianism, and social justice were obvious, and
so was the compatibility of feminism with marriage, sacrifice,
and child rearing.

Marriage needed to be reformed, not thrown out. Historian
Mary Henold notes, "The earliest Catholic feminist writers
believed the church contained within it the seeds of liberation,"
and that included its teaching on marriage and family.[35] While
aware of Friedan and consciousness-raising groups, early Catholic
feminists were, Henold argues, primarily inspired by Vatican II
and lay movements of the 1930s–1960s that "provided opportunities for [single and married] women to lead, theorize, and devote
themselves to reform inspired by the Gospels."[36] The Grail, the
Catholic Worker, and the Friendship House movements were all
part of the Catholic Revival of the early twentieth century. The
all-female Grail movement was a particularly important source
for Catholic feminism. By the 1960s, Grailville was established
as a center to which women came for Christian formation centered on a "family pattern" of life and liturgy.[37] Opportunities for
women to train for lay missionary work abroad, service careers,
and religious education were central. By the end of the 1960s,
the US Grail movement had also become involved in the women's
liberation movement, and the development of Christian feminist
theology.[38] "Feminist theologians Daly, Ruether, and Schüssler
Fiorenza were participating in summer courses on feminist theology, ethics, and worship before such subjects were available in
most seminaries or divinity schools."[39] Though in later years the
group would become known for promoting feminist theology in
its earlier versions, family was part of its radical vision. Catholic
feminists were formed by groups like these to take on new roles
and challenge social norms, including prevailing norms about
family.

In the 1960s, their main target was the theology of the "Eternal
Woman," a ubiquitous concept treated most comprehensively
in an influential 1954 book by German scholar Gertrud von
Le Fort.[40] Le Fort stressed key female attributes of surrender,
sacrifice, and passivity and wrote that the Catholic role model
for women, Mary, "exercises power only by surrendering it."[41]
Thus, "Wheresoever woman is most profoundly herself, she is not
as herself but as surrendered, and wherever she is surrendered,

there she is also bride and mother."[42] This ideology was echoed in popular Catholic publications of the time, which few Catholic women would have been able to avoid. "Literally, woman was to forgo her own personality as part of her sacrifice for others. She was told to strive for 'silence of mouth, mind, and will' and that 'losing herself in other people' was her vocation. . . . Her only self-expression was to be her sacrifice and suffering."[43] Henold notes that mainstream liberal Catholics like Andrew Greeley and the editors of *America* magazine "tried to break away from the eternal woman model yet continued to write within an ideology of female essentialism."[44] They were unable to shake off the influence of the pervasive archetype of the surrendering woman.

Catholic feminists of the 1960s rejected this model of womanhood while maintaining their commitment to marriage in which parents were unified in love for the sake of children and the world. The Grail, Catholic Worker, and Friendship House were important catalysts for some, but more Catholics were formed by less radical movements and moments.[45] For middle-class Catholics, secular and religious books on "sexual" marriage, intimate marriage, and equality in marriage were important. Andrew Greeley was the best-selling apostle of the sexual marriage from the 1970s forward, but similar titles were circulating in the 1960s. For instance, *The Virtue of Sex: Pleasure and Holiness in Marriage* (1966), written by lay philosopher and theologian José de Vinck and endorsed by Thomas Merton, was widely read. De Vinck tries to move away from the theology of the moral manuals to a more positive ethic of sexuality via poetry, literature, and experience. Defending the goodness of sexual passion in remarkably un-gendered prose, the writer concludes, "Let us love with sweet madness and enjoy it in full; let us love with art and ardor, with imagination and fire," not limited by prudishness but by an orientation to lasting love.[46] This valorization of marital sex can seem a tad excessive, but it was a necessary corrective.

Optimism for marriage and family can also be seen in the Christian Family Movement. CFM was brought to the United States in 1967.[47] Attractive mainly to middle-class professional Catholics, it would claim over 100,000 members by 1970. One of its radical features from a cultural and ecclesial perspective was having women and men meet together to talk about serious matters. A study guide from the time is titled "The Family in Revolution" and includes reflections on protest, racism, busing, and affordable housing. Couples were asked to observe what was going on around them, analyze the situation, and agree on shared action. By gathering couples in formative communities and re-focusing marriage and family outward, CFM effectively de-centered sex and downplayed gender roles. Although most of the cake and coffee recommended for meetings was likely prepared by women, the general orientation of the group was more toward social justice through transformation of the family and less on the surrendering Eternal Woman.

The Marriage Encounter Movement, founded in 1962 in Spain, was even more significant in the lives of ordinary Catholics. It influenced hundreds of thousands of couples via weekend retreats that taught the "10 plus 10" method of daily writing, reading, and listening for married couples. Though mainstream in focus, it was revolutionary in its hopes for openness and intimacy in marriage. Fr. Chuck Gallagher, who popularized the movement in the United States, insisted on the revolutionary nature of married love. Naming alienation as the problem of the times, Gallagher claims that Marriage Encounter "grows and flourishes because couples are willing to face the shallowness of their marriages and family relationships and to seek a better way to live."[48] The deeper intimacy they attain enables them to reach outward, because the recognition and love they receive from each other allow them to forgo the more pervasive quests for possessions and power, the very "things that lead to war, poverty and alienation" and instead find "a sense of mission."[49] Intimacy will heal the world.

Ordinary Catholics who were rethinking marriage and family in the 1960s rejected both the Eternal Woman and what they saw as second-wave feminist prioritization of self-assertion and sexual freedom. They sought intimacy, equality, and justice along with church and family. This combination of beliefs is just as evident in the ordinary women studied by Sally Cunneen in 1968 as it is in the theologians and intellectuals. The same women who were frustrated by the pervasiveness of talk about the submissiveness of Mary and the archetypal Eternal Woman, who questioned the need for a new "theology of woman," were deeply interested in renewed attention to developing "a theology of love and marriage" with an orientation toward the world.[50] In this respect, they differed from many of their secular sisters for whom marriage was a central part of woman's problematic status as the "second sex."

Gender Revolution

Focusing on the year 1968 allows us to see Catholic feminism at its early, radical, and hopeful best. Mary Daly was fresh from her third doctorate at Fribourg, writing in the pages of *Commonweal* magazine, teaching at Boston College, challenging the pessimism of Simone de Beauvoir (whose 1949 treatise was titled *The Second Sex*), and taking *The Church and the Second Sex* on a book tour that included a debate with William F. Buckley, among others.[51] It would not be long before she would be "Moving Out" in her own "Exodus" to claim "Space" for women, but for the moment, she was a feminist Catholic reformer with a mainstream Catholic presence.[52]

Another key figure, Elizabeth Farians, was one of the founders of the National Organization of Women (NOW) and the first woman admitted to the Catholic Theological Society of America (CTSA). When she tried to enter the CTSA banquet in 1966, officers threatened to call the police, and it was only with the help of Father Charles E. Curran and others that she ended up at her table.[53] Farians wrote much less than Daly, but was more significant as an activist. She convinced Betty Friedan that NOW needed a task force on religion and led the task force in its "National Unveiling" campaign, which mobilized Catholic women to show up at church with their heads uncovered, a radical act for that time.[54] Later, she would gather a group of women and burn the section of the revised Roman Missal which allowed women to be lectors, but only if they read from outside the sanctuary. The ashes were delivered in a package tied with a pink ribbon to the National Conference of Catholic Bishops together with a poem which ended, "The color of our caste is pink, but the color of our mood is ash."[55]

Both Daly and Farians would soon leave the Catholic Church behind, but in 1968, they were leaders of the Catholic gender revolution and their work was well known. Farians had a major public platform with NOW. *NCR* published a long excerpt from

Mary Daly's *The Church and Second Sex* in March 1968.[56] The basic theological questions that Daly and Farians were raising about women in the church, the portrayal of Mary, male language for God, and women's exclusion from everything from lectoring to preaching to decision making, were the questions of most ordinary Catholic feminists as well.[57] Yet, according to Mary Henold, "Daly's exodus did not cause most Catholic feminists to leave the church. . . . Catholic feminist organizations, networks, and activism grew steadily at this time and were marked by strong identification with Catholicism."[58] Unlike Daly and Farians, most Catholic feminists of the era remained hopeful and stayed.[59]

Why? Sally Cunneen recounts Catholic women's combination of inspiration and frustration with Vatican II. They found the words of some bishops uplifting and were heartened by the inclusion of women observers in the later sessions.[60] But they were angry and frustrated by the tokenism, by the idea that women were supposed to be satisfied with observing rather than speaking and making decisions. Cunneen writes:

> During the Council deliberations, certain lengthy laudatory passages were being prepared on the nature and contribution of women. After listening to fifteen pages of flowery rhetoric, one of the female auditors remarked, "It's very kind of you to be so gracious to women for their ideals but we'd prefer a simple statement saying they are full human persons. In fact all you need to say is, 'And God created them, male and female.'" Even when eminent, progressive theologians wished to throw them verbal bouquets, the women auditors begged them not to bother.[61]

Some Catholic women were inspired to join the feminist group St. Joan's Social and Political Alliance. An early pamphlet proclaims, "We are feminists because we are Catholic."[62] They fought for greater participation for women in the church and reform of canon law.[63] Others never claimed the term "feminist," yet were deeply critical of a church that saw them as "childbearer, laundress, cook, or nun hiding in a cloister. The ideal woman as I see her," wrote one of Cunneen's interviewees, "is one who courageously challenges the Church's 'ideal' woman."[64] But they were also self-critical, aware of their own weaknesses, especially their limited involvement in social and political movements.[65] Awareness of their own limitations fueled their patience with a flawed church and encouraged them to do all they could within it.

Although the work of non-vowed Catholic women was signifi- cant, the "new nuns" of the post–Vatican II era were also a crucial part of the gender revolution. They "entered into the new spirit of the age with the most enthusiasm," embracing change, especially in the form of new ways of living and working in community.[66] Many began advanced theological study for the first time. Their feminism developed through their social justice work. As they came to identify with the liberation of the oppressed, they realized they themselves needed to be liberated.[67] One nun interviewed by Jeanne Pieper in *The Catholic Woman: Difficult Choices in a Modern World* recounts her experience of reading Mary Daly in a group of sisters that became a consciousness-raising group that eventually sponsored weekend retreats centering on femi- nist themes.[68] It was, says Pieper, "the first time we had even a hint of the emerging philosophy of feminist spirituality, our first premonition about where Catholic women might be [headed]."[69]

Thousands of nuns left their religious communities in the 1960s in frustration with the church. But those who stayed did some incredible things, including starting the National Association of Women Religious. Sr. Mary Antona Ebo, FSM, of St. Louis, founded the National Black Sisters Conference in 1968, and Las Hermanas for Hispanic sisters followed in 1971.[70] Though neither of these groups used explicitly feminist language or joined the women's movement in their early days (that would come later), in taking leadership roles in social justice work, they, like most "new nuns," were part of the gender revolution.

Finally, Catholic women intellectual icons of the 1960s had a large impact as writers, speakers, and advocates for the Catho- lic intellectual tradition. Flannery O'Connor wrote stories and essays; Sally Fitzgerald edited *The Habit of Being: Letters of Flannery O'Connor*; Dorothy Day wrote and spoke all over the country; Sally Cunneen was editing *Cross Currents*; and psycholo- gist Sidney Callahan was also a frequent speaker and popular writer. Alongside feminist theologians Daly, Ruether, and Farians, and the hundreds of thousands of ordinary Catholic women joining consciousness-raising groups and fighting for women's participation in the church, their lives stood as refutations of the unjust limitations placed on Catholic women and proof of the potential of women to be interpreters, co-creators, and witnesses of a living tradition.

Missing the Revolution?

I have argued that the Catholic revolution of 1968 in relation to sex, gender, and family was unique and significant, both among intellectuals and ordinary Catholics, especially Catholic women, but the revolution had its limits. Faith-inspired, critical questioning of conservative politics and social norms was common, but most shied away from activism, especially when it came to movements against racism and militarism. Sr. Mary Antona Ebo and Dolores Huerta of the United Farm Workers movement were exceptions. Theirs was a liberationist faith lived out in activism for civil rights and the rights of farmworkers. Ruether, who began her activism in the civil rights movement and whose very first feminist essay links backlash against African Americans with backlash against women's rights, is another exception.[71] So is Dorothy Day. A search through Day's diary in 1968 reveals only one brief, dismissive mention of disputes over *Humanae Vitae*, but plenty of protest and lots of references to figures of the left, including Che Guevara, Abbie Hoffman, Joan Baez, Cesar Chavez, Pete Seeger, Philip Berrigan, and Martin Luther King.[72] But broader studies of the late 1960s reveal the decidedly unradical politics of most Catholic progressives, despite a strong shared and growing sense of social responsibility.[73]

This reality makes it much more difficult to claim a "revolution" in the area of social justice. Here Catholic efforts were tentative and modest. Consider, for instance, the *Notes on Moral Theology* in the late 1960s. The absence of reflection and analysis on key social issues is striking. Contraception was a consistent feature in the *Notes*, whereas war and protest are only occasionally considered, and racism and feminism are inexplicably, unconscionably, and completely absent.[74] Likewise, Catholic groups devoted to progressive reforms related to sex, gender, and family were sympathetic and idealistic but slow to embrace political causes. Reflecting on 1968 means recognizing Catholic failures to be self-critical, to own complicity, to take risks for the sake of vulnerable others. In many ways, "theology"—even theology broadly conceived—did not show up for the social justice revolutions of 1968.

Catholic thinking on sex, marriage, and gender circa 1968 had its share of deficiencies. Looking back, we can see the difficulty most had in escaping the Eternal Woman. We can criticize the middle-class white optic, lack of attention to LGBTQ questions, minimal attention to sexual violence, and disappointingly moderate anger at overwhelming injustice. Mary Daly's Exodus from the Memorial Church at Harvard seems entirely appropriate in contrast.

And yet something about those 1960s Catholics draws me in, intrigues me, and leaves me thinking, "Isn't their sexual revolution more radical than the Summer of Love? Isn't their women's movement more interesting than the movement of Betty Friedan or Simone de Beauvoir? Isn't their embrace and reform of family more radical than rejection of the same?" So, keeping the very real deficiencies in mind, let me end with three high notes from the Catholic revolution of 1968.

1. *Sex may not always be a "grave matter," but it matters.* Sally Cunneen tells about how her women subjects mourned the anti-body theology and legalism they were taught, yet yearned to understand the depth and meaning of sex in their lives. "We are coming to really accept the Incarnate God," said one of Cunneen's married subjects.[75] Sidney Callahan's 1968 book *Beyond Birth Control: The Christian Experience of Sex* finds a way between a sexual revolution focused on technique and performance and theological treatises that make sexual love so exalted and mysterious that it seems completely unrelated to blood and flesh human beings.[76] She locates the gravity of sexual matter in "the long-term sexual community of the couple," which will involve joy, pleasure, sorrow, seriousness, and play over time.[77] For ordinary Catholics and intellectuals, sex matters in more profound ways than it does for the sexual revolution of the 1960s.

Some might argue that a moderate sexual ethic focused on married people is not terribly exciting or worthy of recovery. I am not so sure. Catholic discussion on sexual ethics has, in many ways, been stalled since 1968. We are either locked in a battle over *Humanae Vitae* or, convinced such a battle is pointless, silent, or talking only among ourselves. The silence causes concern. The joys and difficulties of married sex so evident in the work of intellectuals and the words of ordinary Catholics are rarely publicly addressed today. One line in *Humanae Vitae* suggests some of what could have been. "A conjugal act imposed upon one's partner without regard for his or her condition and lawful desires is not a true act of love."[78] This is an important recognition of women's rights in marriage, of the existence of sexual violence in marriage, and of the norm of love. The text goes on to compare the use of contraception to the use of one's partner, an analogy that most Catholics simply do not accept. But in the context of the #MeToo movement and the countless stories of "bad sex" in which women tell about the strong pressures they experience to do what they would rather not do, have we even begun to think about the "bad sex" many Catholics engage in? And have we even begun to talk about what truly mutual and loving sex looks like? What might we contribute to the current moment if we could talk about these things?

   2. *Marriage and family are central to revolution.* What would the Catholic revolution of 1968 be without married couples? Of course, there were incredible single women who also played crucial roles. But how amazing is it that these progressive Catholic couples were at the forefront? They gave witness to the power that can come from two people committed to each other and to changing the world. CFM and Marriage Encounter brought this vision to hundreds of thousands of Catholics. They knew that as powerful as figures like Merton and Day are, if more radical Christian witness is going to spread, it needs to be through family, not against it. It would be worth it to return to the lives of these Catholics, imagining their dinner tables, their living rooms, and their conversations. It might even help us to talk publicly about how sex, love, fidelity, and justice can thrive together.

   3. *Gender liberation at its best is about "freedom for" rather than "freedom from."* But if secular feminists like Friedan and Beauvoir were right to acknowledge that Catholic women bore additional weight from their tradition, they failed to notice that the Christian tradition also gave them a sense of responsibility

for the world. In the 1960s, "new nuns" were embracing social apostolates that required more than silence; lay women in the Christian Family Movement used their voices to focus the energies of their families beyond the home; Daly heard a request to write *The Church and the Second Sex* as a "Summons" or "Call" from the universe; such writers as O'Connor and Cunneen were devoted to their literary and theological craft despite all of the forces telling them to be silent; and Day—a single mother who had chosen her faith over the love of her life—was leading the Catholic Worker movement..

Their feminism owed much more to calling than rights. This is why women like Callahan grew impatient with Friedan and some of second-wave feminism. She wanted to get on with the work. She found the call to do that work in the Christian tradition itself rather than somewhere else.[79] Day wrote in her diary in 1968, "It was the Liturgy which led to both an understanding and to a joy in prayer that revolutionized our lives."[80] Her faith led her to "acknowledgement of our personal sin, which is part of the sin and disorder of the world."[81] The call *from* Christianity led Day beyond the Eternal Woman. And many others—single, religious, and married—who were far less radical, nonetheless spoke of an encounter with the heart of Christianity that left them with a summons to serve. What might current conversations about gender gain from an orientation like this?

In preparing for this talk, I was privileged to spend time with the Catholic sex, gender, and family revolutions of 1968. It was for me, I confess, different from reading the documents of Vatican II. I first read the documents at age twenty-three in graduate school in classes at Weston Jesuit School of Theology. My primary thought was, "This is it? This is what everyone has been talking about?" Of course, I learned to appreciate them by reading them alongside what had come before and understanding the import of subtle changes. But reading these Catholic revolutionaries is different. I can see them in their consciousness-raising groups, at their dinner tables with noisy children and arguing adults, sitting on the floor in their living rooms, at their newspaper desks, in church basements and college lecture halls, and in the streets. I can feel their awakenings. Though their revolutions of sex, gender, and family were not everything they should have been, I want to recapture their energy, the willingness to acknowledge their own failings, and their hopes for the church and the world. And I think their kind of revolution might just contain wisdom that is sorely needed today.

Notes

[1]See, e.g., Anna North, "The Aziz Ansari Story Is Ordinary. That's Why We Have to Talk About It," *Vox*, Jan. 16, 2018, www.vox.com.

[2]William Shannon, ed., *The Lively Debate: Responses to Humanae Vitae* (New York: Sheed & Ward, 1970).

[3]James T. Fisher, *Catholics in America* (Oxford: Oxford University Press, 2000), 144–45.

[4]Ibid., 145.

[5]Robert McClory, *Turning Point: The Inside Story of the Papal Birth Control Commission* (New York: Crossroad, 1995), 72. See also Robert Blair Kaiser, *The Politics of Sex and Religion* (Kansas City, KS: Leaven Press, 1985).

[6]McClory, *Turning Point*, 73.

[7]Ibid. This is a popular version of the principle of totality.

[8]Ibid., 78–79.

[9]Ibid., 91.

[10]After listening to the lay women, one bishop commented, "This is why we wanted to have couples on our Commission." Quoted in McClory, *Turning Point*, 106.

[11]Ibid., 90.

[12]Ibid., 103–4.

[13]Sally Cunneen, *Sex: Female; Religion: Catholic* (New York: Holt, Rinehart, and Winston, 1968), 118–20.

[14]Richard McCormick, *Notes on Moral Theology, 1964–1980* (Washington, DC: University Press of America, 1980).

[15]Ibid., 140.

[16]See, for instance, Bernhard Häring, "The Inseparability of the Unitive-Procreative Functions of the Marital Act," in *Contraception, Authority and Dissent*, ed. Charles E. Curran (New York: Herder and Herder, 1969), 176–92.

[17]See Charles E. Curran and Robert E. Hunt, *Dissent in and for the Church: Theologians and Humanae Vitae* (New York: Sheed and Ward, 1969).

[18]Arthur Jones, *National Catholic Reporter at Fifty: The Story of the Pioneering Paper and Its Editors* (Lanham, MD: Rowman & Littlefield, 2014), 49.

[19]Ibid., 53.

[20]Bob Hoyt, quoted, ibid., 53.

[21]McClory, *Turning Point*, 141.

[22]Ibid.

[23]Cunneen, *Sex: Female; Religion: Catholic*, notes the shift from the early to the late sixties, 121–23.

[24]Perhaps 2 percent of Catholic women currently use NFP, "Guttmacher Statistic on Catholic Women's Contraceptive Use," Feb. 15, 2012, www.guttmacher.org. The pro-NFP Couple to Couple League puts the figure slightly higher at 3 percent. See John Kippley, "How Many?" available at ccli.org.

[25]Cunneen, *Sex: Female; Religion: Catholic*, 115. Respondents found Häring's reasoning casuistic and unconvincing.

[26]Ibid., 108.

[27]Mark S. Massa, SJ, notes that for both liberal and conservative theologians "the older static and classical concepts and arguments from neo-scholastic natural law could no longer provide a believable substructure for Catholic moral teaching." All sides began to write from historically conscious viewpoints, even as they disagreed. Massa, *The American Catholic Revolution: How the Sixties Changed the Church Forever* (Oxford: Oxford University Press, 2010), 48.

[28]Mary Daly, *Beyond God the Father: Toward a Philosophy of Women's Liberation* (Boston: Beacon, 1973), 122.

[29]Mary J. Henold, *Catholic and Feminist: The Surprising Story of the American Catholic Feminist Movement* (Chapel Hill: University of North Carolina Press, 2001), 252–53.

[30]The only anomaly was the Fitzgeralds, who were forces in New York's literary circles. O'Connor's stay at their home in 1949 as she completed her first book is well known. Robert Fitzgerald, a Harvard classics professor, and Sally Fitzgerald edited *Mystery and Manners: Occasional Prose* (1969). Around the time the editor of Farrar, Straus and Giroux asked Sally Fitzgerald to edit O'Connor's letters (later published as *Habit of Being: Letters of Flannery O'Connor*), her husband Robert left her for a younger woman. Elaine Woo, "Sally Fitzgerald: Flannery O'Connor's Friend, Editor, and Literary Steward," *Los Angeles Times*, July 14, 2000, articles.latimes.com.

[31]Leslie Woodcock Tentler, "Souls and Bodies: The Birth Control Controversy and the Collapse of Confession," in *The Crisis of Authority in Catholic Modernity*, ed. Michael J. Lacey and Francis Oakley (Oxford: Oxford University Press, 2011), 293–316.

[32]Sidney Callahan, "Feminism at Fifty," *America*, Dec. 2, 2013, www.americamagazine.org.

[33]Henold, *Catholic and Feminist*, 54.

[34]Ibid.

[35]Ibid., 62.

[36]Ibid., 18.

[37]Marian Ronan, "A Brief History of the Grail in the United States," available at www.grail-us.org, 2.

[38]Ibid., 3.

[39]Ibid.

[40]Henold, *Catholic and Feminist*, 27–28.

[41]Quoted in Henold, *Catholic and Feminist*, 28.

[42]Gertrude von Le Fort, *Eternal Woman: The Timeless Meaning of the Feminine*, new edition (1954; San Francisco: Ignatius Press, 2010), 11.

[43]Henold, *Catholic and Feminist*, 29.

[44]Ibid., 31–32.

[45]Cunneen, *Sex: Female; Religion: Catholic*, 26–27.

[46]José de Vinck, *The Virtue of Sex: Pleasure and Holiness in Marriage* (Gloucestershire, 1966), 245.

[47]Jeffrey M. Burns, *Disturbing the Peace: A History of the Christian Family Movement, 1949–1974* (Notre Dame, IN: University of Notre Dame Press, 1999).

[48]Chuck Gallagher, SJ, *The Marriage Encounter: As I Have Loved You* (New York: Doubleday, 1975), 27.

[49]Ibid., 29, 30.

[50]Cunneen, *Sex: Female; Religion: Catholic*, 37.

[51]Mary Daly, *Outercourse: The Be-Dazzling Voyage* (San Francisco: HarperSanFrancisco, 1992), 93–95.

[52]Ibid.

[53]Henold, *Catholic and Feminist*, 74.

[54]Ibid., 74, 76.

[55]Ibid., 63.

[56]Jones, *National Catholic Reporter at Fifty*, 51. *US Catholic* published an interview with Mary Daly (identified as "a scholar, a well-qualified theologian and a college professor—who also happens to be a lady") in September 1968. Available at www.uscatholic.org.

[57]Cunneen, *Sex: Female; Religion: Catholic*, 12–13.

[58]Henold, *Catholic and Feminist*, 72.

[59]Rosemary Radford Ruether's first feminist essay was not published until 1971, though it was written as a talk in 1968 and titled "Male Chauvinist Theology and the Anger of Women," *Cross Currents* 23, no. 2 (1971): 173–84. She is another feminist who stayed.

[60]Cunneen, *Sex: Female; Religion: Catholic*, 11.

[61]Ibid., 15.

[62]Henold, *Catholic and Feminist*, 84.

[63]The group started in England in 1911 and was brought to the United States in 1965. Cunneen, *Sex: Female; Religion: Catholic*, 13.

[64]Ibid., 14.

[65]Ibid., 16.

[66]Jeanne Pieper, *The Catholic Woman: Difficult Choices in a Modern World* (Los Angeles: Lowell House, 1994), 18.

[67]Henold, *Catholic and Feminist*, 86.

[68]Pieper, *Catholic Woman*, 22.

[69]Ibid.

[70]Henold, *Catholic and Feminist*, 66.

[71]Ruether, "Male Chauvinist Theology and the Anger of Women."

[72]Dorothy Day, *The Duty of Delight: The Diaries of Dorothy Day*, ed. Robert Ellsberg (New York: Image, 2011).

[73]Cunneen, *Sex: Female; Religion: Catholic*, 4.

[74]McCormick, *Notes on Moral Theology, 1965–1980*. The categories for 1968 are: "Of Sin and Death," "The Theology of Revolution," "The Ethics of Heart Transplants," "Morality and the Magisterium," "The Magisterium

and Contraception before 'Humanae Vitae,' " and "The Encyclical 'Humanae Vitae.' "

[75]Cunneen, Sex: Female; Religion: Catholic, 113.

[76]Sidney Callahan, Beyond Birth Control: The Christian Experience of Sex (New York: Sheed and Ward, 1968), 134–35.

[77]Ibid., 154.

[78]Paul VI, Humanae Vitae, www.vatican.va, no. 13. "Pastoral Approaches," from the papal birth control commission, also gives a sense of what might have been.

[79]Callahan, "Feminism at Fifty."

[80]Day, Duty of Delight, 439.

[81]Ibid., 443.

Sex, Secularity, and Cognitive Dissonance

Catholics and Conscience in the Wake of 1968

Daniel A. Rober

Secularization and disaffiliation have been at the forefront of contemporary challenges for Catholic theology precisely inasmuch as they affect the demographics of the church, whose members incarnate that theology from day to day. Most contemporary sociological studies have indicated that issues surrounding sexuality figure strongly in the disaffiliation of Catholics, particularly among youth. This has been increasingly the case with respect to concerns surrounding the LGBTQ community—there is seemingly a declining willingness among many Catholics to handle cognitive dissonance between church teaching and personal conscience (both in terms of one's own behavior and that of others) on sexual matters.

This essay, in its first part, will thus explore cognitive dissonance theory as initially formulated by Leon Festinger and how it relates to questions surrounding Catholics and sexuality. It will then examine the demographic effects of contemporary Catholic attitudes toward these issues, particularly among youth, in critical conversation with the work of Christian Smith, Michele Dillon, and other sociologists. Reflecting on the data laid out in the first part and in conversation with the College Theology Society's 2018 theme of 1968 and its legacy, this essay will in its second part examine what this resistance to cognitive dissonance has to offer for theological anthropology. Pope Francis has taken what I would term a pastoral stopgap approach to some of these matters in *Amoris Laetitia* and elsewhere through an emphasis on mercy, and this has proven unsatisfactory to those who seek a more substantive affirmation of lives and situations that do not conform to traditional sexual norms. I will propose, then, that theological anthropology must reckon with people's desire to be morally consistent and whole—in other words, to avoid cognitive dissonance, as detailed in the first part of the essay. In dialogue with the work of Margaret Farley in this area, I will attempt to articulate how theological anthropology can respond forthrightly—with compassion but also with justice—to the desires of the faithful for a conscience unburdened by such cognitive dissonance.

Michele Dillon has helpfully noted that "a postsecular Catholicism recognizes that, in practice, one cannot separate within-Church processes, including issues of language and authority, from Catholic Church–secular society practices."[1] Dillon's formulation is important because it makes clear that when talking about the church and the secular, one is not speaking about a dichotomy such that the two are in conversation. Rather, the church is embedded in the world, with believers daily experiencing secular reality. As such, there is permeability between issues in the secular world and the way they play out in the church; this has certainly been the case with regard to matters of sexuality.

Cognitive Dissonance

This essay begins with a brief, targeted analysis of cognitive dissonance theory as explicated most notably by Leon Festinger. According to Festinger, "The existence of dissonance, being psychologically uncomfortable, will motivate the person to try to reduce the dissonance and achieve consonance."[2] This in turn leads to a broader avoidance of situations that create dissonance. As Festinger comments in introducing his theory, a certain degree of dissonance is unavoidable: "Where an opinion must be formed or a decision taken, some dissonance is almost unavoidably created between the cognition of the action taken and those opinions or knowledges which tend to point to a different action."[3] Issues arise when that dissonance becomes too much to bear; it is to two relevant instances of dissonance—forced compliance and social support—that this study will now turn.

Forced compliance describes a situation in which "persons will behave in a manner counter to their convictions or will publicly make statements which they do not really believe," thus causing a split between publicly espoused views and privately held ones.[4] This situation usually obtains because of either the exertion of a threat of punishment for noncompliance, on the one hand, or an offer of a special reward for complying, on the other.[5] It thus results in a distinction between professed conviction and action, in a way that might appear to the outsider as moral hypocrisy but is in fact the result of psychological anguish.

Social support, in Festinger's words, means that one is out of sync with other members of a group to which one belongs, such that reduction of dissonance can only be attained if "one can find others who agree with the cognitions one wishes to retain and maintain."[6] Social disagreement within a group, then, can be a source of cognitive dissonance, mitigated by the existence either of objective nonsocial factors militating against the dissonance or other dissident members of the social group.[7] This leads to a kind of conflicted identity, in which one's membership in a group is called into question or undermined by others.

Festinger's theory applies very well to questions concerning Catholics and sexuality. One sees the way in which cognitive dissonance played out before *Humanae Vitae* in Leslie Woodcock Tentler's key study of Catholics and contraception in the 1950s and 1960s, *Catholics and Contraception*. That book probes the real experiences behind the debates leading up to *Humanae Vitae* and helps in many respects to explain why that encyclical was so anticipated and so disappointing to many. Tentler's work is particularly helpful in describing the history and psychological impact of the teaching on contraception, which in addition to its more proximate goals and results "came for growing numbers of Catholics to stand for their Church's unyielding defense of Christian morals in an increasingly pagan world."[8] This resulted in a Catholic religious culture of this period that Tentler describes as "psychically rewarding as well as punitive, nourishing to the mind and senses as well as restrictive of the body, consoling as well as alienating."[9] She describes here an atmosphere of intense psychological pressure surrounding issues of sexuality, containing elements of both forced compliance and issues surrounding social support. This pressure was tied up in the psychological suffering experienced by many Catholics. It exerted itself mainly on the laity and particularly on women, but also extended to the clergy, who by the time of *Humanae Vitae* were themselves in a crisis of confidence brought about by Vatican II's de-emphasis of the priesthood and the subsequent exodus of many priests and seminarians.[10] The issuing of *Humanae Vitae* in 1968 thus stands in a sense as a landmark case of cognitive dissonance, where a situation of high dissonance was exacerbated by the deprivation of a hoped-for reduction of dissonance and move toward consonance.

Mark Jordan has contributed to this discussion in the area of LGBTQ sexuality particularly through his study of Vatican documents on this issue. His focus on rhetoric rather than content, in terms of what he calls "teaching by threatening," supports my discussion of cognitive dissonance theory by illustrating how these documents "are designed to move readers—to move them to opinion, passion, or action."[11] It is, in other words, a form of forced compliance, using rhetoric to scare or shame people into the closet and enforce an atmosphere in the church where open homosexuality is seen as threatening or heterodox. James Alison, who overall takes a more positive view of this matter with regard to Catholicism, has referred to this reality in terms of the "great annihilation of being which has accompanied same-sex desire throughout the monotheistic world and beyond."[12] Both descriptions diagnose a form of cognitive dissonance, and one which, as this essay will go on to show, has had broad direct and indirect effects on contemporary Catholics.

Analysis of Tentler, as well as of Jordan and Alison, demonstrates how Festinger's cognitive dissonance theory can helpfully explicate Catholic experiences of sexuality. The language of Catholic sexual teaching and particularly its implementation within the culture of the church have corresponded strongly to Festinger's description of forced compliance as well as the need of social support for dissent. The following section turns to recent sociological data that demonstrate how this reality has played out demographically.

Examining the Sociological Data

Data from both sociological studies and those working with young people have indicated the importance of sexuality in trends toward secularization and disaffiliation. In his study *Young Catholic Americans*, Christian Smith identified a large number of lapsed Catholics among young people.[13] Among the trends identified in the study, the issue of premarital sex looms large. According to the study, reactions ranged from feelings of guilt—intellectual agreement contradicted by action—to feelings of contention and frustration.[14] As the authors conclude, "A basic incongruence exists between the central assumptions and values of emerging adult culture and those of the Catholic Church," evinced particularly by changing attitudes among subjects over the five-year period of the study.[15]

Smith's study also finds that Catholic emerging adults have been growing more liberal on issues relating to gay rights relative to non-Catholic peers and at an accelerating rate. This is consonant with work by Robert Putnam that indicates reaction to "culture wars" and their issues as a major factor in trends toward secularization within the United States.[16] Inasmuch as religion or Christianity becomes associated with a set of political positions that are either unpopular to begin with or rendered so through association with other positions and figures, they become less credible particularly with young people.

Elizabeth Drescher describes how fully half of the Catholics she spoke to her in study about disaffiliation felt as if they were pushed out of the church.[17] The stories she describes concern issues surrounding sexuality or linked to it, such as in vitro fertilization and divorce.[18] Drescher notes interestingly that the Nones from Catholic backgrounds dealt with in her study did not so much drift as did many former mainline Christians, but rather experienced something more like a breakup, with citations of examples such as leaving an abusive marriage or getting over an addiction.[19] Drescher also demonstrates with respect to Catholics how the existence of other dissident members of the social group—such as liberal Catholics who vocally protest church teaching on sexuality—reduces but does not totally eliminate cognitive dissonance.

The more recent study *Going, Going, Gone* organizes the young people it surveyed into three groups: the injured, drifters, and dissenters. The first and third categories are of particular interest for this study of cognitive dissonance. The injured are those who have undergone "negative experiences associated with faith and religious practice, both familial and ecclesial."[20] For these young people, cognitive dissonance was tied up in the disjunction between expected outcomes of prayer and church attendance and reality. Dissenters, for their part, experience the belief system of the church, particularly on sexual teachings, as a source of cognitive dissonance.[21] The authors of the study support the case for thinking in terms of cognitive dissonance with their conclusion that the individuals who disaffiliate typically have a "sense of being happy and free or relieved by the decision to disaffiliate with the Church or from belief."[22]

Based on the data and the broader historical issues involved, it strongly appears as if Catholic reaction to issues surrounding sexuality has tracked with the culture at large while also displaying evidence of grappling with loyalty to the church. Catholics have thus followed along with the culture in many ways, but not by way of abandoning the church; rather, they have struggled and sought to find ways to make their positions cohere more closely with their Catholic identity. The failure of this to work for many of them has been a source of cognitive dissonance and pain.

These sociological studies thus build on the prior discussion of Festinger, Tentler, Jordan, and others by showing how demographic data have pivoted at least in part on Catholic teaching surrounding sexuality since 1968. Correlation and causation are thus related here in a way that reflects the nuance of individual situations. Choices to disaffiliate, particularly among Catholics, are, as Drescher shows, painful ones frequently taken after all other options for staying have been exhausted. The data particularly show the importance of social support in resisting cognitive dissonance, and the higher likelihood of disaffiliation if such social support is not present.

Implications for Today

It is easy to pinpoint 1968 and *Humanae Vitae* as touchstones of the relationship of the church to the "sexual revolution," but the reality is more complex and indicative of what Stephen Schloesser has called the impact of "biopolitics" on church life. According to Schloesser, the church was unprepared for changes in Western culture surrounding sexuality, which he calls the "most important epistemic shift of the twentieth century."[23] These new issues were framed in categories different from those the church had been accustomed to using in the political sphere, and they played up the lack of power that women in particular had within church decision making.[24]

Pope Francis has pioneered a new approach to these issues, centered on the Synod on the Family and the post-synodal apostolic exhortation, *Amoris Laetitia*.[25] For Francis, the touchstone has been mercy, namely, making people feel welcome whatever their status and life choices, and reminding them that God and the church love them. As a tonal shift, this has been significant, but on a substantive level it mostly represents an attitude that was widely available if one knew where to look. Brian Robinette has described *Amoris Laetitia* in particular as "neither reactionary to the ideals of self-fulfillment in contemporary society nor supportive of them in their current form."[26] Francis has thus approached this matter somewhat "sideways" relative to widely held sets of positions, an approach that has been alternately exciting and frustrating for those who hold to them.

Michele Dillon's new work in this area adds important insights to this discussion. For Dillon, sexuality and gender pose a dilemma for the contemporary church in that "how the Church frames these issues impacts individual, personal and social relationships, and public culture in ways beyond their theological significance."[27] The discourse, according to Dillon, has alternated between supposedly secular idioms such as natural law and sharp dichotomies such as John Paul II's contrast of cultures of life and of death.[28] This certainly applies, for Dillon, with respect to contemporary sexual teaching, where broad calls for non-discrimination against gays, for example, are "attenuated by the Church's teaching" and condemnation of same-sex relationships.[29]

The above conversation suggests that the challenge posed to Catholic magisterial teaching on sexuality by contemporary sociological trends among Catholics does not represent something that can be answered simply by tweaking existing language in a more pastoral direction, but rather one that requires new grounding that speaks to contemporary insights about experience, particularly the experience of women and of LGBTQ persons. Mercy, in other words, has been for Pope Francis a way of avoiding a harsh form of justice that seeks to condemn. At the same time, though, it is necessary to ask whether that vision of mercy is in turn asking the church to think more broadly of what justice might look like.

Sexuality, Secularization, and Theological Anthropology

What implications do these developments have for theological anthropology? I argue that the above evidence suggests a strong desire for wholeness and of avoiding tensions within oneself. Contemporary society, I argue, has accepted the idea that people do not have to live with high levels of cognitive dissonance. One of the effects of the 1960s with respect to sexuality has been opening up spaces in which people are free to live without such cognitive dissonance. This is somewhat distinct from the idea of "privatization." As Jeffrey Weeks has pointed out, sexuality has never really been a fully "private" matter, but people have been able to find mental, emotional, and physical spaces to avoid guilt over their sexual behavior in a way that was not possible in the past.[30]

The challenge, then, for formulating a Catholic theological response to the secular regarding sexuality is to examine how the church can help people achieve a healthy consonance. It seems clear that advocates of the current teaching believe that they are promoting the most positive and life-giving course for people. However, as data show, not only are people often finding this not to be the case, they are finding it damaging and indeed traumatizing. The negative effects of this situation are clear from what has been presented. Although there are some who might find a kind of romantic attraction in the resistance of Catholicism to the modern world, this resistance comes at the expense of the happiness and consonance of many Catholics.

Applying cognitive dissonance theory to theological anthropology, then, leads to the question of how the church can facilitate people finding consonance and wholeness. This wholeness, of course, is never complete, given precisely that the church acknowledges people's ultimate orientation toward God's grace. Dissonance, however, takes away from people's happiness and fulfillment by placing them under psychological pressure. As Margaret Farley has put it, "Insofar as the church acts in a way that is destructive of its own community, it is simply less able to participate in society."[31] This statement was made in the particular context of how theologians are disciplined, but it can be constructively connected to her definition elsewhere of justice as implying that "*persons and groups of persons ought to be affirmed according to their concrete reality, actual and potential.*"[32] I would like to read this part of Farley's work in terms of her previous work on commitment with its emphasis on attaining wholeness within relationship. On this account, part of human happiness is seeking just relationships that bring people toward wholeness within themselves and with others. Wholeness is not an end or summation of what humans seek to achieve in their lives, but it is a prerequisite.

Farley's work on commitment is also helpful in this context because it is increasingly clear that one's relationship to the church is indeed perceived in today's society as a commitment much like one's other voluntary commitments such as those to one's spouse or friends. Farley speaks in that work of a "way of fidelity" that involves more than simple duty.[33] Fidelity, on Farley's account, is learning to be faithful even when the original vision of our commitment seems to have fallen away: "The *wager* of fidelity is in our choice to believe in the original vision now when we no longer see it."[34] This way or wager, then, offers a beginning for envisioning a Catholic identity that overcomes cognitive dissonance in a positive manner. Being a faithful Catholic is not simply an adherence to a set of norms or mores but rather a relationship that, like any continuing commitment, is subject to change and possible dissolution should the level of cognitive dissonance become too extreme. This vision itself helps to complicate the language and attitudes described above, by Jordan in particular, which have fostered strong levels of cognitive dissonance, and offers a possible positive path forward.

Farley's account of wholeness and fidelity challenges those who think about the church, sexuality, and secularization to adopt a substantially different framing fundamentally compatible with the approach Pope Francis has taken but pushing it further. On first glance, Farley and Francis seem to indicate a move away from sin or prohibition as the category for thinking about matters of sexuality and toward a holistic approach that asks needed questions about how they help or harm human flourishing. This is not permissiveness but rather contextualization and compassion for people's lived situations and experiences—a pastoral accompaniment that Francis has proposed on numerous occasions. Farley's work importantly adds, however, substantive questions about how people seek wholeness and how their commitments foster that wholeness. Applied to people's journeys of faith, Francis's pastoral contextualization and Farley's criteria of wholeness and fidelity challenge theologians to seek a "way of fidelity" for Catholics that does not simply tolerate cognitive dissonance but overcomes it in constructive ways.

Beyond Cognitive Dissonance

An adequate way forward would mean neither a blithe acceptance nor an entrenched resistance to the "sexual revolution," construed as a product of the 1960s. Indeed, Jeffrey Weeks has critiqued this interpretation, arguing that "the various proponents" who criticize the 1960s and the idea of the sexual revolution "find in the period a convenient scapegoat for changes whose sources are actually diverse and often lie elsewhere."[35] Hugh McLeod has also complicated narratives about European secularization and American religiosity based on this model, indicating they reflect different ways of being secular and religious.[36] There is, I think, reason to believe that correlation implies causation with respect to these matters relating to disaffiliation and secularization. Other factors are certainly involved, among which I would single out economic factors, but one cannot properly understand disaffiliation and secularization without strong reference to sexuality.

Reversing demographic trends is neither a likely outcome nor an effective way of thinking about what the church and its theology ought to be like. The question of cognitive dissonance, however, goes far beyond demographics and into broader questions of what helps people live just and happy lives. Building a church community in which people feel that wholeness is possible because of rather than in spite of that community would seem to be a prerequisite for any positive renewal. The last part of this essay indicates the beginning of what such an accounting might involve.

Notes

[1]Michele Dillon, *Postsecular Catholicism* (New York: Oxford University Press, 2018), 13.

[2]Leon Festinger, *A Theory of Cognitive Dissonance* (Stanford, CA: Stanford University Press, 1957), 3.

[3]Ibid., 5.

[4]Ibid., 84.

[5]Ibid., 85.

[6]Ibid., 177.

[7]Ibid., 179.

[8]Leslie Woodcock Tentler, *Catholics and Contraception* (Ithaca, NY: Cornell University Press, 2004), 9.

[9]Ibid., 13.

[10]Ibid., 236: "The birth control crisis further weakened the already shaken self-confidence of a great many clergy."

[11]Mark Jordan, *The Silence of Sodom* (Chicago: University of Chicago Press, 2000), 22.

[12]James Alison, *Faith beyond Resentment* (New York: Crossroad, 2001), xi.

[13]Christian Smith, *Young Catholic Americans* (New York: Oxford University Press, 2014), 114.

[14]Ibid., 117.

[15]Ibid., 118.

[16]Robert Putnam and David Campbell, *American Grace* (New York: Simon & Schuster, 2010), 130–31.

[17]Elizabeth Drescher, *Choosing Our Religion* (New York: Oxford University Press, 2016), 74.

[18]Ibid., 76–77.

[19]Ibid., 79.

[20]Robert J. McCarty and John M. Vitek, *Going, Going, Gone* (Winona, MN: St. Mary's Press, 2018), 14.

[21]Ibid., 21.

[22]Ibid., 27.

[23]Stephen Schloesser, "Dancing on the Edge of the Volcano," in *From Vatican II to Pope Francis*, ed. Paul Crowley, SJ (Maryknoll, NY: Orbis Books, 2014), 4.

[24]Ibid., 19.

[25]Pope Francis, *On Love in the Family* (*Amoris Laetitia*), March 19, 2016, w2.vatican.va.

[26]Brian D. Robinette, "*Amoris Laetitia* and the Nones," in *Amoris Laetitia: A New Momentum for Moral Formation and Pastoral Practice*, ed. Grant

Gallicho and James F. Keenan, SJ (Mahwah, NJ: Paulist Press, 2018), 91.

[27]Dillon, *Postsecular Catholicism*, 67.

[28]Ibid., 72.

[29]Ibid., 75.

[30]Jeffrey Weeks, *Sexuality and Its Discontents* (London: Routledge & Kegan Paul, 1985), 24–25.

[31]Margaret Farley, "The Church in the Public Forum," *CTSA Proceedings* 55 (2000): 98.

[32]Margaret Farley, *Just Love* (New York: Continuum, 2006), 209, emphasis in original.

[33]Margaret Farley, *Personal Commitments* (Maryknoll, NY: Orbis Books, 2013), 50.

[34]Ibid., 64.

[35]Weeks, *Sexuality and Its Discontents*, 19.

[36]Hugh McLeod, *The Religious Crisis of the 1960s* (Oxford: Oxford University Press, 2007), 255.

Humanae Vitae, Menstruating Bodies, and Revolution from Within

Doris M. Kieser

From menarche until menopause, female bodies typically menstruate. The ways by which menstruation is individually managed and socially perceived are myriad, yet all are situated in the reality of bleeding, sexual, and reproductive bodies. In this essay, I explore menstruation and female sexual bodies in the Roman Catholic tradition, particularly in light of Pope Paul VI's 1968 encyclical *Humanae Vitae (HV),* promulgated amid the sea change following the Second Vatican Council.[1] The relatively peaceful revolution that characterized the church's movement through the twentieth century and into the twenty-first sits within the broader context of shifting Western social values and structures: advancing science and technology, marginalization of religious authority, women (primarily white and Western) moving into new realms of power, a turn to the person in moral and personal insight, recognition of oppressions such as sexism and racism, and an evolving global economy. Together, these factors empowered Catholic women, those most affected by *HV,* to effect a revolution of their own regarding their reproductive bodies.

In the fifty years following the 1968 encyclical, the menstrual workings of the female body remain alien to official Catholic teaching. Growing social recognition of menstruation as a key aspect of female sexuality[2] acknowledges that females the world over have been simultaneously invisible and scrutinized for their bleeding, which has abetted patriarchal control of their bodies.[3] This seemingly paradoxical pattern can be traced throughout the history of Catholic teaching regarding sexuality, birth control, and reproduction. However, within and following the watershed era of *HV,* this patriarchal pattern has been disrupted by the voices of women.

Perhaps the most striking trait of the various participants in the *academic* debate over *HV* is that they were overwhelmingly male clerics. In a 1960s and '70s discussion about birthing/not birthing, sex, marriage, and the church, while women had clearly spoken to the issues, for example, Sidney Callahan and Rosemary Radford Ruether,[4] their voices were muted in the end: men were instructing women on the management of their bleeding, menstrual bodies. The revolution that followed the omission of women's actual embodied experiences from the final teaching, however, was the turn to women's embodied experiences, by women, as the centerpiece of feminist theological discussions of sexuality.[5]

The Backdrop

From within a changing context of social and moral normativity, Pope Paul VI responded to Pope John XXIII's call for the church to speak authoritatively on reproductive matters, marital sexual expression, birth control, and the moral limits of science and technology. He first diversified John XXIII's original commission to study the questions, and in 1968 he issued his judgment in *Humanae Vitae,* arguably the most conspicuous modern magisterial teaching on sexuality. The magisterium, theologians, and the church community together engaged in the so-called "lively debate" that Pope Paul himself recognized as useful to and healthy within the church at large.[6]

The crux of the teaching in *HV* was its insistence that God has willed there to be two inseparable aspects of marital sexual intercourse: unitive and procreative (12). The equal primacy of union and procreation, and the divine mandate of their inseparability, constituted new teaching.[7] Because God has willed this inseparability, any physical impediment to either in sexual intimacy and/or procreation was morally unacceptable. Artificial modes of birth control would impede the procreative aspect and were thus deemed intrinsically morally evil (14). These methods could include: hormonal (e.g., birth control pills); medical (e.g., tubal ligation/vasectomy); barrier (e.g., condoms, diaphragms); or some combination thereof (spermicide/condoms, IUDs). Natural Family

Planning (NFP), which at that time was broadly understood as the rhythm method, was deemed acceptable (16). More recent and effective methods include: thermal (basal temperature); Billings, Creighton, and Two-Day Methods (cervical mucus); sympto-thermal (temperature and mucus); Lactational Amenorrhea (post-partum infertility while breast-feeding); and Standard Days Method (ovulation calculation using CycleBeads).[8] Regarding the reliability of the methods, the Centers for Disease Control currently cite a collective, typical-use failure rate of 24 percent for various fertility-awareness based methods, in contrast with the typical-use failure rates of other contraceptives: intrauterine contraception: 0.2–0.8 percent; hormonal methods: 0.05–9.0 percent; barrier methods: 12–28 percent.[9] It is unsurprising that in the 1960s, prior to the development of methods of fertility awareness more reliable than the rhythm method, women whose menstrual cycles were difficult or impossible to chart accurately were enthusiastic about trying hormonal contraception. It is also understandable that the document's removal of the moral consideration of contraception from the entirety of its situational application and conscientious discernment was a concern both for scholars and Catholic couples.

The Missing Menstrual Body

Two dominant theological perspectives emerged in discussions about the teaching: those supporting the church's continued rejection of artificial birth control and acceptance of NFP, as consistent with Catholic tradition,[10] and revisionists critiquing the continued ban on artificial birth control as overly physicalist and lacking contextual awareness of married love.[11] In this theological discussion, however, there was only nominal attention to actual menstruating and ovulating bodies. There was reference to the reproductive cycle and recourse to its infertile times as a means of birth control, noting mucus watching and temperature taking, and to the sometimes-unpredictable cycle that requires regula-tion via hormonal intervention.[12] But there was little mention of the peculiarities, health, or integration into full lives of actual bleeding, menstruating bodies,[13] despite sufficient evidence that many Catholic women experienced these factors as significant concerns.[14] Approximately 3,000 practicing Catholic couples in

the United States and Canada (reported primarily by women) had responded to lay commission members Patty and Pat Crowley's scholarly survey regarding their marital experiences with the rhythm method. The few unreservedly positive recollections of its use in marriage offered by respondents were overshadowed by detailed descriptions of couples' struggles with irregular periods and demeaning experiences, e.g., feeling "like a human thermometer."[15] And although these data were presented to all of the commission members as the voices of those experiencing pregnancy planning firsthand, and were reportedly influential in the drafting of the final report of the commission,[16] they went unheeded in the encyclical and beyond.

The exclusion of actual experiences of menstruation and reproduction rendered the ensuing debate theoretical and limited the discussion of the reproductive cycle solely to the context of marriage and facilitating or avoiding conception. The failure to identify and integrate the phenomena of menstruation and pregnancy *as experienced* into the sexual teachings of the church eliminated women's bodies from any positive description of human sexuality and invited ongoing hierarchical control. Mary Daly wrote pointedly about this phenomenon at the time: theological discourses that idealized and ossified constructions of *female* and *woman* as collective categories rather than individual realities facilitated males' perception and control of actual female bodies.[17]

Humanae Vitae, Natural Family Planning, and the Revisionists

Humanae Vitae noted that it is morally inoffensive for married couples to "take advantage of the natural cycles immanent in the reproductive system and engage in marital intercourse only during those times that are infertile" (16). The document failed, however, to name the experiential realities of menstruation, pregnancy, and birthing (the *female* reproductive cycle) that inform sexual and reproductive experiences. Yet for most females past puberty, menstruation or its lack is the most obvious indicator of their reproductive status and health;[18] thus its absence from the discussion is somewhat curious.

By referring to spacing of births by recourse to infertile periods narrowly as "natural," the document further implied that reproductive cycles are oriented to couples, relevant only to marriage, and useful primarily to space pregnancies. Although it is true that the document was intended for married couples looking to space births, still, it did not explicitly recognize that menstruation and fertility are distinctly *female* phenomena, whose onset is typically long before marriage (around the ages of twelve or thirteen in North America).[19] As far as *HV* is concerned, female bodily awareness is introduced late in menstruants' lives via NFP: long past menarche and long after they have been subjected to social biases and taboos about the menstruating body, its need for regulation and disguise, market-driven assumptions about sexual bodies, and judgment as to menstruants' competence or social acceptability.[20] At the time, *HV's* message seemed simply to have dismissed the reproductive realities facing Catholic women. Today, its message seems almost archaic: by the time of marriage, contemporary females are typically already sexually active,[21] have long been using some form of artificial contraception as a means of making their menstrual bodies socially acceptable and sexually available,[22] and are often uninterested in beginning to chart their naturally occurring reproductive cycles.[23] "Family planning" situates menstrual awareness late in menstruants' lives, and only within the context of marital reproduction: a woman's body is considered only in relation to a man's.

Also, *HV's* insight into allowing natural reproductive cycles to space births was necessarily limited and incomplete. Its attention to reproductive bodies seemed a general reference to an ideal female body, whose cycle was presumed steady, universal, and invisible. Those of us who have, will, or do menstruate know this perception to be a fantasy, which effectually deems magisterial perceptions of actual menstruating bodies as *less than ideal* and menstrual irregularities as *abnormal* in the reproductive cycle.[24]

Although some couples do find NFP helpful for marital intimacy, more find it hindering. As reported in the Crowley survey, many women were suffering due to their irregularities, concomitant health issues, fear of pregnancy, and stilted or abusive marital relations. For instance: "The slightest upset, mental or physical, appears to change the cycle and thereby renders this method of family planning useless. Our marriage problem is not financial. ... But my husband has a terrible weakness when it comes to self-control in sex and unless his demands are met in every way when he feels this way, he is a very dangerous man to me and my daughters."[25] Such real experiences of menstruation, and their social ramifications, made clear the necessity of women's voices in crafting church teaching, to avoid a sanitized and obscured understanding of reproduction and bodies, intimacy and patriarchal violence.[26] These realities further nullify the assumption that the only impediment to using NFP is an ethical one: the "periodic continence" that requires "complete mastery" over one's desires and passions (21, 25). Rather, females often do not have the luxury of agency in their sexual encounters. Willful ignorance of real female experiences and normalized hierarchical control over bodily diversities yielded a doctrine and theology that effectively minimized concern for the health and well-being of actual menstrual bodies.

As the revisionists pointed out and critiqued, the document rests on a particular interpretation of natural law (NL), which itself relies on two assumptions. The first assumption is that "nature" somehow determines morality. In this case, nature pertains to the functional purposes of reproductive organs/genitals and the immoral frustration of those purposes by artificial means (11). This assumption belied the more complex history of theological engagement with natural law.[27] The second assumption is that the "natural faculty and functional purpose" of genitals (reproduction) must never intentionally be impeded. The reproductive body is designed by God, into which we have no business intervening (12, 18). Thus marital sexual intercourse was morally judged in each individual act as either closed or open to the possibility of procreation based on the "unnatural" intervention, or not, of artificial contraception (14). This understanding of NL regarding sexuality and reproduction, which saw artificial birth control as a perversion of the faculty natural to the body, without regard for the persons acting, their intentions for the act, or its consequences, was denounced by the revisionists.[28]

Yet many married couples attested to the multifaceted purposes of sexual expression, like intimate emotional connection and free self-giving.[29] Thus another critique from the revisionist thinkers regarded the moral reading of NL as strictly confined to discrete acts of natural sexual expression in marital relationships, without concomitant consideration of the broader relational context of those acts: it constituted an ethical *physicalism*. Charles E. Curran and Richard McCormick disputed *HV*'s reading of NL as a reasonably discernible collection of moral maxims based on what is natural in the world, as opposed to a system of thinking that leads to reasonable discernment of facts and, thereby, moral judgments in particular circumstances.[30] They accused the document of employing a classicist worldview that resisted the historical consciousness of human evolution.

Although the revisionists' charge of physicalism in *HV* was merited, insofar as physicalism isolates individual acts from their contexts, still, this charge and the revisionist arguments against it were limited by their own lack of attention to actual menstruating bodies and ethical consideration of harm to them. Again, when referenced at all, *female* collectively seemed to presuppose reproductive cycles and capacities as predictable, marital, and uniform realities.

Neither did revisionist and pro-birth control positions account for the menstruating body as a sign of health and well-being among actual females. Rather, there appeared an assumption that controlling and regulating female bodies and procreation hormonally was a good that was also the will of God. Because the position was grounded in classic theological categories of natural law, intrinsic and moral evils, objective moral truths regarding procreation, and the principles informing moral decision making, it missed the mark regarding female health and well-being by overlooking some of the experiential data necessary to moral thinking.[31] At that time, the moral question about the health of women regarding the experimental ingestion of what turned out to be grossly excessive doses of hormones, particularly among already devalued females (for example, Puerto Rican and Haitian women), went unconsidered.[32] The discussion of controlling the abstract notion of fertility, rather than attending to real females' health and fertility, detracted from the well-meaning intention to liberate women from excessive childbirth.[33]

Menstruation and Revolution

Humanae Vitae and its supporters, and its revisionist detractors, politely circumvented the realities of menstruating females, seemed oblivious to reproductive cycles prior to marriage, and relegated menstruants and menstruation to the fringe of sexuality. But the ambiguity of these realities was and is front and center for those in their midst: bleeding can be messy, uncomfortable, liberating, joyful, complex, and expensive to manage, both socially and individually.[34]

Any non-menstrual account of reproduction and birth control that favors classic theological arguments regarding what constitutes the natural, the role of women in the home, family, and church, and the limits (or not) of human engagement with technology, even for what are likely complex reasons, fails actual females. The methodological and procedural omission of explicit menstrual experiences in addressing the issue of birth control cannot but skew the moral content away from menstruating bodies and toward abstract theorizing:[35] it preempts the experiences of the persons affected by its conclusions, and the procedural suppression of relevant data biases the conclusions away from those most affected by the outcome.

Regarding NFP, had the teaching demonstrated zeal for females to know and understand their reproductive bodies, the particularity of menstruation would have necessarily informed the conversation about menstrual and reproductive awareness for all females. Menarche, menstruation, and menopause would each be recognized (perhaps even celebrated) for their diversity among menstruants and their signposting of human reproduction. As it stood, the intricacies of menstrual awareness were (and are) absent.

By subsuming menstrual awareness under the NFP label, *HV* neatly sidestepped females' autonomy regarding their bodies, choices, and agencies by denouncing any artificial birth control as contrary to the will of God, ultimately rejecting the testimonies of real females subject to the whimsy of "nature" in reproduction. By focusing on a physicalist critique of the teaching in support of contraception, the revisionist project undertook no hermeneutical suspicion for the wellness of menstruating bodies that might be required regarding cycle regulation. One might have asked why we were not teaching females to know their bodies, first and foremost, around menarche, before the discussion of birth control and NFP took place. Promoting the goodness of female bodies and menstrual awareness, for their own sakes, might have encouraged all females to deepen their understanding of their own bodies as a point of health and well-being.[36]

A repercussion of theological inattention to menstruating bodies in the development of Catholic doctrine and theology is a gaping distance between women's diverse perceptions of themselves and the church's characterizations of them. The revolution that turned on *HV* and the introduction of a variety of reliable methods of birth control was enacted by women's call for their bodies to be respected for exactly what they were, and are—diverse, complex, lovely, bloody, creative—rather than to be idealized, sanitized, and jeopardized for the sake of a disembodied discourse about fertility and reproduction. The opportunity in the 1960s and '70s for the magisterium to engage more robustly the lives and experiences of females, so clearly placed before them, and to initiate a frank and respectful dialogue about human sexuality, was not taken.

Today, rather than a robust and sound magisterial theology of human bodies, including those that menstruate, we have a binary and ideological theology of the body that permeates official church teaching. Here, real bodies are given over to fantasies of idealized bodies, particularly female bodies. Menstrual bodies remain taboo, unmarried sexual bodies remain invisible, and non-binary bodies remain incomprehensible within a theology of the body inattentive to people's actual sexualities and experiences. But the voices of feminist theologians, mothers, sisters, and daughters, and many others have continued to rise. The practical outcome of a non-menstrual theology is that today 70–80 percent of practicing Catholic couples in the United States use some form of artificial contraception.[37] The rejection of the teaching on birth control by scores of Catholics is an indication that, by not attending to the *realities* of menstruation and reproduction, the revolution the church was hoping to avoid by maintaining its teachings was exactly what transpired.

Notes

[1]Pope Paul VI, *Humanae Vitae*, 1968, www.vatican.va.

[2]For example: Abigail Radnor, " 'We're Having a Menstrual Liberation': How Periods Got Woke," *The Guardian*, November 11, 2017, www.

theguardian.com. I do not, however, equate *female* solely with menstruation and reproduction; rather, I explore them to highlight their absence in
magisterial teachings.

[3]The implications of both the Jewish and Christian perceptions of blood,
menstrual blood, purity, and patriarchal control of female bodies are clearly
immense. Due to space limitations, I will not explicitly explore these topics
in depth here. For reference, see Tina Beattie, *God's Mother, Eve's Advocate*
(London: Continuum, 2002), 19–98.

[4]Sidney Callahan, "Procreation and Control," in *The Catholic Case for
Contraception*, ed. Daniel Callahan (London: Arlington Books, 1969), 41–64;
Rosemary Radford Ruether, "Birth Control and the Ideals of Marital Sexual-
ity," in *Contraception and Holiness: The Catholic Predicament*, ed. Thomas
D. Roberts (New York: Herder and Herder, 1964), 72–91.

[5]For example: Lisa Sowle Cahill, "Catholic Sexual Ethics and the Dignity
of the Person: A Double Message," *Theological Studies* 50, no. 1 (1989):
120–50; Margaret A. Farley, *Just Love: A Framework for Christian Sexual
Ethics* (New York: Continuum, 2006); Aline H. Kalbian, *Sex, Violence, and
Justice: Contraception and the Catholic Church* (Washington, DC: Georgetown University Press, 2014).

[6]See William H. Shannon, *The Lively Debate: Response to* Humanae
Vitae (New York: Sheed & Ward, 1970).

[7]In contrast to *Casti Connubii,* in which procreation was primary and
unity secondary. Pope Pius XI, 1930, nos. 54–56, www.vatican.va.

[8]Re thermal: Planned Parenthood, www.plannedparenthood.org; re Billings and Creighton: Billings Ovulation Method, www.billings.life, Creighton Model Fertility Care System, www.creightonmodel.com; re Two-Day:
Institute for Reproductive Health, Georgetown University, www.irh.org; re
sympto-thermal: Serena Canada, www.serena.ca; re Lactational Amenorrhea
and Standard Days Method: Institute for Reproductive Health, Georgetown
University, www.irh.org.

[9]Division of Reproductive Health, National Center for Chronic Disease
Prevention and Health Promotion, "Contraception," www.cdc.gov.

[10]For example: "The Minority Papal Commission Report," in *The Catholic
Case*, ed. Callahan, 174–211; Germain Grisez, *Contraception and the Natural
Law* (Milwaukee: Bruce Publishing, 1964).

[11]For example: "The Majority Papal Commission Report," in *The Catholic
Case*, ed. Callahan, 149–73; Charles Curran, "Personal Reflections on Birth
Control," in *The Catholic Case*, ed. Callahan, 19–29.

[12]Richard McCormick, "Anti-Fertility Pills," *Homiletic and Pastoral Review*
62, no. 8 (1962): 697–99.

[13]Excepting medical professionals. See Dr. John Ryan's detailed account in
support of Pius XII's "Discourse to Members of the Congress of the Italian
Association of Catholic Midwives," October 9, 1951, in *Family Limitation:
Modern Medical Observation on the Use of the "Safe Period"* (New York:
Sheed and Ward, 1956).

[14]Cited in Robert McClory, "The Survey," 1965–66, in *Turning Point* (New
York: Crossroad, 1995), 86–95.

[15] McClory, *Turning Point*, 90.

[16] Ibid., 96–108.

[17] Mary Daly, *The Church and the Second Sex* (New York: Harper & Row, 1968). In particular, Chapter 4 concerning "Theological Distortions," "Eternal Feminine," "Mary," "God's Plan," and "Woman's Nature."

[18] American Academy of Pediatrics and American College of Obstetricians and Gynecologists, "Menstruation in Girls and Adolescents: Using the Menstrual Cycle as a Vital Sign," *Pediatrics* 118, no. 5 (2006): 2245–50.

[19] Brian Bordini and Robert L. Rosenfield, "Normal Pubertal Development: Part II: Clinical Aspects of Puberty," *Pediatrics in Review* 32, no. 7 (2011): 281–92.

[20] Doris M. Kieser, "The Female Body in Catholic Theology: Menstruation, Reproduction, and Autonomy," *Horizons* 44, no. 1 (2017): 1–27.

[21] Anjani Chandra, Casey Copen, and William D. Mosher, *Sexual Behavior, Sexual Attraction, and Sexual Identity in the United States: Data from the 2006–2010 National Survey of Family Growth, National Health Statistics Report, No. 36* (Hyattsville, MD: National Center for Health Statistics, 2011), www.cdc.gov.nchs.

[22] Joyce C. Abma and Gladys M. Martinez, *Sexual Activity and Contraceptive Use among Teenagers in the United States, 2011–2015, National Health Statistics Report, No. 104* (Hyattsville, MD: National Center for Health Statistics, 2017), www.cdc.gov.nchs.

[23] Ingrid Johnston-Robledo, Kristin Sheffield, Jacqueline Boigt, and Jennifer Wilcox-Constantine, "Reproductive Shame: Self-Objectification and Young Women's Attitudes toward Their Reproductive Functioning," *Women & Health* 46, no. 1 (2007): 25–39.

[24] Tomi-Ann Roberts, Jamie L. Goldenberg, Cathleen Power, and Tom Pyszczynski, " 'Feminine Protection': The Effects of Menstruation on Attitudes towards Women," *Psychology of Women Quarterly* 26 (2002): 131–39.

[25] McClory, *Turning Point*, 91.

[26] Ibid., 86–159.

[27] For example, Jean Porter, *Natural and Divine Law: Reclaiming the Tradition for Christian Ethics* (Ottawa, ON: Novalis, St. Paul University, 1999).

[28] Charles E. Curran, "The Aftermath of *Humanae Vitae*," in *Catholic Moral Theology in the United States: A History* (Washington, DC: Georgetown University Press, 2008), 102–30.

[29] McClory, *Turning Point*, 86–95.

[30] Curran, "Aftermath," 104–7; McCormick, "Notes on Moral Theology, 1978: *Humanae Vitae* and the Magisterium," *Theological Studies* 40, no. 1 (1979): 80–97.

[31] Michael G. Lawler and Todd A. Salzman address this issue explicitly regarding *Humanae Vitae* in "The End of the Affair? 'Humanae Vitae' at 50," *National Catholic Reporter*, May 21, 2018, www.ncronline.org (adapted from "Experience and Moral Theology: Reflections on Humanae Vitae Forty Years Later," *INTAMS Review* 14 [2008]).

[32] Re: the development of hormonal birth control pills and Puerto Rican women as test subjects, see Laura Briggs, "Demon Mothers in the Social

Laboratory: Development, Overpopulation, and 'The Pill,' 1940–1960," in *Reproducing Empire: Race, Sex, Science, and US Imperialism in Puerto Rico* (Berkeley: University of California Press, 2002), 109–41. This point is contrary to the hand-wringing expressed for the imagined neuroses and psychoses affecting females on the contraceptive pill. Barberi and Selling point to the influence of Dr. Wanda Poltawska's perception of hormonal birth control and female neuroses on Karol Cardinal Wojtyla in the crafting of his "Krakow Memorandum." In 1968, Wojtyla called a birth control commission of his own in Krakow, which is purported by Barberi and Selling to be foundational to *Humanae Vitae*. Michael J. Barberi and Joseph A. Selling, "The Origin of *Humanae Vitae* and the Impasse in Fundamental Theological Ethics," *Louvain Studies* 37 (2013): 369, 378.

[33]For example, the "Theologians' Statement" in disagreement with *HV*, which outlines objections to the teaching's ecclesiology, methodology, and conclusions, and was eventually signed by over 600 theologians, raises no concerns for female bodies in general, or particular aspects of reproduction. See *The Catholic Case*, 67–70.

[34]Tomi-Ann Roberts and Patricia L. Waters, "Self-Objectification and That 'Not So Fresh Feeling': Feminist Therapeutic Interventions for Healthy Female Embodiment," *Women & Therapy* 27 no. 3/4 (2004): 5–21.

[35]Cristina L. H. Traina, *Feminist Ethics and Natural Law: The End of Anathemas* (Washington, DC: Georgetown University Press, 1999), 140–68.

[36]Kieser, "The Female Body," 1–27.

[37]Rachel K. Jones and Joerg Dreweke, *Countering Conventional Wisdom: New Evidence on Religion and Contraceptive Use* (New York: Guttmacher Institute, 2011), based on the 2006–8 *National Survey of Family Growth*, United States.

Leaping toward an Embodied Hope

Emily Pennington's Feminist Eschatology and Joan Didion's *Slouching towards Bethlehem* (1968)

David von Schlichten

Joan Didion's (b. 1934) *Slouching towards Bethlehem* (hereafter referred to as *Slouching*) is a 1968 collection of essays offering a trenchant, troubling portrait of a nation falling apart as it struggled to find its center.[1] Pulsing through her collection is a sense that America has reached an eschaton, the end of one era, and stands on the windy cliff of an uncertain, precarious future. Didion's diagnosis is that Americans have lost their center—a core identity, narrative, and ethos—frequently without even realizing that the loss has occurred. As a result, many Americans, self-deluded, have defaulted to escapes through reductive understandings of religion and culture, often in conjunction with drug abuse. For Didion, millions of people in the late 1960s had some sense of identity, but it was a fractured, shallow, misdirected one that ended up being no enduring identity at all.

As we in 2018 struggle with an array of issues—anthropogenic climate change, ubiquitous accounts of sexual assault, pervasive drug abuse, a shallow pursuit of spirituality removed from its theological moorings, and divisive political chaos in which facts and truths are regarded as malleable and disposable—Didion's portrait of 1968 mirrors our own era. Reading her classic work can help us see our own crisis of loss-of-center in new ways.

Didion offers little hope in *Slouching*, but we in the church have faith that hope abides. Along those lines, I propose that Emily Pennington's feminist eschatology is particularly apt as a treatment for this loss-of-center and its resulting self-delusion, alienation, and superficiality. I begin by explicating *Slouching* and showing how it helps illumine the problems of today. Next, I explain how Pennington's feminist eschatology is especially germane to addressing the issues Didion raises.

Didion's Diagnosis: Loss-of-Center Begetting Self-Delusion, Alienation, and Superficiality

Slouching, Joan Didion's first nonfiction book, received wide acclaim as a brilliant example of literary journalism in which writers relate factual events by using techniques normally reserved for fiction, such as detailed scene description and dialogue. Didion would go on to publish about twenty works in various genres, most notably *The Year of Magical Thinking* (2005), a memoir about her husband's death and her daughter's chronic illness, for which she won the National Book Award.

The theme of loss-of-center and its consequences is evident early on in *Slouching*. Many of the essays describe life in California, where she lived and where she thought America's epidemic of alienation and anomie was especially pronounced. In the first essay, "Some Dreamers of the Golden Dream," her opening sentence is "This is a story about love and death in the golden land, and begins with the country."[2] For her, California is a land people come to with the hope of realizing their dreams, only to become disillusioned. David L. Ulin writes, "Here Didion exposes the underside of the great Golden State myth: that it is a land of reinvention, in which we escape the past to find ourselves."[3] Didion describes the topography and climate of the San Bernardino Valley, including its hot winds, as harsh and thus contributing to a harsh life for its inhabitants. She writes, "There has been no rain since April. Every voice seems a scream. It is the season of suicide and divorce and prickly dread, wherever the wind blows."[4]

This essay and, indeed, the book in general repeatedly explore this bleak world of California, which, for Didion, is simultaneously unique and illustrative of the rest of the nation. As she relates in "Some Dreamers of the Golden Dream," California is where a woman named Lucille Miller's troubled marriage culminates in her going to prison for murdering her husband. Didion also writes about California's fixation on celebrities, such as in her cynical description of Joan Baez's school of nonviolence in the essay, "Where the Kissing Never Stops." In "Marrying Absurd," she depicts the shallow weddings in nearby Las Vegas. Throughout these pieces, she presents people searching for love and truth but ending up with loneliness and answers that taste good but offer little nourishment.

Because the most stunning depiction of the loss-of-center and its consequences is in the title piece, I will focus on it. "Slouching towards Bethlehem" describes the drug culture among hippies living in San Francisco's Haight-Ashbury district. Haight-Ashbury had become famous as the epicenter of the hippie movement. Despite the movement's positive results, such as an emphasis on harmony and a sharp critique of capitalism, by the time Didion visited Haight-Ashbury, the district had deteriorated into rampant drug abuse and poverty. She describes the area's denizens as obsessed with getting high and tripping on acid while they claim that doing so is a grand, countercultural statement or a means to enlightenment. An especially chilling snapshot of this world comes near the end of the essay:

> When I finally find Otto he says "I got something at my place that'll blow your mind," and when we get there I see a child on the living-room floor, wearing a reefer coat, reading a comic book. She keeps licking her lips in concentration and the only off thing about her is that she's wearing white lipstick.
> "Five years old," Otto says. "On acid."[5]

With her signature restraint, Didion offers little in the way of commentary on this horrific absurdity. No commentary is needed.

Didion describes this essay—the longest in the book—as "the most imperative of all these pieces to write and the only one that made me despondent after it was printed."[6] The despondency arose from the failure of most readers to understand that the essay was not just about a few people in that dying district but was describing a national crisis of which the people in the essay were simply examples. As she explains early in the piece,

It was not a country in open revolution. It was not a country under enemy siege. It was the United States of America in the cold late spring of 1967, and the market was steady and the G.N.P. high and a great many articulate people seemed to have a high sense of social purpose and it might have been a spring of brave hopes and national promises, but it was not, and more and more people had the uneasy apprehension that it was not. All that seemed clear was that we had aborted ourselves and butchered the job. . . . San Francisco was where the social hemorrhaging was showing up.[7]

That the hippie movement in Haight-Ashbury had all but died by the time Didion arrived—some of the residents actually held a "Death of Hippie" funeral procession in October 1967—did not matter for Didion because the devolution of the region reflected larger dynamics that spread from California to New York. Regarding how readers responded to the essay, which was generally by focusing solely on Haight-Ashbury, she writes, "I had never gotten a feedback so universally beside the point."[8]

Actually, that so many readers missed the point supports Didion's central theme, that many people in America at the time lacked a center and so often tragically misunderstood who they were and how to connect meaningfully with others. As Ulin notes, "For Didion . . . it's another chance to explore the yawning gap between who we are and who we think we are, between those stories we tell ourselves and the ways we actually live."[9]

A striking example of this gap between who people think they are and who they actually are is in Didion's depiction of spirituality and religion, which she largely conveys as ineffective because most people's engagement with them is superficial. When she mentions the occasional Christian group or church, it is always in passing, the implication being that Christianity has little profound bearing on most people's lives. Didion repeatedly notes her subjects' interest in Eastern religion, which was trendy at the time, but here, too, is a lack of deep connection. For instance, she quotes a song about Krishna by Howard Wheeler and Michael Grant and then recounts Grant explaining that he is helping to spread the spiritual movement by teaching people a particular chant he learned from a Swami. In the next scene, though, a man named Max tells Didion, "You can get a high on a mantra . . . But I'm holy on acid."[10] In general, repeatedly what dominates among the people she interviews in the Haight-Ashbury is not any profound engagement with religion or spirituality, but drug dependency. There is an interest in meditation and yoga and chanting, but what overshadows all of these spiritual practices is smoking weed and tripping on acid. These people may think that they are deeply spiritual and the champions of a noble counterculture, but Didion presents them as lost in a world of drugs. They do not have the center they think they have.

Even so, within this miasma of drug-addled self-delusion are occasional moments of recognition that something profound has been lost and that hope has vanished. For instance, one person, Chet, declares, "God died last year and was obited by the press."[11] Another person, Steve, says:

> California is the beginning of the end . . . I feel it's insane . . . this chick tells me there's no meaning to life but it doesn't matter, we'll just flow right out. There've been times I felt like packing up and taking off for the East Coast again . . . At least there you expect that it's going to *happen* . . . Here you know it's not going to.

When Didion asks what is supposed to happen, Steve replies, "'I don't know . . . Something. Anything."[12]

The title of the essay and collection, which alludes to William Butler Yeats's poem "The Second Coming," focuses on a sense of loss-of-center and a bleak outlook for future. Yeats wrote his oft-quoted poem in 1919, shortly after World War I, describing a world in which all had fallen apart. The poem ends with a prophecy that some even greater horror has yet to arrive. The Second Coming, for Yeats, is not the hopeful return of Christ but the advent of a slouching, rough beast. Indeed, Yeats wrote those lines while a certain soldier and failed artist was conceiving of an unprecedented savagery that he would beget within a generation. Similarly, Didion offers little hope for the future. It thus makes sense that she opens the book by quoting Yeats's poem in its entirety.

Given that "The Second Coming" has enjoyed a resurgence

in prominence, Didion's use of Yeats beckons us in 2018 to compare her period to our own. Ed Ballard reported in the *Wall Street Journal* on August 23, 2016, that "some of Yeats's most resonant lines have been quoted in news sources more often in the first seven months of 2016 than any other year in the past three decades," largely in response to Brexit and the presidential campaign here in the United States.[13] Just as Didion saw Yeats's poem as particularly relevant to her era, many of us see the poem as particularly relevant to our own. She lived in a Yeatsian moment, and so do we.

Part of the appeal of "The Second Coming" is that the imagery is general enough that one can apply it to periods in history in which it seems that everything is truly falling apart. Some of the lines relate to many a decade, yet there are those times when chaos and bleakness are especially sharp, such as immediately after World War I, or fifty years later, 1968, and one hundred years later, 2018.

Reading *Slouching* can help us see 2018 more clearly by challenging our perceptions in at least three ways. First, Didion's careful attention to California reminds us of the importance of geography and culture. With its distinctive landscape and climates and idolatry of celebrity, California stands out and is also a microcosm of the nation as a whole. We in 2018 would do well to study more carefully the culture and climate of different parts of the country, including California (where celebrity is still all-important and where fires rage with increasing ferocity), and how regions in our nation are both distinctive and representative of our entire nation. Indeed, as we will see in Emily Pennington's feminist eschatology, attention to particularity, especially embodiment, is important for understanding the current human crisis and God's response to it.

Second, reading *Slouching* underscores how we humans can easily delude ourselves and thus end up alienated from others and clinging to the superficial as if it is of ultimate importance. Her work exhorts us to find a center and to help others do likewise. To find that center one must learn about larger historical, social, and theological contexts. A bit of religion here and drugs there will not do. As Didion writes, the young people caught up in Haight-Ashbury "are less in rebellion against the society than ignorant of it, able only to feed back certain of its most publicized self-doubts."[14]

Third, Didion makes a strong case for the power of carefully constructed, restrained words to distill an era. Central to her genius is her combination of exquisitely precise description and emotional restraint as she describes shocking scenes, such as the one of the five-year-old on acid. She notes that many of the hippies regard words as often unnecessary. She writes, "Because they do not believe in words—words are for 'typeheads' . . . and a thought which needs words is just one more of those ego trips—their only proficient vocabulary is in the society's platitudes." She insists that being able to "think for oneself depends upon one's mastery of the language."[15] In an age of screaming tweets and yelling pundits, we would benefit richly from studying this controlled, thoughtful, meticulous master of prose.

Of course, Didion's book is only one view of America. The reality, as the 2018 College Theology Society convention showed, is that 1968, like every year, was complex, even contradictory. There was more than a lack of a center. The year 1968 also brought us meaningful music, important developments in the church, and advocacy for gender equity, such as in the protest against the Miss America Pageant. Mr. Rogers, who had an obvious center, introduced the world to his neighborhood that year.

Further, if we stop with *Slouching*, we have a kind of eschaton with a rough beast approaching and no new Jerusalem descending, but Emily Pennington's feminist eschatology offers in a striking way the hope that Didion lacks, including by addressing cogently the loss-of-center that Didion laments.

Pennington's Hope: Feminist Eschatology as Embodiment

Emily Pennington points out that "eschatology and feminist theology have a complicated relationship."[16] Generally, eschatology is, of course, future-oriented and also emphasizes the spiritual over the material and the next world over the present one. Such a focus downplays the importance of resolving oppression in the present, including sexism against women. The logic goes that we do not need to worry ourselves about the present because God will fix it all at the end. Further, Pennington contends, this type of eschatology is rooted in patriarchy. She recalls Catholic feminist theologian Rosemary Radford Ruether's observation that the spiritual has long been associated with men, while the material has long been associated with women. So then, an eschatology that features the triumph of the spiritual over the material implies a triumph of the masculine over the feminine. As Pennington indicates, Ruether asserts, "Redeemed life is perfected spiritual masculinity. Women can become 'perfect', whole, and spiritual only by rejecting everything about themselves that, both culturally and biologically, was identified as specifically female."[17]

In addition, as theologians such as Carol Christ have pointed out, eschatology usually emphasizes force. For the end to be brought about, an omnipotent God must override the free will of creation to "fix" or "rescue" it.[18] God, then, "neither requires nor desires creaturely assistance or acceptance."[19] Such an understanding of God arises from and reinforces a hierarchical, patriarchal theology. God is ultimately the powerful ruler who will force his will on the world. Consequently, Pennington observes, feminist theologians have eschewed eschatology in favor of a theology that devotes attention to experiencing God in the present and addressing current injustices.

Pennington critiques the eschatology of other theologians as drawing too heavily from patriarchy and as dwelling either too much on a future detached from the present (as is the case of most eschatologies) or on the present to the neglect of the future (as is the case of feminist eschatologies). In addition, essential for Pennington is a theology, including an eschatology, that highlights the oppression of women, most notably how their bodies have been abused, neglected, and devalued:

> A primarily presentist stance was seen to present a limited hope, for embodied relationality, fluidity, and sensuality were never able to be experienced in their fullness. An alternative response was therefore deemed necessary; a response in which the concerns of feminist theologians could not only be affirmed but also used to significantly rethink eschatology. I thus sought to contribute a new perspective whereby traits associated with women's embodied existences emerged as inseparable from, abundant in, and revelatory of the eschatological future for all.[20]

Pennington emphasizes relationality, fluidity, and tactility as key components of her feminist eschatology. By relationality, she means God collaborating with humanity toward the eschaton. By fluidity, she means that, even at the eschaton, there can be a dynamism to bodies and experiences in the constant, eternal relationship with God and one another. By tactility, she means that the eschaton can contain positive experiences of touch among our bodies.[21]

Although we can and should work toward relationality, fluidity, and tactility in the present, Pennington insists that this theology must, in fact, be eschatological because these qualities will never be fully realized until the eschaton, given that humans will always fall short of the ideal. However, this point poses the challenge of how that realization will be achieved. Eschatology generally contends that God will ultimately force that realization into being, an understanding at odds with the anti-hierarchical and collaborative emphases of feminist theology. Borrowing from Letty Russell and Jürgen Moltmann, Pennington proposes that eschatology must envision creation in partnership with God as part of dependence on God. Moltmann contends that our insistence that God must somehow force our obedience reflects our narrow human understanding of free will and God's ability to collaborate with us. God works with us, rejecting our rejections of God in a way that still somehow allows our partnership with God, guiding us toward this full realization of liberation for all.[22]

Thus, feminist theology, with its validation of women's experiences, attention to the plight of the oppressed, and eschewal of hierarchies, can and must have an eschatological component that values all those emphases. Relationality, fluidity, and tactility become the end toward which God guides us in collaboration with us.

This feminist eschatology provides an antidote for the loss-of-center that Didion helps us see more clearly in 2018 through her description of 1968. Rather than people living in self-delusion, alienation, and superficiality, struggling to find meaning in all the wrong realms, they can instead receive hope from Pennington's feminist eschatology, which highlights God working in relation, that is, collaboratively, and with fluidity and tactility to help all human beings focus on true, genuine relationships with God and one another in a way that leads to loving cohesion for all. Pennington pushes beyond self-delusion by grounding the person in divine relationality. She pushes beyond alienation in the same way while offering a well-grounded sense of fluidity that takes seriously the dynamism of women's bodies and bodies in general and how God lovingly responds to that dynamism. Finally, she pushes beyond superficiality with an eschatology rooted in theological categories and traditions but primarily centered on the experience of women and how their bodies have been mistreated.

There is nothing shallow or facile about Pennington's theology. This is not an opiate or a flirtation with Eastern religion but a comprehensive theology that embraces human experience, especially that of women, in profound ways.

Especially important is Pennington's attention to context and embodiment. Didion also is acutely aware of specific settings, as in her careful depiction of California's climate and culture, even while recognizing the universal found in the particular. Attention to setting is a kind of embodiment and is thus a point of connection between Didion and Pennington. However, although Didion often regards that geographic and cultural embodiment as bleak, Pennington focuses on the positive side of embodiment, both for the present and the eschatological future.

Although there is much in Pennington's eschatology that is worthwhile, a problematic feature is that it values over all else the experience women and girls have had regarding their bodies. She declares that her starting point is with this bodily experience and that she is therefore justified in ignoring other important theological categories and traditions that do not serve her purpose. Thus, "certain doctrines that are connected to eschatology, such as Christology, Incarnation, final judgement, and the parousia were not explicitly addressed or utilised."[23] In her attention to female embodiment and her neglect of important theological categories, she ventures dangerously close to idolatry. Nevertheless, her study of embodiment and her focus on relationality, fluidity, and tactility can be helpful in the face of the loss-of-center Didion diagnoses.

More work, then, should be done to develop a fuller feminist eschatology that truly takes seriously both the present plight of women and the eschatological future and that addresses these important concerns about embodiment while also addressing the significant theological categories listed above that Pennington disregards.

Moving Forward with the Center Holding

Didion's *Slouching towards Bethlehem* heightens our sensitivity to the problem of a loss-of-center that begets self-delusion, alienation, and superficiality. Pennington's feminist eschatology moves us toward relationality, fluidity, and tactility that reject hierarchy and dominance and devotes significant attention to both present injustices and the eschaton. Despite its shortcomings, Pennington's feminist eschatology can lead us to healing by grounding us in meaningful relationships with God and one another that take seriously our bodily dynamism and loving touch. May we reach a point where the center does indeed hold.

Notes

[1] Joan Didion, *Slouching towards Bethlehem* (New York: Farrar, Straus and Giroux, 1968). The book takes its name from a phrase in the final line of the William Butler Yeats poem "The Second Coming," in *The Collected Poems of W. B. Yeats* (Ware, Hertfordshire, UK: Wordsworth Editions Limited, 1994), 158.

[2] Didion, *Slouching*, 3.

[3] David L. Ulin, "What Happened Here?" *Columbia Journalism Review*, March/April 2010, 52.

[4] Didion, *Slouching*, 3.

[5] Ibid., 127.

[6] Ibid., xiii.

[7] Ibid., 85.

[8] Ibid., xiv.

[9] Ulin, "What Happened Here?" 53.

[10] Didion, *Slouching*, 120.

[11] Ibid., 104.

[12] Ibid., 98.

[13] Ed Ballard, "Terror, Brexit and US Election Have Made 2016 the Year of Yeats," *Wall Street Journal*, August 23, 2016, www.wsj.com.

[14] Didion, *Slouching*, 123.

[15] Ibid.

[16] Emily Pennington, "Does Feminism Need the Future?: Rethinking Eschatology for Feminist Theology," *Feminist Theology* 21, no. 3 (2013): 220.

[17] Rosemary Radford Ruether, *Sexism and God Talk* (London: SCM Press, 2002), 67.

[18]Pennington, "Does Feminism Need the Future?" 222, quoting Christ, *She Who Changes: Re-Imagining the Divine in the World* (New York: Palgrave, 2003), 90.

[19]Ibid.

[20]Emily Pennington, *Feminist Eschatology: Embodied Futures* (New York: Routledge, 2017), Kindle edition, 204–5.

[21]Ibid., chaps. 2–4.

[22]Ibid., 227–30.

[23]Ibid., 251.

"You Say You Want a Green Revolution?"

Eugene and Abigail McCarthy
and Catholic Agrarianism

William J. Collinge

Late in 1967, Senator Eugene McCarthy, Democrat from Minnesota, became the first opponent of the Vietnam War to declare candidacy for the presidency. His surprising performance in the New Hampshire Democratic primary on March 12, 1968, in which he came close to defeating incumbent President Lyndon Johnson, started a chain of events that led to Johnson's unexpected withdrawal from the race on March 31. Eugene McCarthy did not win the presidency, and the war did not end until 1975, but, looking back nearly fifty years later, Lawrence O'Donnell concludes his book on the 1968 election, "No one did more to stop the killing in Vietnam than Senator Eugene McCarthy."[1] McCarthy and his wife, Abigail, had roots in the Catholic agrarian movement of the 1930s and 1940s, and, while by 1968 Eugene McCarthy was no longer an agrarian, there are significant links between his early agrarianism and the themes of his presidential campaign and even with the politics of today.

Eugene McCarthy (1915–2005) was a farm boy from Watkins, about seventy-five miles west-northwest of Minneapolis. His father, Michael McCarthy, was no agrarian; "To Dad McCarthy," Abigail wrote, "a farm was business property, something you owned and managed but did not live on."[2] The McCarthys' agrarianism derived instead from the Benedictine monks of Saint John's Abbey in Collegeville, where Eugene attended prep school and college, graduating from Saint John's University in 1935.

Abigail Quigley McCarthy (1915–2001) hailed from Wabasha, in southeastern Minnesota, and graduated from the College of St. Catherine in 1936.[3] After she and Eugene were married in 1945, they settled on eighty acres in Watkins that they had purchased from Eugene's father. They called it St. Anne's Farm.

Catholic Agrarianism

"Gene ... was caught up in the vision of the Catholic rural life movement whose ideal was the land as a source of freedom and security and as a base of community," Abigail wrote.[4] She notes the mainstream agrarianism of the National Catholic Rural Life Conference (NCRLC), now Catholic Rural Life, whose initial concerns were the strengthening of rural parishes and rural Catholic families (she does not note that it had added a second focus on the impact "of Catholic social teachings on the rural life of the nation as a whole").[5] "But the agrarianism that we were interested in went beyond that. It was spoken of at the time as the 'Green Revolution' and was thought of as a revolt against the system."[6]

The term "Green Revolution" was coined as an alternative to the "Red Revolution" of Communism by the best-known and most radical of the Catholic agrarians in the United States, the French immigrant Peter Maurin (1877–1949), co-founder, with Dorothy Day, of the Catholic Worker movement.[7] Maurin was shaped by the European Catholic response first to industrialism and then to the Depression, understood as a final crisis of the industrial capitalist order. European social Catholicism looked back to the order of guilds and communal villages, such as the one in which Maurin had been born. Maurin's "Green Revolution" proposed to supplant industrialism and urbanism with a society reconstructed around farming communes, which he also called "agronomic universities." These would be centers of "cult, culture, and cultivation," combining features of monasteries, schools, and peasant villages. There people would learn to support themselves from the land and from craft industries and also would be nurtured spiritually by prayer and intellectually by study of the Catholic tradition.[8]

Though the McCarthys admired the Catholic Workers, the

Workers were not the most direct influence on their agrarianism. That role belonged to Fr. Virgil Michel (1890–1938), by all accounts, including the McCarthys', the intellectual leader of Saint John's University at the time. Michel respected Maurin, describing him to his abbot as "ein Original [a 'character'] of the first order" but one who "has a wealth of ideas and projects."[9] The two spent long hours in conversation, Day says, and Maurin introduced Michel to the personalist philosophy of Emmanuel Mounier.[10] However, Michel kept some distance from the more radical aspects of Maurin's program and did not use the term "Green Revolution."

Michel was the leading advocate in the United States of a link between liturgy and social action. In Michel's words, "Pius X tells us that the liturgy is the indispensable source of the true Christian spirit; Pius XI says that the true Christian spirit is indispensable for social regeneration. Hence the conclusion: The liturgy is the indispensable basis for Christian social regeneration."[11] The link between liturgy and social regeneration was the mystical body of Christ, the union of the faithful, in which are found "organic fellowship coupled with full respect for human personality and individual responsibility."[12] Michel thus opposed individualism in liturgy and in society. In liturgy, individualism was reflected in worshippers' concentration on their individual relationships with Christ and on private prayers during Mass. In society, "It has meant that each man is for himself alone, and need have no consideration for anyone else. It has resulted in the avaricious pursuit of material profit and gain for its own sake—the spoils always going to the strongest, the most fortunate, often the most unscrupulous."[13]

Michel championed the agricultural cooperative movement as a natural approximation to the supernatural community of the mystical body. However, it could be perfected only through the grace of Christ, and thus it "needs the help and the inspiration of the liturgical movement."[14] In turn, the cooperative movement can be a means of extending the grace of the liturgy into ordinary life. In general, agricultural life was a natural approximation to the life of grace, one that led more easily to "the true Christian life, the liturgical life," than did urban life.[15] The back-to-the-land movement, "bringing people back closer to nature," is therefore important "for any genuine Catholic revival. The latter is necessarily a revival in terms of an intelligent participation in the corporate supernatural life of Christ, and for this a more truly natural life is indispensable."[16]

Emerson Hynes (1915–1971), a student of Michel, develops this last point at length in a two-part article, "Land and Liturgy." Besides the McCarthys themselves, Hynes, a classmate of Eugene's at Saint John's and his closest friend, was the strongest personal link between the early agrarianism and the 1968 campaign.[17] "Their lives were intertwined [at Saint John's] and never really separated again," Abigail said.[18] Hynes returned to teach at Collegeville, where he continued to write for decentralist and agrarian publications. In 1959, the newly elected Senator Eugene McCarthy invited him to become his legislative assistant. Throughout McCarthy's years in the Senate, he consulted Hynes on agricultural and other issues. Hynes's son Michael recalled that his father "was always true to the vision and true to the principles and I think McCarthy needed that kind of guidance . . . and that's why he loved Emerson and kept him on."[19] Shortly into the 1968 campaign, Emerson Hynes was disabled by a massive stroke.

The subtitle of the first part of Hynes's article shows the connection with Michel's thought: "Fuller Natural Life the Basis for Supernature."[20] Hynes extols a romanticized version of farm life in arguing that "the entire environment of life on the land disposes the person toward the liturgy in a special manner."[21] He gives four reasons: (1) The farmer "perceives so thoroughly the order in the environment in which he works that he cannot help but reflect upon the Author of it." (2) "The rural man tends to be free from worldliness" and to take the long-range view of things. (3) "The farmer is a man of faith," a faith founded "in wisdom which comes from an intimate knowledge of nature." (4) The farmer is "blessed with peace," a relationship with nature more peaceful than the competitive struggles of the commercial world.[22] In short, the entire end of rural life is natural health. Liturgy, in turn, aims at supernatural health, the fullness of human perfection. "Liturgy and land, each in its own plane, seek to bring about the perfection of the whole man."[23]

Hynes argues that the liturgical movement and rural life need each other. The liturgical movement must draw on the relative health of rural families and parishes if it is to "bring back to true

Christian life a people who have strayed so far."[24] And rural life needs the liturgy. In a decidedly unromantic turn, Hynes claims that "today farming is less a way of life and ever more and more a strictly business proposition."[25] Indeed, "The commercial farmer is no less than simoniacal."[26] He concludes, "The liturgy and perhaps only the liturgy can . . . bring the farmer to the realization of his true vocation: mother of the land for the glory of God and for the needs of himself and the hungry."[27]

According to Abigail McCarthy, "One of [the] apostles [of the Green Revolution] in whom we were much interested was Willis Nutting who later wrote *Reclamation of Independence.*"[28] Nutting (1900–1975) proclaimed a Green Revolution and acknowledged the inspiration of Maurin, but he did not hold to Maurin's ideal of a village or monastic community.[29] Standing in the Jeffersonian tradition of the yeoman farmer and the homesteader, Nutting calls for an "Americanism" in which "a man should stand or fall by his own efforts, and should neither be shielded from the consequences of his own errors nor deprived of the rewards of his successes."[30]

Nutting often sounds like a modern American libertarian, opposing minimum wage laws, collective bargaining, and the New Deal, and holding that government planning cannot succeed because we lack adequate knowledge of people's choices. But he parts company with libertarians in holding that the ideals of freedom and pursuit of wealth are incompatible. Freedom is not the absence of restriction in following one's desires, but a person's ability to make "for himself . . . those great decisions by which the main course of his life is directed and by which his character is formed."[31] But by exalting unlimited competition in the pursuit of wealth, we have brought about a system in which a few people control natural resources and the means of production, and the great majority work for them in the specialized tasks praised by Adam Smith. With such specialized skills they cannot support themselves; they are dependent on an employer for a living and in turn upon "a vast economic System of production, communication, distribution, and finance which covers the whole nation and even the whole world."[32] The attempt to keep the system functioning, Nutting argues, leads inevitably to collectivism and totalitarianism. The "reclamation of independence" comes about when "each family can provide for itself many of its actual necessities" from its own land and skills, and "those necessities which a family cannot provide by its own efforts can be produced within the local community."[33] "His argument was one Gene fully concurred with," Abigail writes.[34]

The McCarthys on the Farm

Writing as E. J. McCarthy and Mrs. E. J. McCarthy, the McCarthys published a facing pair of articles, jointly titled "A Year on the Land," in the September 1947 issue of *Land and Home*, a publication of the NCRLC. Eugene's article begins with the smallholder's joy of ownership. "The exhilaration of spirit, the sense of rightness, of security which I felt when I first stepped over the boundary fence onto the land which now was mine made the old rational arguments of the naturalness of ownership seem very unconvincing and certainly unnecessary."[35] It is "a proper place to bring a wife to establish a family."[36]

Reminiscent of Michel and Hynes, he parallels the farm year with the liturgical year from Lent to Advent, planting to fallow time. "In Advent, as in the other seasons of the liturgical year, the work and spirit of the farmer's work year is marvelously adjusted to that of the Church."[37] Eugene's tendency toward abstraction surfaces as, near the midpoint of the article, the first person singular disappears and "the farmer" becomes the subject of the narrative.

Mrs. McCarthy contrasts the farm woman's life with the unhappiness and loneliness of urban women, isolated from their husbands' worlds and bearing a disproportionate share of the manual labor at home. By contrast, "The country woman plans and works with her husband—she rules the home *with* him, not in his stead."[38] She focuses on the peace of farm life, the absence of noise and distraction, and holds that farm life affords the possibility to offer true hospitality. Guests are not in the way; they can fit into the routines and join in the common work. "And the best talking men and women do is that around a big table after they have broken bread together."[39] In country life, she concludes, "A sense of proportion and a hierarchy of values become a part of one as they were never a part before."[40]

In her memoir, Abigail affirms that the articles reflected "what our year on the farm had meant to both of us and to each of us."[41] She writes, "We were very serious about building a home life based on the Benedictine ideal of mixed prayer and work, of lives which combined both intellectual and manual work," and of the practice of hospitality.[42] But the memoir shows that life was not as serene as the article portrays; it is full of stories of difficulties with neighbors and tradesmen and of Abigail's isolation.

The McCarthys had hoped to revive a recently closed Catholic high school in Watkins and build a community of lay teachers around it. But Archbishop John Gregory Murray made it clear that "he would rather have no school than a school conducted by the laity."[43] The McCarthys could not support themselves from the farm alone, and when a teaching position at the College of St. Thomas in Saint Paul opened up, Eugene quickly accepted. By the time the articles in *Land and Home* were published, they had been off the farm for a year.

Away from Agrarianism

The McCarthys had intended to resume farming. By 1949, however, Eugene had become a member of the US House of Representatives. At St. Thomas, Eugene had encountered a Catholic political philosophy quite different from the anarchism of Maurin and the quasi-libertarianism of Nutting. Next door to the McCarthys in St. Thomas faculty housing lived Heinrich Rommen, a lawyer and political theorist who was a refugee from the Nazis. When Eugene was at Saint John's, according to Abigail, "Identification of modern evils had been clear enough, but the solutions seemed to lie in a return to what had been lost. Underlying this was the thinly veiled attitude that the government was at best a necessary evil."[44] Rommen shared with the agrarians an insistence on personal freedom and individual rights and with Maurin and Michel an emphasis on the importance of local communities and institutions. But he placed great importance on the state and developed a scholastic theory of it similar to that of his contemporary Jacques Maritain. The state is based on human personal and social nature and exists in order to promote the common good of the society.[45] Suspicious of excessive centralization, Rommen defended the principle of subsidiarity ("the end value of the intermediary organizations and their right to realize their ends in the *ordo* of the state")[46] and was enthusiastic about the separation of powers in US government. Nevertheless, "His concern for social justice meant that he envisaged a role for the welfare state greater than that acceptable even to many Democrats."[47] According to Larry Merthan, a colleague of both men, "Rommen . . . was the first political theorist he'd been exposed to in person, and McCarthy devoured it all."[48]

Rommen stressed the importance of active participation in the political process, as did Marshall Smelser, a younger colleague, who introduced McCarthy to Minnesota Democratic-Farmer-Labor politics. In 1948, McCarthy was elected to the Congressional seat representing Ramsey County. "Although my running for Congress was not a fulfillment of long held hopes and careful planning," he wrote in his memoirs, "it seemed at the time, as it does in retrospect, to have been an orderly progression from study and reflection on political and social problems and thought."[49]

1968

McCarthy served in the House of Representatives from 1949 to 1959 and in the Senate from 1959 to 1971. As a member of the Senate Foreign Relations Committee, he began to see the inconsistency between the Johnson administration's optimistic projections for the war in Vietnam and the war's actual progress, which resulted in ever-increasing commitments of US troops. He had long been disturbed by the expansion of executive power, and he came to believe that the administration was usurping the Senate's constitutional role in foreign policy. On November 30, 1967, McCarthy announced his candidacy for president.

It was an antiwar, not agrarian, campaign cast in just-war terms. As to just cause, he said, we cannot trust the administration's statements of its aims. The means by which we are fighting the war are extremely destructive. And "It is no longer possible to prove that the good that may come with what is called victory, or projected as victory, is proportionate to the loss of life and property and to other disorders that follow from this war."[50] But in describing his opposition to the war as a "judgment of individual conscience,"[51] he evokes the personalism of his earlier years.

Personalism unified the campaign more broadly. "If there is one central theme to my campaign," McCarthy said in Milwaukee on March 25, "it is the president's duty to liberate individuals so they may determine their own lives, to restore their mastery and power over individual life and social enterprise which has been so seriously eroded by the growing impersonality of our society and by the misuse of central power."[52] It also marked the way McCarthy conducted his campaign, for better and worse. He proclaimed that 1968 would be a year "of the people of this country so far as politics is concerned, not of political leadership, not of organized politics, but a politics of participation and a politics of personal response on the part of the citizens of this country."[53]

McCarthy's domestic policy combined personalism with an emphasis on the limits of centralized power and the importance of intermediate institutions. This joined the communitarianism of Maurin and the Benedictines with Rommen's insistence on subsidiarity and separation of powers. In addressing the problem of inner city poverty and unrest, the central domestic issue of the 1968 campaign, McCarthy rolled out an ambitious proposal of new "civil rights," such as Rommen would have approved: (1) to a decent job with a guaranteed minimum income; (2) to adequate health care; (3) to education sufficient to develop one's full potential; and (4) to "a decent house in a neighborhood which is part of a community."[54] As Dominic Sandbrook summarized it, McCarthy's program aimed at "the diffusion of power and responsibility throughout the community in order to 'release the black people and the poor of this country from bondage.'"[55]

Foreign wars and urban poverty remain serious issues for American politics, and McCarthy's antiwar stance and his "new civil rights" would find resonances in some segments of today's Democratic Party. A McCarthy campaign today might supplement these themes with themes of McCarthy's earlier agrarianism, joining an emphasis on reviving rural communities, characteristic of Donald Trump's 2016 campaign, with an emphasis on environmentally sustainable agriculture, as advocated by Maurin, Michel, and some present-day Democrats.

During the 1968 campaign, McCarthy underwent an apparent personal crisis that led to his leaving Abigail and the Senate and assuming the role of an erratic outsider.[56] But he deserves to be remembered for his refusal to separate politics from morality and his courageous stance against an immoral war. After McCarthy's death, Albert Eisele reiterated, "Eugene McCarthy showed that it is possible for one man to make a difference in a democratic society, and that not even the immense power of the presidency can withstand the opposition from a public aroused by a man who speaks out against what he sees as an immoral action by government."[57] Might we hope for such a politician fifty years later?

Notes

[1]Lawrence O'Donnell, *Playing with Fire: The 1968 Election and the Transformation of American Politics* (New York: Penguin, 2017), 427.

[2]Abigail McCarthy, *Private Faces/Public Places* (Garden City, NY: Doubleday, 1972), 108.

[3]The Abigail Quigley McCarthy Center for Women, at St. Catherine's, is named after her. This essay was first presented in Whitby Hall, where Abigail studied in the 1930s and taught in the late 1940s.

[4]Abigail McCarthy, *Private Faces/Public Places*, 109. Garry Wills provides an incisive survey of the cultural milieu of postwar Minnesota Catholic agrarianism, with reference to the McCarthys, in "Relicts of a Catholic Renaissance," *New York Review of Books*, October 10, 2013, 37–38.

[5]David S. Bovée, *The Church and the Land: The National Catholic Rural Life Conference and American Society, 1923–2007* (Washington, DC: Catholic University of America Press, 2010), 128.

[6]Abigail McCarthy, *Private Faces/Public Places*, 109.

[7]Peter Maurin favored organic farming methods and thus would have opposed the unrelated "Green Revolution" of the 1960s, led by Norman Borlaug and featuring high-yield seeds and intensive use of chemical fertilizers and pesticides.

[8]William J. Collinge, "Peter Maurin's Ideal of Farming Communes," in *Dorothy Day and the Catholic Worker Movement: Centenary Essays*, ed. William Thorn, Phillip Runkel, and Susan Mountin (Milwaukee: Marquette University Press, 2001), 385–98.

[9]R. W. Franklin and Robert L. Spaeth, *Virgil Michel: American Catholic* (Collegeville, MN: Liturgical Press, 1988), 116.

[10]Dorothy Day, "On Pilgrimage," *The Catholic Worker*, October 1953, catholicworker.org. See Emmanuel Mounier, *A Personalist Manifesto,* translated by Monks of Saint John's Abbey (New York: Longmans, Green, 1938). Maurin asked Virgil Michel to oversee this translation.

[11]Virgil Michel, *The Social Question: Essays on Capitalism and Christianity*, ed. Robert L. Spaeth (Collegeville, MN: Office of Academic Affairs, Saint John's University, 1987), 8.

[12]Ibid., 5.

[13]Michel, "The Cooperative Movement and the Liturgical Movement," *Orate Fratres* 14, no. 4 (February 18, 1940): 152.

[14]Ibid., 158.

[15]Michel, "City or Farm," *Orate Fratres* 12, no. 8 (June 12, 1938): 367–68.

[16]Ibid., 369.

[17]See Jeanne Lorraine Cofell, "Closest to the Heart—The Life of Emerson Hynes: A Biographical Study of Human Goodness with a Focus on the College Years" (EdD diss., School of Education of the University of Saint Thomas, 2014), ir.stthomas.edu.

[18]Abigail McCarthy, *Private Faces/Public Places*, 72.

[19]Cofell, "Closest to the Heart," 125.

[20]Emerson Hynes, "Land and Liturgy," *Orate Fratres* 13, no. 12 (October 29, 1939): 540.

[21]Ibid.

[22]Ibid., 541–42.

[23]Ibid., 544.

[24]Hynes, "Land and Liturgy (II)," *Orate Fratres* 14, no. 1 (November 26, 1939): 14.

[25]Ibid., 17.

[26]Ibid.

[27]Ibid., 18. In "Consider the Person," *Catholic Rural Life Bulletin* (May 1939): 9–12, 28–29, Hynes applies Mounier's personalist philosophy to agricultural life.

[28]Abigail McCarthy, *Private Faces/Public Places*, 109.

[29]A biography of Willis Nutting may be found on the University of Notre Dame website, ethicscenter.nd.edu.

[30]Willis Dwight Nutting, *Reclamation of Independence* (Nevada City, CA: Berliner and Lanigan, 1947), 177.

[31]Ibid.

[32]Ibid., 34.

[33]Ibid., 70.

[34]Abigail McCarthy, *Private Faces/Public Places*, 109.

[35]E. J. McCarthy and Mrs. E. J. McCarthy, "A Year on the Land," *Land and Home*, September 1947, 30.

[36]Ibid.

[37]Ibid., 31.

[38]Ibid.

[39]Ibid.

[40]Ibid.

[41]Abigail McCarthy, *Private Faces/Public Places*, 132.

[42]Ibid., 118.

[43]Ibid., 128.

[44]Ibid., 140.

[45]Heinrich Rommen, *The State in Catholic Thought: A Treatise in Political Philosophy* (St. Louis: B. Herder, 1945), 306–11.

[46]Ibid., 302.

[47]Dominic Sandbrook, *Eugene McCarthy: The Rise and Fall of Postwar American Liberalism* (New York: Knopf, 2004), 41.

[48]Albert Eisele, *Almost to the Presidency: A Biography of Two American Politicians* (Blue Earth, MN: Piper, 1972), 76.

[49]Eugene McCarthy, *Up 'Til Now: A Memoir* (San Diego: Harcourt Brace Jovanovich, 1987), 5.

[50]"Address of Senator Eugene J. McCarthy, Conference of Concerned Democrats, Conrad Hilton Hotel, Chicago, Illinois, December 2, 1967," in Eugene J. McCarthy, *The Year of the People* (Garden City, NY: Doubleday, 1969), 287.

[51]Ibid.

[52]Quoted in Eisele, *Almost to the Presidency*, 305.

[53]Eugene McCarthy, speech during 1968 Indiana primary campaign, quoted in Eisele, *Almost to the Presidency*, 311.

[54]"Speech by Senator Eugene J. McCarthy, Sargent Gymnasium, Boston University, Boston, Massachusetts, April 11, 1968," in *The Year of the People*, 303–5.

[55]Sandbrook, *Eugene McCarthy*, 196. The source of the embedded McCarthy quotation is not clear.

[56]On McCarthy's "long exile" after 1968, see Sandbrook, *Eugene McCarthy*, 257–92.

[57]Albert Eisele, "Eugene McCarthy: Poet and Patriot," *Commonweal*, April 21, 2006, 11, quoting *Almost to the Presidency*, 445.

PART III

CONTEMPLATION, ACTION,

AND REVOLUTION

Proximity, Disruption, and Grace

Notes for a Pedagogy
of Racial Justice and Reconciliation

Christopher Pramuk

I sometimes begin graduate courses in theology with a poem by Wendell Berry titled "An Embarrassment." It begins with a fairly innocent if awkward scene around a dinner table, when the meal has been served and everyone waits to see who might be willing to offer grace. It concludes with a disarmingly poignant insight about all attempts to do what we dare to do in our profession: namely, to speak about God. Berry likens the act of offering grace to a man who, "at a sedate party," suddenly removes his clothes and takes his wife passionately in his arms.[1] Though doing theology is not precisely the same as prayer, to dare to say a word about God, to God, and from God, is, as I take Berry to mean, a dangerously intimate business. To try to speak in "sedate" company of that most vulnerable of relationships is to risk embarrassment, at least, if not misunderstanding and blushing humiliation. Our efforts may rise like graceful fireworks only to fall like ash, landing, as Berry suggests, "with a soft thump." The point is, the College Theology Society (CTS) has long been for me a wonderfully congenial and collegial space in which to take the risk. The CTS is "sedate company," appropriate to the subject of our vocation, but not *too* sedate. If there's any group before which I would feel comfortable "removing my clothes," so to speak, theologically, it would be the CTS.

All theology is contextual. Even more, all theology is confessional, insofar as it implicates each of us in a life story, a habitus, a

God-haunted way of proceeding. Not unlike offering the blessing around the dinner table, the doing of theology, whether in print or in the classroom, calls us to "give an account" publicly for the hope that is in us (1 Pet 3:15). The theme of this year's College Theology Society gathering—"'You Say You Want a Revolution': 1968–2018 in Theological Perspective"—is both evocative and provocative because it invites each of us to locate our own vocations within the broad horizon of the developments that have transformed theology in this remarkable half-century. Thus, I have framed what follows largely in autobiographical terms, but in such a way that I hope you will find resonances between your own theological journeys and the questions and movements that have so deeply shaped mine. The stories of "graced encounters across the color line" that I share in the second half of the essay relate to my attempts to teach and write on the topic of racial justice and reconciliation. But those efforts make little sense to me outside a deeper context and dynamism of "proximity, disruption, and grace," a dynamism, both personal and communal, that I explore in the first half of the essay. In other words, I am interested not only in *what* we teach and attempt to say about God, about race, about social justice, and faith, but also in *how* the relational context within and from which we dare to share with others the reasons for our hope profoundly affects the impact of our teaching.

An Era of Social and Ecclesial Revolution

I was born in 1964, in an era that Thomas Merton called a "season of fury."[2] I remember Larry Cunningham, my doctoral director at the University of Notre Dame, describing the 1960s as a time when "the whole country was having a nervous breakdown." As the fourth of six children in my family, I can remember plenty of times my parents seemed to be having a nervous breakdown. How they managed to hold us together, I am not sure. We certainly had our share of domestic madness, but the truth is, I was insulated from the most dramatic events that buffeted the lives of so many Americans during the 1960s. I have no memory of Martin Luther King Jr.'s death—I was three years old—no memory of demonstrations or riots. More than civil rights or Vietnam or even Watergate, which I do remember—Nixon's grim face on the living room television set is not something a child easily forgets—my youth was largely shaped by benevolent social forces: Little League, for example, weekly piano lessons, and the church. If I was not on the baseball field, I was at the piano, trying to learn the latest songs by Billy Joel, or at church rehearsing with the folk choir, learning songs by the St. Louis Jesuits for Mass the following Sunday. In other words, I was the son of middle-class privilege, an inheritor of the American dream, more or less blind to what Malcolm X would call, in the year of my birth, and not long before his death, the American nightmare.[3] Though my childhood was not without its own forms of suffering, one could say, to borrow from Audre Lorde, that I lived in the Master's House, and I still do.[4]

I grew up in Lexington, Kentucky, in a white suburban neighborhood where I had almost no contact with any people of color. In my mid-twenties, I moved to Colorado and was quickly plunged into more diverse environments. Though Kentucky is a border state, and Lexington a big university town, the culture is inescapably southern. As a teenager, one of my favorite things to do was to leave the confines of the suburbs and drive with my friends out to the two-lane country roads bordering the horse farms and tobacco fields beyond the city limits. These rural roadways, lined with antebellum fieldstone walls and freshly painted white wooden fences, were utterly enchanting to me, transporting me into a kind of twilight zone of contemplation. I remember a strange feeling of alarm and sadness when my father casually remarked to me, as we were driving out Old Richmond Road, that slaves had built those fieldstone walls I so admired. It was like the slow puncturing of a balloon, the idyllic innocence of a revered landscape suddenly problematized. Less than three miles from my childhood parish there was and still is a thriving African American Catholic church. I am sad to say that until my mid-twenties I had no idea that black Catholics existed. There are some four million Catholics of African descent in the United States. I did not know them. I could not even see them. Nor was I ever taught the extraordinary history of black Catholic sisters, priests, and lay parishioners across the country, who kept the faith so often in the face of breathtaking racism and discrimination.[5] "The problem of the twentieth century," W. E. B. Du Bois wrote in 1903, "is the problem of the color line,"[6] but like many white

Catholics of my generation, the problem was almost entirely invisible to me.

Of course, you do not really know the bubble in which you are living until someone bursts it. The veil began to lift for me not in the classroom but, perhaps ironically, in the church. Since my childhood, in predominantly African American churches in three different cities, I have been welcomed like a brother, and I have often felt something like the movement of the Spirit stirring deep within my heart, as if saying to me: here are my beloved children on whom my favor rests. Can you see them? Will you share their joys and sorrows? The black Catholic tradition reshaped my whole sense of what it means to be Catholic. And yet for all its cultural and racial blind spots, the ubiquitously white Catholic environment of my youth as I remember it was nevertheless suffused with a spirit of genuine openness and engagement with the world, the revolutionary spirit of Vatican II.

My teachers, many of them good diocesan priests and committed religious sisters, were trying to figure things out in the wake of the council at the same time that I was trying to figure things out. Who am I? To whom do I belong? To what end will I use my gifts? And so it was for the church: Who are we? What is our place in the world as a community of faith? Do we belong to ourselves alone, or is the Spirit calling us to share in the joys and hopes of all people, especially those most afflicted, those hidden in plain sight among us? Somehow the revolutionary vision of *Gaudium et Spes* got infused into my bones, my deepest sensibilities as a Catholic. Maybe it was those subversive St. Louis Jesuits! Or, just as likely, it was the Sisters of Divine Providence who taught at my grade school. Many of them, very young themselves, witnessed to me and my classmates a fierce fidelity to the church's mission in the world that I recall with wonder.[7] Of course, I would later study and absorb into my own Catholic sensibilities other revolutionary movements: feminist and environmental theologies, Latin American, black, and Latino liberation theologies, the witness of Pedro Arrupe, and much later, the Jesuit martyrs of El Salvador. At the University of Notre Dame I had the enormous privilege of studying with Fr. Gustavo Gutiérrez, Fr. Virgil Elizondo, of blessed memory, Sr. Cathy Hilkert, Mary Doak, Matt Ashley, Tim Matovina—a veritable cloud of witnesses in the evolution of my faith, my spirituality, my theological imagination.

But long before I encountered these great teachers, I have my mother to thank for introducing me, at the age of fifteen, to Thomas Merton. More than any other influence, Merton taught me that I could be faithfully Catholic and capaciously curious about other peoples and religious traditions. Indeed, they had something essential to teach me about the mystery of God. There was a music in Merton's writings that broke open my theological imagination, preparing me for later encounters with Karl Rahner and Gustavo Gutiérrez, Malcolm X and James Baldwin, Thich Nhat Hanh and Etty Hillesum, Abraham Joshua Heschel, and more recently, Jewish feminist theologian Melissa Raphael. In Merton, I discovered the feminine face of God, "Hagia Sophia," who breathes in all things, "like the air receiving the sunlight." She is, writes Merton, "the Child who is prisoner in all the people, and who says nothing."[8] Much later, in Melissa Raphael, I would contemplate the female face of God in Auschwitz, the divine Shekhinah, who accompanies the people in their exile and despair.[9] In short, under Merton's tutelage I grew up believing that the "the gate of heaven is everywhere," as he discovered at the corner of Fourth and Walnut, in Louisville, "in the center of the shopping district,"[10] or it is nowhere at all. Either the Christian of the future will be a mystic, as Rahner famously declared, or the Christian will be nothing at all.[11]

Merton is a theologian in the sense that Evagrius used that term to describe "one whose prayer is true, one who sees deeply into the mysteries of God."[12] As Metz would say of the theology of his beloved teacher Rahner, Merton's theology, too, is "a mystical biography of religious experience, of the history of a life before the veiled face of God, in the doxology of faith."[13] And I have tried to bring that sensibility—call it mystical, or contemplative if you prefer—into all my writing and teaching as a theologian. "The world is charged with the grandeur of God,"[14] says Hopkins. My questions became: Are you awake? Are you listening?

Racism, Hope-Building, and the Imagination

In her extraordinary study of women's memoirs in Auschwitz, a book called *The Female Face of God in Auschwitz*, Melissa Raphael suggests that there has been too much asking, "*Where* is God?" in our tumultuous times, and not enough "*Who* is God?"

in our times.[15] In whom is God most urgently being revealed to us? Where is the divine image being hidden, violated, desecrated under our watch? Can we hear Her presence crying out to us in marginalized peoples and cultures, in the cry of the suffering Earth? Though theology has changed dramatically in the last fifty years, the root questions have not changed much at all save the urgency with which we turn our awareness, let us hope not too late, to the suffering planet. Today the writings of another poet and prophet from Kentucky, Wendell Berry, are as crucial to me as the writings of Merton and Metz.[16] Like the Taos Indians of New Mexico or the Lakota Sioux of Standing Rock, Berry reclaims an indigenous metaphysic of creation, or what Pope Francis has called an integral ecology.[17] The protests at Standing Rock show us theology's silence in the half century since Rachel Carson published *Silent Spring*. Our students are paying close attention to the issues coalescing around Standing Rock, but are we?[18]

All of these root questions boil down to the question of hope: What reasons can we give for the hope that is in us? The systematician in me wants to critically examine systems and structures of power that exclude and marginalize to expose, resist, and dismantle those systems. The artist, the musician, the poet in me wants to lift up persons and communities and earthen landscapes that stir in me a sense of divine presence and light in the midst of darkness, a hope against despair in the heart of contradiction. And the theo-poet in me understands that hope is always the fruit of imagination. Where others want to close the book on divine and human possibilities, the poets, mystics, and prophets open the book again, showing us the possibility of many more pages. We still need the systematicians, the sociologists, the economists, the scientists. To paraphrase James Baldwin, where I tend to emphasize the "unprecedented miracles" that human beings are and are capable of becoming, the sociologist, the economist, the critical race theorist remind me not to overlook the "disasters" we have become.[19] How much of my contemplative gaze is shaped by the circumstances of my birth, education, privilege? I do not know how to begin answering this dreadful question. I do know that I constantly need to be asking it.

A chief aim in writing *Hope Sings, So Beautiful* was to join my voice with other Catholic theologians who have inspired me and whose work provides an entry point into conversations around racial justice: Jon Nilson, Shawn Copeland, Jamie Phelps, and Bryan Massingale, to name a few.[20] The book builds from the premise that racism is the symptom of a profound poverty of imagination, including our theological imagination, that is, how we remember and practice our elemental images of God. And a disease of the imagination demands not only moral, ethical, or political responses but also responses that nourish, enlarge, and free the imagination. In Ignatian terms, each of the book's nine chapters offers a "composition of place," drawing from witnesses who have broken open my images and experiential sense of the divine: Howard Thurman, Sr. Thea Bowman, Billie Holiday, Georgia O'Keeffe, Jonathan Kozol, Stevie Wonder, Etty Hillesum, Malcolm X, the Taos Indians, the slave songs and spirituals. All speak to something more than our heads, more than *ideas* about race; they speak to the whole person and open the heart.[21] Throughout the book I also weave elements of my own life story and that of my family. Eight years ago my wife and I adopted two children from Haiti. Thus for eight years the color line has passed through my own family. While that experience has brought much joy, it has also brought sorrow. Both the joy and the sorrow I have come to accept as part of a single fabric, which I would call the mystery of grace.

The remainder of my observations focus on this mystery. Theologically, *Hope Sings, So Beautiful* builds on the theology of grace—an invitation to explore "graced encounters across the color line," and the commitment to create new relationships of understanding, truth-telling, and hope-building across the color line. By "graced" I mean having the character of a gift from God. Such gifts are paradoxical: they can disturb and console at the same time. Grace *interrupts* our habitual ways of seeing, judging, and acting from day to day, revealing truths that have been hidden from our sight.[22] A "graced encounter" is an illumination that leaves us without adequate words to respond, save perhaps "thank you." Grace issues in wonder and amazement, for, as the famous hymn by former slave trader John Newton goes, "I once was lost but now am found, was blind but now I see." As theologians know, grace can break through in the pages of a book, in the witness of another author, living or dead, whose insights may interrupt and disturb, yet at the very same time, inspire wonder. Above all, as Pope Francis insists, grace breaks through in the living encounter with the other, through proximity, drawing near, closeness. To truly encounter another person or community requires resisting what Pope Francis calls the "culture of the adjective,"[23] those convenient labels that hold different communities at arm's length, in a categorical box, to avoid risking the vulnerability, the messiness, the complicity of real encounter. "In life, God accompanies persons," says Pope Francis, "and we must accompany them, starting with their situation."[24]

What follows is an attempt to explore, however tentatively, three "graced encounters" that I have experienced since my book's publication. The first concerns the massacre at Mother Emmanuel AME Baptist Church in Charleston, South Carolina, which occurred in June 2015; the second involves the classroom, and moments of disruption and grace that I have shared with my students; the third has to do with my adopted son Henry, now nine years old, and how being his father has shaped my understanding of what inhabiting a black or brown body might mean in America. I conclude with a brief postscript from James Baldwin.

Graced Encounters across the Color Line

Scene I: Charleston

Recently I flew to Charleston for a long weekend to participate in a retreat on Thomas Merton at Mepkin Abbey, a Trappist monastery on the outskirts of the city. While there, I also spent time with local organizations, including the monks, who, in the wake of the massacre of nine members of the historic Mother Emmanuel AME Church, have been working a great deal in the area of racial justice and reconciliation. The opening evening of the retreat was held in downtown Charleston, just blocks from Mother Emmanuel. As we drove past the church, my host slowed the car to a stop, and together we sat for a while in silence. It felt like hallowed ground, perhaps in the way that Gettysburg, or Golgotha, is hallowed ground.

Mepkin Abbey is situated on a former slave plantation. At the property's edge near the woods, signs indicate a path to a slave cemetery on the property. On the retreat's second day, just before sunrise, I set out for a two-mile hike through corn and cotton fields in the half-light along a rough path through the woods until I came upon an iron arch opening into the slave cemetery. I arrived just as the treetops were starting to glow with the dawn light. The whole landscape breathes what Metz calls "dangerous memory."[25] Even the trees, draped with what locals call "resurrection moss," form a kind of mystic canopy over everything. They seem to hold the presence of the dead. And I could almost hear the slaves singing in the field.

> *I wanna die easy when I die*
> *I wanna die easy when I die*
> *I wanna die easy when I die*
> *shout salvation as I rise*
> *I wanna die easy when I die*
> *when I die. . . .*
> *Wade in the water*
> *Wade in the water children*
> *Wade in the water*
> *God's gonna trouble the water . . .*

In his extraordinary slave narrative, Frederick Douglass describes hearing his fellow slaves singing as they made their way between the fields and the farm house after nightfall, making "the dense old woods, for miles around, reverberate with their wild songs, revealing at once the highest joy and the deepest sadness." "Every tone," he writes, "was a testimony against slavery, and a prayer to God for deliverance from chains. The hearing of those wild notes always depressed my spirit, and filled me with ineffable sadness. I have frequently found myself in tears while hearing them."[26] When I teach Douglass's slave narrative, we begin by reading aloud together the first few pages, slowly, taking turns around the circle. In those pages, Douglass details the faintest memories of his mother coming to hold him in the middle of the night when he was but a few years old. Separated from him as an infant and sold to another plantation twelve miles away, the penalty she risked for "not being in the field at sunrise,"[27] he notes, was a severe whipping. Nevertheless she came. A woman "disappeared" from all other US history accounts, the memory of her nocturnal visits remained burned into his consciousness, her love for him imprinted, it seems, on his very flesh. The flesh memory of his mother's love would pulse in him his whole life long. Though lost, she was found again, in his fierce witness to humanity, to justice, to the abolition of slavery.

The music in Douglass's writing breaks open the heart, and if we allow it, our theological imagination. The dim memory of his mother, the young boy's yearning to know things that most of us take for granted, like the date of his birthday, or the identity of his father (fellow slaves whispered that the white slave master was his father): these questions of identity and belonging resonate across time and distance. Their terrible beauty begins to take hold of my students, to seize their imaginations, even from the first day of class. When I introduce the spirituals on the second or third day of class, one of the first things that students notice is the longing for the mother expressed in so many of the sorrow songs, a yearning that is not too difficult, I think, for any human being to recognize.

> *Sometimes I feel like a motherless child*
> *sometimes I feel like a motherless child*
> *Sometimes I feel like a motherless child*
> *a long way from home.*[28]

Catholic theologian David Tracy, in his still monumentally important work of 1981, *The Analogical Imagination*, describes the "classic" as follows: "When a work of art so captures a paradigmatic experience of [an] event of truth, it becomes in that moment normative. Its memory enters as a catalyst into all our other memories, and, now subtly, now compellingly, transforms our perceptions of the real."[29] For anyone who has experienced the power of Frederick Douglass's writings, the power of the spirituals and sorrow songs—for anyone who has listened to Billie Holiday's devastating rendition of "Strange Fruit" and really allowed it to get under their skin—any "pastoral scene of the gallant South"[30] proves impossible to behold in the same way. Our "perceptions of the real," as Tracy has it, are forever changed. The magnificently restored plantation houses, for example, a big tourist attraction in today's rural South, can no longer be enjoyed without at once "seeing" the bodies of black men hanging from their fragrant trees, and the visage of slave women whipped raw, chained to the hitching post just this side of the mansion's grand entrance.

This is not to suggest we must always remain prisoners of our nation's blood-soaked past. It is to suggest that the past, as hard as we try to "disappear" it, is always contained in the present, like the bodies of the dead who become the earth. The classic, says Tracy, "confronts and provokes us in our present horizon with the feeling that 'something else might be the case.' "[31] The spirituals possess a revelatory power: they unveil—apocalyptically—in the deepest theological sense of that word—the truth of our common humanity, which we have severed from ourselves, from the social body, as like a vital organ or limb. To say it another way, with Johann Baptist Metz, our theological reason, our theo-*logos*, is at its very heart an anamnestic reason, a reason that remembers, a reason ever shadowed by our remembrance of the cross, by the faces of the dead. The questions remain: Precisely *whose* dead haunt our theological imagination? *Which* cloud of witnesses informs and shapes our liturgical-anamnestic consciousness?[32]

These uniquely American spirituals and sorrow songs offer even more. When you hear them as if rising up from the fields and forests, in secret, under the hush arbors at night, you feel a oneness with the Earth itself, the memory of the suffering Earth, who does not forget the least of her creatures. Like the resurrection moss that hangs like a mist over Mepkin Abbey's fields and forests, the whisperings of primordial kinship with the Earth haunt Langston Hughes's poem, "The Negro Speaks of Rivers."[33] The history of Mepkin Abbey's lands haunts the monks whose work is, in part, the work of penance and of reparation—of *tikkun olam*, the repairing of the world, the healing of the social body. "What have you done?" the Lord said to Cain. "The voice of your brother's blood cries out to me from the ground" (Gen 4:10).

Nine members of Mother Emmanuel AME lost their lives on June 17, 2015. The following morning, June 18, Pope Francis released *Laudato Si': On Care for Our Common Home*. Under the shadow of Charleston, I first read Francis's words:

> We are not faced with two separate crises, one environmental and the other social, but rather one complex crisis which is both social and environmental. . . . There can be no renewal of our relationship with nature without a renewal of humanity itself . . . . The violence present in our hearts, wounded by sin, is also reflected in the symptoms of sickness evident in the soil, in the water, in the air and in all forms of life.[34]

After Charleston, the question is not simply how a young white man like Dylann Roof could have so violated the sacredness of life and the good faith of strangers. The harder question is, What kind of a culture could produce a Dylann Roof? What sort of a society could legislate its way free of responsibility for the deaths of Tamir Rice, Sandra Bland, Alton Sterling, Philando Castile, Laquan McDonald, and Sam DuBose? Behind the dying words of Eric Garner—"I can't breathe, I can't breathe"—are ten thousand more voices crying out a painful truth that white Americans may find difficult to register. The culture that produced Dylann Roof and the Flint water crisis will produce many more horrors like these, so long as we refuse to wade into the dark waters of our times, truly listen and learn from one another, and pray God to give us the courage and imagination to create something new in this moment of our history.

A last image from Charleston: at the funeral for Reverend Clementa Pinckney, the slain pastor of Mother Emmanuel, President Obama preached on the theme of grace. He dared to suggest that "as a nation, out of this terrible tragedy, God has visited grace upon us, for he has allowed us to see where we've been blind. We may not have earned it, this grace," he continued, "with our rancor and complacency, and short-sightedness and fear of each other—but we got it all the same. He gave it to us anyway. He's once more given us grace. But it is up to us now to make the most of it, to receive it with gratitude, and to prove ourselves worthy of this gift."[35] And then, to the surprise of everyone, Mr. Obama began to sing the beloved hymn "Amazing Grace," written by John Newton, a former slave trader. Newton, it is worth remembering, wrote with great remorse of his former occupation: "[My] confession . . . comes too late. . . . It will always be a subject of humiliating reflection to me that I was once an active instrument in a business at which my heart now shudders."[36] Grace is disruptive like that. Grace doesn't change the truth, as if magically or mythologically making everything all right again. Grace reveals the truth, sometimes apocalyptically, and then the next move is ours. It is in the acceptance of the truth, and the willingness to "prove ourselves worthy of this gift," that we are set free.

Scene II: Disruption and Grace in the Classroom

Several years ago I developed a first-year seminar for undergraduate freshmen called "Black Literature and Faith." The course was premised on the conviction that the classics of African American literature, music, and art are a powerful lens through which to examine religious faith expression in the United States and the relationship between faith and social justice. I was somewhat reluctant to teach the class knowing the material would surface painful realities for students of every racial background, if for different reasons. I also wondered about the receptivity of students, particularly students of color, to a white professor teaching the class. My reluctance was affirmed when we, the course participants, were quickly thrown outside our comfort zones.

About four weeks into the semester, an argument broke out between two students, an African American female and a Caucasian male, during a discussion around various definitions of racism. The young black woman was making the case that racism as such is tied to social power. Black people can be prejudiced toward whites but not racist, since blacks lack the social power to implement prejudice against whites in any systematic way. The white student objected vigorously, arguing that racial prejudice in any form is racism and is inexcusable. He said it makes him crazy when blacks complain about police as if the whole law enforcement system was racist. "Look," he said, now shouting, "my uncle has been a cop for 20 years. You have no idea what he's up against every day." She shouted back, "*Don't you get it?* When I see a cop in my rear view mirror my whole body literally starts to shake. It's a matter of survival. I don't have the luxury to ask whether this or that officer is a racist. There's zero room for error. I'm trying to make it through another day alive."

Now in the middle of all this, I am asking myself, "OK, what should I do here? Should I intervene, break it up, call a time-out?" I took a deep breath, muttered a silent prayer, and said nothing. The argument raged on. But what happened next was extraordinary. In a pause between their angry back and forth, very tentatively a number of other students began to step into the circle. One by one, they affirmed both of their classmates, suggesting that each had legitimate points. To a person, the interventions were careful, thoughtful, and kind, and the racial breakdown was not what one might expect. A black female student affirmed the white male student's perspective; a white female affirmed the black female's position. Everybody seemed to take a collective breath. I stayed silent. Then, the white male student apologized. Looking across the table, he said, "I'm sorry I shouted at you; I shouldn't have done that." She responded, "It's OK; I'm sorry, too." Finally, I spoke. "This is really, really hard," I said. "But it's real. And it's right where our country seems to be right now. So as hard as it is, it's really important that we don't run from this conversation."

Following class, I replayed the scene over and over again in my head and wondered about my students' willingness to risk the vulnerability of that encounter. And from that day forward, a palpable change occurred in the class: a sense that we could tackle just about any discussion with honesty. Of course, much more remained to unpack together *conceptually*, such as various definitions of racism; but *relationally*, something fundamentally shifted in the classroom. Indeed the students frequently referred to "The Argument," often with humor, as an important breakthrough. I have no better word for what happened than "grace," the kind of grace that breaks down defenses so that we might better grasp the life-world of others. Admittedly, I have often wondered what would have happened if the argument had broken out earlier in the semester, before the group had developed some degree of trust. Would it have unfolded differently, perhaps disastrously?

It occurs to me that we all began the course more or less held captive by what Pope Francis calls the "culture of the adjective": the white professor, the black or Latina or white students; those deemed "first-generation" versus "privileged," determined by appearance or manner of speaking. "There is a distasteful habit, is there not," observes Pope Francis, "of following a 'culture of the adjective': this is so, this is such and such, this is like... No!"

he continues, "This is a child of God. Then come the virtues or defects, but [first] the faithful truth of the person and not the adjective regarded as the substance."[37] Proximity, nearness, closeness, says Francis,

> is the key to truth . . . . Can distances really be shortened where truth is concerned? Yes, they can. Because truth is not only the definition of situations and things from a certain distance, by abstract and logical reasoning. It is more than that. Truth is also fidelity. It makes you name people with their real name, as the Lord names them, before categorizing them or defining "their situation."[38]

Here is the great gift and burden of the classroom: over time the labels simply cannot hold.

If our goal as people of faith, as teachers, as theologians, is growth in understanding others so as to be able to "name people with their real name," we have to find ways to cross not only the physical but also the categorical barriers that divide us. How do we create spaces to draw near and listen deeply through the pain, as my students did in this class?[39] My chief concern with race discourse is how it tends to be practiced in academic circles. The terms "white privilege" and "white supremacy" are powerful and necessary descriptors in the work of racial justice. But how we utilize these terms is crucial. To be clear, I am not talking about protecting white fragility. I am talking about how such terms, if used without care, without relational context—dare I say, without love—can effectively block meaningful dialogue with the very persons we hope to reach.[40] We have to be careful," as Pope Francis insists, "not to fall into the temptation of making idols of certain abstract truths. They can be comfortable idols, always within easy reach; they offer a certain prestige and power and are difficult to discern. Because the 'truth-idol' imitates, it dresses itself up in the words of the Gospel, but it does not let those words touch the heart."[41]

Francis's warning can be difficult for me as an academic. It means stepping out from behind ideas and notions, however valuable, and making room for the mystery of the whole person who sits in front of me, irrespective of skin color, a person with a name, a history, a story. It means showing up ourselves as whole persons, sharing our own joys and sorrows, blindnesses and biases, struggles and mistakes. To the degree we model respect for the whole person in the classroom, it gives our students permission and courage to do the same. This calls for trust, understood also as mercy, or better, the cultivation of what Merton calls a "climate of mercy"—an atmosphere allowing risk and imperfection, stumbling expression and misunderstanding, which are precursors for authentic mutual exploration and growth. The presumption behind the commitment to mercy as a pedagogical first principle is that no two individuals enter the conversation at the same developmental stage in the journey of life and in the web of social relationships. To some extent all of us are stumbling pilgrims on the journey, feeling our way forward in the dark.

A few years ago I taught a class, The Black Catholic Experience, inspired, in part, by the memory of Sr. Thea Bowman.[42] My students and I attended Mass together at two different black Catholic churches in inner-city Cincinnati neighborhoods, both less than five miles from campus. About the experience, one student wrote in his journal: "I have seen a different side of my faith that I did not know anything about. I have learned about the embarrassment that blacks felt when the Jim Crow laws were in effect; I have heard the music that made me *feel* some of the same oppression that African Americans in my own Church were feeling." A female student wrote, "I've learned that you cannot understand a culture by simply reading about it in a textbook—you need to fully immerse yourself, both cognitively and physically, to be a part of it." Did we change the structural dynamics of racism and segregation in the city of Cincinnati? Not by a hair's breadth. But I would never underestimate the impact of those experiences on my students' imaginations, students black and white, the flowering of new possibilities never considered before. As one student put it, "No matter where you come from or what you look like, you are welcome here. We are part of each other's story."

If proximity is a precursor to grace, then surely one of the best gifts we can give students is to take them into unfamiliar communities outside of their comfort zone. Many universities are islands of privilege in the middle of impoverished neighborhoods, reinforcing cultural blindness and outsider gaze. Who are the communities right now in my city, perhaps right next door to my university, with their backs against the wall? Who agonizes over the safety of their children? Who longs to eat the scraps that fall from our table? In sum, it is not enough for white people like me to love black music, black theology, black culture, and not to love, befriend, and defend actual black and brown people; it is not enough to sing the occasional Negro spiritual in class or at my church and consider myself sanctified. Some years ago I heard Dominican Sr. Jamie Phelps put the question this way: "What work are we doing to cultivate the image of God in people of color?" To respond to that question calls for systemic critique *and* personal encounter, the work of justice *and* reconciliation, political solidarity *and* intimate accompaniment, from heart to heart.

Scene III: The Breakfast Table

Pope Francis's cautionary reflections on the "culture of the adjective" bring to mind this era's unrivaled king of categorical broadsides, the current President of the United States. Recall how on January 11, 2018, in a closed-door meeting on immigration, the president referred to Haiti and a number of African nations as "shithole" countries.[43] The following morning, January 12, which happened to be the eighth anniversary of a massive earthquake in Haiti that killed some 300,000 people, I am sitting across the breakfast table from our son Henry, who came to us from an orphanage just outside Port-au-Prince twelve days after the quake. His smile could light up a football stadium. Still stewing over the president's remarks from the day before, I look at Henry, eating his waffles, and I suddenly notice his t-shirt. In large block letters covering the shirt's front, it proclaims: "I CAN'T HEAR YOU OVER THE SOUND OF HOW EPIC I AM." A good countermessage, I thought, to the ignorant and racist words of the president. But my consolation was bittersweet. I had to wonder, and not for the last time: Is Henry welcome to be Henry, in his own skin?

It is not accidental that Henry has struggled a lot under the cloud of the Trump presidency. What has helped him and our family a great deal are people who recognize how EPICALLY BEAUTIFUL he is, with all his gifts and his struggles, no less and no more beautiful than our biological children. It truly does take a village to raise a child. Every person who in the last eight years has loved Henry, who has seen the child of God and not "the adjective regarded as the substance," I thank and I cherish. They include teachers and coaches, therapists and friends, strangers and family members. Clearly, I have skin in the game in a very personal way. But the truth is, we all have skin in the game. Henry cannot stay forever inside the warm glow of his parents' love, nor their white privilege. Here is the great promise and the great burden of America: my son's future well-being belongs to all of us. And so I ask myself, do I have faith in America? Is Henry—a dark-skinned boy, twice the size of his peers in second grade—welcome to be Henry in his own skin?

In the video produced for Starbucks' recent nationwide racial sensitivity training with employees, an African American father shares his pain about the current state of race relations in the United States. His confession casts Langston Hughes's poem, "The Negro Speaks of Rivers," in an even more darkly anamnestic light. In the video, he says:

> It brought me such despair, the day I recognized I had to explain this to my son. That this muddy river of racism, he was still gonna have to walk through it. We hadn't dammed it, we hadn't dried it up. It was still there for him to go through. And I've got to somehow tell him, "Okay—off you go."

Though I cannot know everything about what it means to inhabit the skin of an African American father, as a father myself, as Henry's father, I can know something. We all can, I believe, if we look and listen deeply through the eyes and ears of the heart. The culture of the adjective diminishes us all, but disproportionately it destroys the lives of children of color. We must be faithful to the "*truth of the person and not the adjective regarded as the substance.*"

The Unpaid Promissory Note

Four years after the assassination of Dr. King, James Baldwin published a remarkable essay titled "Martin and Malcolm,"[44] a meditation on loss and grief and rage in the wake of Martin's and

Malcolm's deaths. The essay's moral power turns on the question every person of color must have asked in the wake of King's death, a question many still ask today. As Baldwin frames it, "To what extent am I prepared to gamble on the good faith of my countrymen?"[45] Under the shadow of King's death, "an unforgivable indignity, both personal and vast," Baldwin nakedly confesses his own struggle for faith: faith in human beings, faith in God, faith in white people, faith in America, and whether the good faith of people of color, the promissory note of American democracy, will ever be returned to them in kind. The essay concludes with both a plea and a veiled warning, identifying a wound that still throbs deep and wide beneath the staid surfaces of American life.

> If I still thought, as I did when Martin and Malcolm were still alive, that the generality of white Americans were able to hear and to learn and begin to change, I would counsel them, as vividly as I could, to attempt, now, to minimize the bill which is absolutely certain to be presented to their children. . . . If I were you, I would pause a long while before deciding to use what you think of as your power. For we, the blacks, have not found possible what you found necessary: we have not denied our ancestors who trust us, now, to redeem their pain.[46]

If I still thought that the generality of white Americans were able to hear and to learn and begin to change: here, it seems to me, Baldwin exposes the stubbornly vexatious heart of the race question that continues to interrogate our work as teachers and theologians.

For my part, I can only confess that if I did not believe that "the generality of white Americans" were capable of change, not least my white students, I wouldn't last two weeks, much less twenty years, in the classroom. Not every day, of course, but day after day, in the "fullness of time," as it were, I have come to know the classroom as a sacred space, a space for grace, where the work of deep listening, learning, and transformation can and does break through. Teaching, no less than theology, is an act of faith, and though the fruits of our labors are not often seen directly, they bear out over time in who our students become. In the meantime,

I believe that every effort we make, whenever it is done from love, both reconciles the pain of the ancestors and plants genuine seeds of hope for the next generation, for children and young people of all races. The veil is pulled away, if even for a moment, and a small part of that tear in the fabric of the beloved community is made whole again.

Notes

[1]Wendell Berry, *Leavings: Poems* (Berkeley, CA: Counterpoint, 2010), 16–17. Jewish poet and philosopher of religion Rabbi Abraham Joshua Heschel often used the word "embarrassment" to characterize faith and the attempt to describe it. Etty Hillesum, in her war-time diaries, wonders, "But is there indeed anything as intimate as man's relationship with God?" See Etty Hillesum, *An Interrupted Life: The Diaries (1941–1943) and Letters from Westerbork* (New York: Henry Holt, 1996), 105.

[2]Thomas Merton, *Emblems of a Season of Fury* (New York: New Directions, 1963).

[3]Malcolm X, "The Ballot or the Bullet," April 3, 1964, *Malcolm X Speaks: Selected Speeches and Statements*, ed. George Breitman (New York: Grove, 1965), 23–44.

[4]Audre Lorde, "The Master's Tools Will Never Dismantle the Master's House," in *Sister Outsider: Essays and Speeches by Audre Lorde* (Trumansburg, NY: Crossing Press, 1984), 114–23.

[5]Foundational texts used in my teaching that history include Cyprian Davis, *The History of Black Catholics in the United States* (New York: Crossroad, 1995); M. Shawn Copeland, ed., *Uncommon Faithfulness: The Black Catholic Experience* (Maryknoll, NY: Orbis Books, 2009); Albert Raboteau, *Canaan Land: A Religious History of African Americans* (New York: Oxford, 1999); Bryan Massingale, *Racial Justice and the Catholic Church* (Maryknoll, NY: Orbis Books, 2010); United States Conference of Catholic Bishops, *Plenty Good Room: The Spirit and Truth of African American Worship* (1991). Also effective are compilations of short oral histories of individual black Catholics and black Catholic churches in local communities, such as those gathered by the Office of African American Catholic Ministries of the Archdiocese of Cincinnati, in *Tracing Your Catholic Roots: 1990–2009*, at www.catholiccincinnati.org, as well as connecting with local Black Catholics who can share their stories directly with students as guest speakers.

[6]W. E. B. Du Bois, *The Souls of Black Folk* (New York: Oxford World's Classics, 2007), 3, 15.

[7]See others' accounts of indebtedness to women religious before, during, and after Vatican II in *Thank You, Sisters: Stories of Women Religious and How They Enrich Our Lives*, ed. John Feister (Cincinnati: Franciscan Media, 2009).

[8]Thomas Merton, "Hagia Sophia," in *Emblems of a Season of Fury*, 63.

[9]Melissa Raphael, *The Female Face of God in Auschwitz: A Jewish Feminist Theology of the Holocaust* (New York: Routledge, 2003).

[10]Thomas Merton, *Conjectures of a Guilty Bystander* (Garden City, NY: Doubleday, 1966), 156–57.

[11]"Tomorrow's devout person will either be a mystic—someone who has 'experienced' something—or else they will no longer be devout at all." Cited in *Karl Rahner: Spiritual Writings*, ed. Phillip Endean (Maryknoll, NY: Orbis Books, 2004), 24. Endean cautions that we misinterpret Rahner [and Merton] if we take such statements to mean "that future Christians must be like John of the Cross." For both Merton and Rahner "we need to lose the sense of elitism associated with talk of the mystical" (ibid.).

[12]See Christopher Pramuk, *Sophia: The Hidden Christ of Thomas Merton* (Collegeville, MN: Michael Glazier/Liturgical, 2009), 21, citing A. M. Allchin. For a compact exploration of Merton's Wisdom-haunted theological imagination, see Christopher Pramuk, *At Play in Creation: Merton's Awakening to the Feminine Divine* (Collegeville, MN: Liturgical, 2015); idem, "Theodicy and the Feminine Divine: Thomas Merton's 'Hagia Sophia' in Dialogue with Western Theology," *Theological Studies* 77 (2016): 48–76, and references therein.

[13]Johann B. Metz, "*Karl Rahner—ein theologisches Leben*," cited in Harvey D. Egan, "Theology and Spirituality," in *The Cambridge Companion to Karl Rahner*, ed. Declan Marmion and Mary E. Hines (New York: Cambridge University Press, 2005), 14.

[14]Gerard Manley Hopkins, "God's Grandeur," in *Gerard Manley Hopkins: The Major Works* (Oxford: Oxford University Press, 1986), 128.

[15]Raphael, *The Female Face of God in Auschwitz*, 54; on exploring Raphael's work with students, see Christopher Pramuk, "Making Sanctuary for the Divine: Exploring Melissa Raphael's Holocaust Theology," *Studies in Christian-Jewish Relations* 12, no. 1 (2017): 1–16.

[16]For example, Wendell Berry, *The World-Ending Fire: The Essential Wendell Berry* (Berkeley, CA: Counterpoint, 2018).

[17]Pope Francis, *Laudato Si': On Care for Our Common Home*, at w2.vatican.va, especially nos. 137–55. For the resonances between Merton's "sapiential epistemology" and Pope Francis's integral ecology, see Christopher Pramuk, "Contemplation and the Suffering Earth: Thomas Merton, Pope Francis, and the Next Generation," *Open Theology* 4 (2018): 212–27.

[18]Rachel Carson, *Silent Spring* (New York: Houghton Mifflin, 1962). While the fields of eco-theology and eco-justice have burgeoned in the last fifty years, more Catholic theologians today—in the United States led by pioneering feminist theologian Elizabeth Johnson—are reclaiming what we might call an indigenous metaphysic of creation, or reimagining, in mystical-evolutionary terms, what Pope Francis terms an integral ecology. See Elizabeth Johnson, *Ask the Beasts: Darwin and the God of Love* (London: Bloomsbury, 2014); idem, *Creation and the Cross: The Mercy of God for a Planet in Peril* (Maryknoll, NY: Orbis Books, 2018); Anthony Annett, Jeffrey Sachs, and William Vendley, *The Significance of Laudato Si'* (Mahwah, NJ: Paulist, 2018). Contemplative theologians like Douglas Christie, much in the

way of Merton, seek to retrieve the ancient wisdom of the Eastern desert fathers and mothers in reorienting our vision to the rhythms of the natural world. See Douglas E. Christie, *The Blue Sapphire of the Mind: Notes for a Contemplative Ecology* (New York: Oxford, 2013); Monica Weis, *The Environmental Vision of Thomas Merton* (Lexington: University Press of Kentucky, 2011).

[19]"Incontestably, alas, most people are not, in action, worth very much; and yet every human being is an unprecedented miracle. One tries to treat them as the miracles they are, while trying to protect oneself against the disasters they become." James Baldwin, "Martin and Malcolm," *Esquire*, April 1972, 94.

[20]Christopher Pramuk, *Hope Sings, So Beautiful: Graced Encounters across the Color Line* (Collegeville, MN: Michael Glazier/Liturgical Press, 2013).

[21]On the "method of catholicity" I employ, with both Merton and Ignatian spirituality as implicit guides, and also the link between racism and the imagination, see *Hope Sings*, xxi–xxv.

[22]My method in *Hope Sings* is also much indebted to Johann Baptist Metz, whose political theology is built on the categories of memory, narrative, and solidaristic hope. Metz adopts the phrase "dangerous memory" to describe the disruptive or interruptive power of Jesus's death and resurrection, and by extension, the remembrance of all the forgotten victims of history. "The shortest definition of religion: interruption." See his *Faith in History and Society: Toward a Practical Fundamental Theology*, trans. J. Matthew Ashley (New York: Crossroad, 2007).

[23]Pope Francis, Homily for Holy Thursday Chrism Mass, March 29, 2018, w2.vatican.va/content.

[24]Anthony Spadaro, "A Big Heart Open to God: The Exclusive Interview with Pope Francis," *America* 209 (September 30, 2013), 26. Of course, behind this vision of accompaniment and graced encounter is a profoundly incarnational, sacramental, and Ignatian sensibility, a memory and experience of God who comes to us "in all things," a grace that overflows all boundaries.

[25]Metz, *Faith in History and Society*, 182–85.

[26]"Narrative of the Life of Frederick Douglass," in *The Classic Slave Narratives*, ed. Henry Louis Gates (New York: Signet, 2012), 324–25.

[27]Ibid., 316.

[28]Compare these lines to the harrowing scenes at the US southern border of children separated from their parents ("illegal aliens" that are "infesting" our country) and kept in holding facilities for children of "tender age," as the current administration terms these shelters. See Garance Burke and Martha Mendoza, "At Least Three Tender Age Facilities Set Up for Child Migrants," Associated Press, June 20, 2018.

[29]David Tracy, *The Analogical Imagination: Christianity and the Culture of Pluralism* (1981; New York: Crossroad, 1998), 115.

[30]Billie Holiday, "Strange Fruit" (Commodore, 1940), composed by Lewis Allan, a.k.a. Abel Meeropol, 1939; Pramuk, *Hope Sings*, 53–66. The documentary *Strange Fruit* (dir. Joel Katz [San Francisco: California Newsreel, 2002]) chronicles the song's historical genesis and its often contentious reception when Holiday performed it live.

[31]Tracy, *The Analogical Imagination*, 102.

[32]See Christopher Pramuk, "Black Suffering/White Revelation," *Theological Studies* 67 (2006): 345–77. This question links Metz's European political theology, shadowed by the memory of Auschwitz, with North American black liberation theology, haunted by the history and enduring effects of slavery. Both trajectories interrogate Western theology's historical amnesia with respect to what Metz calls the "unreconciled dead."

[33]*The Collected Poems of Langston Hughes* (New York: Vintage Classics, 1994), 23. The poem could not be excerpted here due to permissions restrictions.

[34]*Laudato Si'*, nos. 139, 118.

[35]President Barack Obama, "Remarks by the President in Eulogy for the Honorable Reverend Clementa Pinckney," June 26, 2015, at obamawhitehouse.archives.gov.

[36]John Newton, *Thoughts Upon the African Slave Trade* (1787), cited in spartacus-educational.com.

[37]Pope Francis, Homily for Holy Thursday Chrism Mass.

[38]Ibid.,

[39]Jon Nilson has consistently and courageously asked himself and other white Catholic theologians to ask themselves the same question. See his *Hearing Past the Pain: Why White Catholic Theologians Need Black Theology* (Mahwah, NJ: Paulist Press, 2007); and Jon Nilson, "Confessions of a White Catholic Racist Theologian," *Origins* 33 (2003): 130–38.

[40]See *Hope Sings*, 1–5, where I try to argue this point from multiple sides, with as much complexity and nuance as it deserves.

[41]Pope Francis, Homily for Holy Thursday Chrism Mass.

[42]See Charlene Smith and John Feister, *Thea's Song: The Life of Thea Bowman* (Maryknoll, NY: Orbis Books, 2012); Christopher Pramuk, "To Live Fully: The Witness of Thea Bowman," *America*, June 24, 2014, 25–26; idem, "O Happy Day: Imagining a Church beyond the Color Line," *America*, August 18, 2003, 8–10.

[43]See Josh Dawsey, "Trump Derides Protections for Immigrants from 'Shithole' Countries," *Washington Post*, January 12, 2018.

[44]James Baldwin, "Martin and Malcolm," *Esquire*, April 1972.

[45]Ibid.

[46]Ibid.

Bernard Lonergan on the Revolution in Catholic Theology

Donna Teevan

In 1972 Bernard Lonergan gave an address titled "Revolution in Catholic Theology."[1] In this lecture and others around that time, Lonergan argues that in the twentieth century "theology is undergoing a profound change, one comparable in magnitude to the change that occurred in the Middle Ages."[2] The elements of this change are laid out in several papers that were originally given as lectures or published as articles in or around 1968.[3] In these papers, Lonergan contends that "the contemporary issue is, not a new religion, not a new faith, but a belated social and cultural transition,"[4] one that calls for a reassessment of theology's foundations.

The themes in Lonergan's work at this time have much in common with how Sandra Yocum Mize characterizes the period of 1965–1974 in her history of the College Theology Society. The headings for her chapter on 1965–1974 include "Vatican II as a Metaphor for Change"; "Teaching College Theology in a Time of Revolution"; "A New Breed of Students"; "Turning to the Subject"; "Personalist Touch, Existential Quandary"; "Method"; "Theology and Its Authorities"; and finally, "From Personal Freedom to Political Liberation."[5] Lonergan does not detail the actual events taking place at this time but chooses instead to dig into what he saw as the underpinnings of this transition as they pertain to Catholic theology. He identifies four: (1) the shift from a normative, even classicist notion of culture, to an empirical, historically conscious understanding of it; (2) developments in modern philosophy that incline toward greater existential concerns and concreteness; (3) the growing influence of modern science with its emphasis on verifiability; and (4) the introduction of new interdisciplinary interlocutors for Catholic theology, such as religious studies and the social sciences, as well as the urgent need for theology to contribute to its more traditional conversation partners in the humanities. Although Lonergan noted that he "cannot prophesy,"[6] much of what he identified as significant has led to important developments in theology, some of which are still ongoing.

The Shift to an Empirical, Historically Conscious Understanding of Culture

In his 1968 essay "Belief: Today's Issue," Lonergan argues that what Catholic theology is struggling with in his day is "a belated social and cultural transition."[7] He defines "the social" aspect of this transition as that which pertains to a way of living and "the cultural" dimension as related to "the meaning we find in our present way of life, the value we place upon it, or, again, the things we find meaningless, stupid, wicked, horrid, atrocious, disastrous."[8] He describes this understanding of culture as empirical rather than classicist because it recognizes cultures as multiple and as created by human beings rather than as singular, normative givens. Whereas classicists saw human beings as personally responsible for their individual lives, as Lonergan observes, the modern person knows that human beings have a collective responsibility for the world. The situation of Catholics of his time, as he sees it, is one of "disorientation, disillusionment, crisis, surrender, and unbelief."[9] He attributes this state of affairs to the fact that until Vatican II, Catholics were sheltered from some of the challenges of the modern world which they were now experiencing with full force.

In another 1968 article, "Theology in Its New Context," Lonergan again contends that the changes to which theology was responding in the 1960s reflect "not a new revelation or a new faith, but a new cultural context."[10] He insists that in this encounter with the culture of the times, it is vital that theology accurately interpret the cultural factors at work in the world. He then goes on to list the changes in theology that have taken place in this new context. Theology was deductive but now is empirical, in the sense that Scripture and Tradition were understood to provide data rather than premises. The new context demands an awareness of historical evolution and development that was lacking in the old dogmatic theology's understanding of history.

The vocabulary and conceptual framework of the new theology draws not from Aristotle's philosophy but from biblical words and images, as well as from historicist, personalist, phenomenological, and existential thought. This new conceptual apparatus attends more fully to the concrete person as "incarnate subject" and to what Lonergan calls "the constitutive role of meaning in human living."[11] Meaning is important because human beings make themselves and their world through acts of meaning. The freedom of humankind to choose the meanings that shape human living is what Lonergan calls "the realm of freedom and creativity, of solidarity and responsibility, of dazzling achievement and pitiable madness."[12] This "realm" of the human person is also where human beings encounter God and where God is at work in the world. It is here that theology has an important role to play, for theology is called "to mediate God's meaning into the whole of human affairs" and thus to influence the cultural context with a concern that includes all human beings, not just Catholics.[13] In undertaking the task, theology must use the tools of newer disciplines such as the social sciences as well as the more traditional ones.

At this point, Lonergan calls for a new foundation for theology and argues that this foundation should be "the method that will generate the revision of conclusions, laws, principles of tomorrow."[14] This list of revisions might lead one to conclude that he advocates a theological method modeled on the natural sciences, but he argues that theology is reflection on religion and that at the heart of religion is conversion. Reflection on conversion leads theology to its new foundation. As he puts it, the new type of foundation is found "not in objective statement but in subjective reality."[15] He describes this foundation as "concrete, dynamic, personal, communal, and historical."[16]

In late 1973 and into 1974, Lonergan again turned to the issue of revolution in Catholic theology, except at this point he punctuated the topic with a question mark. In a lecture series at the University of Toronto and then again at Yale University, he explores the question: "Revolution in Catholic Theology?"[17] His first lecture continues his emphasis on the historical and personal in an exploration of "a new pastoral theology," a result of Vatican II, which he characterizes as a pastoral council. He is emphatic that what is involved in this new pastoral theology is much more than the application of the universal to particular situations. With relevance to the whole of theology, this new pastoral theology attends to the individual, personal, the communitarian, and the historical. He notes too that this new theology "places orthopraxis above orthodoxy," although the two are closely bound. Unlike the theology of the past which derived its terms from metaphysics, this new theology derives its basic concepts from "immediate human experience as brought to light by intentionality analysis."[18] Nonetheless, Lonergan contends that metaphysics is not to be discarded but to be critically grounded. He concludes by arguing that "the very development of doctrine calls for a doctrinal pluralism, for there are as many manners of teaching the same basic message as there are distinct classes dividing each of the many cultures of mankind."[19] Here again he highlights the significance of an empirical rather than a classical notion of culture.

Modern Philosophy's Greater Existential Concerns and Concreteness

In one of his 1968 lectures, Lonergan states that he saw Catholic theology "disengaging itself from Aristotle and deriving new categories from personalist, phenomenological, existentialist, historicist and transcendental types of philosophic thought."[20] He welcomed these new developments and, perhaps because of his openness to change, he was asked to address students at Loyola College (Montreal) who were experiencing the unrest present on many campuses in 1968. As he explains it, "It has been found, I am told, that existential philosophy has exerted an unfortunate influence on student behavior, and I have been asked to elucidate the matter."[21] In the essay he delivered, titled "Existential Crisis," he asserts that such a crisis can arise in one of two ways. The first, which he associates with Europe and its experiences in the two

World Wars, "arises from a conflict between the individual's need to exist authentically and the objective situation in which he finds himself."[22] The second, which he associates with Canada and the United States, is one in which "youth suspects the authenticity of their elders, refuses to accept their way of life, is determined to reshape things in some quite different, if unspecified manner."[23] Note that in both cases, the issue is authenticity, not the corrosive effect of a modern philosophy. What follows in his essay offers advice concerning the specific situation in 1968, but he concludes that existential crises generally arise from social ills, or from a lack in the educational process, or from some combination of both. There is more than a hint in his analysis that the difficulties being experienced might be better understood through an examination of the social situation and an appreciation for how powerful the human desire for authenticity actually is.

The Growing Influence of Modern Science with Its Emphasis on Verifiability

Already in the 1950s, Lonergan was exploring the relation between Thomist thought and modern science as part of his efforts to bring Catholic theology into conversation with modern science.[24] His 1957 book *Insight* reveals the depth of his interest in empirical method.[25] He develops a generalized empirical method, one that applies not just to sense data but to the data of consciousness. It should not be surprising then that in explaining the title for his Toronto/Yale lectures, "Revolution in Catholic Theology?" Lonergan states that the revolution he has in mind is not a political revolution, but the kind of revolution set out by Thomas Kuhn in his now classic *The Structure of Scientific Revolutions*. Lonergan, like Kuhn, focuses on the kind of achievement that changes "the whole face of things" and begins a new period of "normal science" in which this new way of understanding is applied to problems that can now be understood more fully and deeply.[26]

Although Lonergan never advocated a model of theological method based simply on the natural sciences, he did assume that theology is grounded in the same human intelligence as science and that it can learn from the sciences. During this period of

1968–1974, Lonergan repeatedly contended that modern science (1) is quite different from the science of Aristotle; (2) depends on its method, a self-correcting process of learning; (3) demands specialization, which creates a need for collaboration; and (4) offers conclusions that are not ultimately final but only the best scientific opinion of the day and thus open to revision. Lonergan offers both an appreciation for the natural sciences and a healthy awareness of where things go wrong when science becomes scientism or when science is valued only for the technological advances it provides.

During this period, Lonergan also dealt with practical matters rooted in scientific developments. One especially associated with 1968 was the promulgation of *Humanae Vitae*.[27] The Canadian bishops consulted with Lonergan prior to their meeting in Winnipeg to discuss the encyclical. In a letter dated September 1968, he points out that traditional Catholic teaching on this topic was based on Aristotelian biology, now known to be inaccurate.[28] He focuses not on questions of dissent from *Humanae Vitae* but on its problematic grounding in an Aristotelian rather than a modern biological understanding of the relation between insemination and conception. He also points out *Humanae Vitae*'s neglect of what modern phenomenology brings to light about marital intercourse as an expression and sustainer of love. In this way, Lonergan brought the revolution in Catholic theology, in its scientific and philosophical aspects, to bear on a practical matter much debated in his time.

New Interdisciplinary Interlocutors for Catholic Theology

Lonergan most clearly displays his thinking on theology and its conversation partners in a 1968 lecture, "Theology and Man's Future," delivered at St. Louis University. His lecture begins with a statement about the university's changing role in the world.

For the university has ceased to be a storehouse whence traditional wisdom and knowledge are dispensed. It is a center in which ever-increasing knowledge is disseminated to bring about ever-increasing social and cultural change. It has a grave responsibility for the future of man.[29]

He goes on to explore the impact of five disciplines on Catholic theology at this time: history, philosophy, religious studies, method, and communication.

As is evident in all of his writings during this period, Lonergan emphasized the impact that modern historical scholarship has had on Catholic theology, not just in the study of patristics and medieval theology—or even biblical scholarship—but on every aspect of theology. He observes that "a great revolution was needed—and it is not yet completed."[30] Lonergan sometimes uses "history" as shorthand for "historical consciousness" and for theology's need to take into account the development of doctrine. He argues that "to put the matter historically, to follow Aquinas today is not to repeat Aquinas today, but to do for the twentieth century what he did for the thirteenth."[31] Aquinas, according to Lonergan, sought to "baptize" elements of Greek and Arabic culture, and his contemporaries in theology have an analogous task: to baptize key elements of modern culture, though not uncritically.

With regard to philosophy, he argues, here as elsewhere, that contemporary Catholic theology must accept the inadequacy of Aristotelian philosophy to respond to every problem or task now at hand, given the ancient philosopher's lack of modern scientific knowledge. This inadequacy does not lessen theology's need for philosophy, but in fact makes the need even more urgent. Lonergan describes theologians' primary need simply: "to know what [they are] doing when they are doing theology."[32] In other words, "Theologians have minds and use them, and they had best know what they are doing when they use them."[33]

Explicitly influenced by Vatican II and its concern with ecumenism, interreligious dialogue, and the growth of atheism, Lonergan identifies religious studies as one of the disciplines that theology must now engage. He envisions Catholic theology as maintaining its own identity while being in conversation with other religions and thus in dialogue with the discipline of religious studies. For theology to have an impact on modern culture, which Lonergan wants, requires interaction not only with the traditional disciplinary partners of theology but also with all of the human sciences. The post–Vatican II world of ecumenism and interreligious dialogue especially demands engagement with the discipline of religious studies, a field that draws heavily on the social sciences.

In particular, Lonergan sees religious studies as of interest to the theologian because it explores God's grace in various places throughout the world. He also appreciates religious studies' rejection of classicist assumptions.[34] Nonetheless, he makes clear that theology must remain distinct from religious studies because theology deals with God and all things in relation to God, whereas religious studies, as he understands it, concerns human beings in their dealings with God or gods and goddesses and, at least in some models, operates similarly to the natural sciences (to such a degree, in fact, that it could even fall into reductionism). Religious studies cannot replace theology, Lonergan insists, because "the divine is not a datum to be observed by sense or to be uncovered by introspection."[35]

The fourth discipline Lonergan discusses is "method," which brings him to the topic of modern science, previously discussed. The fifth and last discipline is communications. Here Lonergan acknowledges the church's mission to proclaim the gospel and mentions once again the impact of shifting from a classicist to an empirical notion of culture in thinking about how to do this work. This modern understanding of culture appreciates how numerous the world's cultures are and how complex the task of communicating is. It is here, and later, more thoroughly in *Method in Theology*,[36] that Lonergan frequently refers to the importance of meaning and the need for hermeneutics. At this point in his work, he is also more attentive to the role of feeling in both Christian life and theology. The Christian message, he writes, has to touch "the manifold fabric of everyday meaning and feeling that directs and propels the lives of" men and women.[37]

After describing the impact of other disciplines on theology, Lonergan then turns to what theology has to offer other disciplines. Here he invokes John Henry Newman's well-known argument that if one significant part of knowledge is omitted, the whole of human knowing is distorted. Thus, it is vital that theology participate in interdisciplinary conversations with both the sciences and the humanities. Lonergan observes that by modeling themselves after the natural sciences, the human or social sciences risk the loss of what is human or social about them. He sees the human sciences as needing to avoid reductionism and what he calls "philosophic fads." He argues that theology has much to offer the human sciences in that theology engages important aspects of various philosophies (rather than adopting any one of them in its entirety). It also has centuries of experience grappling with matters of meaning and values. He goes on to say that theology has something to offer the humanities as well. Citing modern humanism's tendency "to ignore God and to ridicule religion, when it is not militantly atheistic," Lonergan insists that authentic humanism is inherently religious.[38] The human being has a capacity for self-transcendence and a need to find fulfillment in being in love with God. Theological expertise in these matters can assist the humanities in grounding themselves in a more authentic humanism.

Social Transformation:
An Intended Outcome of the Revolution

Lonergan's 1968 papers reveal his thinking about what a few years later he called the revolution in Catholic theology. In general, his writings attended to what he saw as the social and cultural shifts that necessitated a long overdue Catholic theological encounter with modernity. Although Lonergan embraced modernity, he has a sophisticated understanding of the task of the *aggiornamento* initiated by Vatican II and an appreciation for the past as well as the present, along with a deep concern for the future:

> *Aggiornamento* is not desertion of the past but only a discerning and discriminating disengagement from its limitations. *Aggiornamento* is not just acceptance of the present; it is acknowledgment of its evil as well as of its good; and, as acknowledgment alone is not enough, it also is, by the power of the cross, that meeting of evil with good which transforms evil into good.[39]

Lonergan's writings from this period make clear his vision of theology not just as faith seeking understanding but as faith seeking an understanding that will transform the world.

Lonergan's "Revolution in Catholic Theology" lecture (not the lecture series) was presented in some form at a College Theology Society event in 1972, according to Sandra Yocum Mize's *Joining the Revolution in Theology.* Yocum Mize observes that the two respondents to Lonergan's paper both objected to the abstractness of what he proposed, with its focus on hermeneutics and on culture as the context of all knowing. One respondent, William Murnion, argued that the revolution in Catholic theology is to be found instead in the "practical" activities of the Berrigans, Dom Helder Camara, and Bishop Gumbleton. The other respondent, Austin B. Vaughan, stated that he would have preferred to see Lonergan "paying more attention to the 'life of the Church' rather than the 'mental processes of theologians.' "[40] Although there is some merit in these critiques, Lonergan's papers in the 1960s and 1970s demonstrate his awareness that these shifts have important implications for the well-being of the church and indeed of the larger world.

To better appreciate Lonergan's thinking about theology's potential impact on the world, it is helpful to understand Lonergan's distinction between infrastructure and superstructure as well as his distinction between religion and theology.[41] For Lonergan, "Theology stands to religion, as economics does to business, as biology to health, as chemistry to [d]uPont industries. . . . Theology pertains to the cultural superstructure, while religion pertains to its day to day substance."[42] Putting it another way, he quips that "most saints were not theologians, and most theologians were not saints."[43] Religion or religious living for Lonergan is part of the infrastructure. Theology cannot replace actual authentic religious living, but it can inform it (and vice versa). Lonergan perceived very well the many challenges of his day and understood that Catholic theology required nothing short of a revolution to operate effectively in its time and thus make its contribution to an authentic transformation of the world.

Notes

[1]Bernard Lonergan, "Revolution in Catholic Theology," in *A Second Collection: Papers by Bernard J. F. Lonergan, SJ*, ed. William F. J. Ryan and Bernard J. Tyrrell (London: Darton Longman and Todd, 1974 [Reprint edition, Toronto: University of Toronto, 1996]), 231–38. *A Second Collection* has been released in a revised and augmented edition: *The Collected Works of Bernard Lonergan*, ed. Robert M. Doran and John D. Dadosky, vol. 13, *A Second Collection* (Toronto: University of Toronto Press, 2016). Citations in this essay refer to the original edition.

[2]Bernard Lonergan, "Revolution in Catholic Theology," in *A Second Collection*, 237.

[3]Most of the relevant papers are in *A Second Collection*, but others are in *The Collected Works of Bernard Lonergan*, ed. Robert C. Croken and Robert M. Doran, vol. 17, *Philosophical and Theological Papers, 1965–1980* (Toronto: University of Toronto Press, 2004).

[4]Lonergan, "Belief: Today's Issue," in *A Second Collection*, 98.

[5]Sandra Yocum Mize, "Theology as Liberation, Revolution, Freedom (1965–1974)," in *Joining the Revolution in Theology: The College Theology Society, 1954–2004* (Lanham, MD: Rowman & Littlefield, 2007), 89–109.

[6]Lonergan, "Revolution in Catholic Theology," in *A Second Collection*, 237.

[7]Lonergan, "Belief: Today's Issue," in *A Second Collection*, 98.

[8]Ibid., 91.

[9]Ibid., 93.

[10]Lonergan, "Theology in Its New Context," in *A Second Collection*, 58.

[11]Ibid., 61.

[12]Ibid.

[13]Ibid., 62.

[14]Ibid., 64.

[15]Ibid., 67.

[16]Ibid.

[17]Lonergan, "Revolution in Catholic Theology?" in *Philosophical and Theological Papers, 1965–1980*.

[18]Ibid., 237.

[19]Ibid., 239.

[20]Lonergan, "Theology and Man's Future," in *A Second Collection*, 143.

[21]Bernard Lonergan, "Existential Crisis," in *The Collected Works of Bernard Lonergan*, ed. Robert C. Croken, Robert M. Doran, and H. Daniel Monsour, vol. 20, *Shorter Papers* (Toronto: University of Toronto Press, 2007), 258.

[22]Ibid., 259.

[23]Ibid.

[24]Frederick E. Crowe, *Lonergan* (Collegeville, MN: Liturgical Press, 1992), 54. For a look at how Lonergan's thought relates to theological questions regarding evolution, see Cynthia Crysdale and Neil Ormerod, *Creator God, Evolving World* (Minneapolis: Fortress Press, 2013).

[25]Bernard Lonergan, *The Collected Works of Bernard Lonergan*, ed. Frederick E. Crowe and Robert M. Doran, vol. 3, *Insight* (Toronto: University of Toronto Press, 1992).

[26]Lonergan, "A New Pastoral Theology," in *Philosophical and Theological Papers, 1965–1980*, 222.

[27]*Humanae Vitae*, www.vatican.va.

[28]"Letter on Humanae Vitae," www.bernardlonergan.com.

[29]Lonergan, "Theology and Man's Future," in *A Second Collection*, 135.

[30]Ibid., 136.

[31]Ibid., 138.

[32]Ibid., 137–38.

[33]Ibid., 138.

[34]Lonergan, "The Absence of God in Modern Culture," in *A Second Collection*, 107.

[35]Ibid.

[36]Bernard Lonergan, *The Collected Works of Bernard Lonergan*, ed. Robert M. Doran and John D. Dadosky, vol. 14, *Method in Theology* (Toronto: University of Toronto Press, 2017).

[37]Lonergan, "Theology and Man's Future," in *A Second Collection*, 141.

[38]Ibid., 144.

[39]Lonergan, "The Absence of God in Modern Culture," in *A Second Collection*, 113.

[40]Yocum Mize, *Joining the Revolution in Theology*, 101–3.

[41]For a fuller exploration of the infrastructure and superstructure that is grounded in Lonergan's work yet goes beyond him, see Robert M. Doran, *Theology and the Dialectics of History* (Toronto: University of Toronto Press, 1990).

[42]Lonergan, "Belief: Today's Issue," in *A Second Collection*, 97.

[43]Ibid.

Prophecy and the Paschal Imagination

Sandra Schneiders's Challenge to Ecclesial Spirituality

B. Kevin Brown

In June 1968, Sandra Schneiders arrived in Paris to begin her licentiate in sacred scripture. That month "the student revolution reached its peak," spilling out of Paris's Latin Quarter, just as the effects of the Second Vatican Council (Vatican II) were beginning to be felt in biblical studies.[1] "These two historical developments," she writes, "combined to energize the wholehearted espousal of historical critical work by Catholic biblical scholars."[2] However, as Schneiders continued her studies, she realized that historical criticism alone could not answer her questions regarding Christian spirituality. Historical critical research has remained a part of Schneiders's work. But she has pushed beyond it to ask how the biblical text serves as "a privileged locus of the transforming encounter between God and the believer."[3] This essay argues that Schneiders's work in theology, biblical studies, and Christian spirituality, which is rooted in her own spirituality as a ministerial woman religious,[4] challenges the church to adopt what I identify as a prophetic ecclesial spirituality.

The argument develops in three parts. First, I maintain that the intersection of three events, occurring around 1968, shaped Schneiders's spirituality as a ministerial religious. I argue, second, that Schneiders's own spirituality shaped her work in the areas of biblical hermeneutics, Christian spirituality, and theology, which when read together suggest that Christian spirituality is prophetic in nature. Finally, I address how her work challenges the church, here understood as the community of disciples continually born into history by Jesus and the Spirit, to adopt a prophetic ecclesial spirituality, and I outline what such a spirituality entails.

The Paschal Imagination

In 1968, a friend drove Schneiders to the airport for her flight to Paris and offered her one piece of advice: "Don't ever refuse an invitation."[5] Schneiders recalls, "If ever in my life I had heard a recipe for moral, theological, and vocational shipwreck, that bit of advice was it. . . . Catholic life at that point in history and *a fortiori* religious life, could almost have been formulated as the inverse of his advice: Never accept an invitation."[6] Immediately on her arrival, she was showered with invitations to encounter new people, cultures, art, and political thought. But she also received two additional invitations: Vatican II's summons to religious communities to renewal and the challenges of liberation theologies, especially feminist theology. A survey of Schneiders's work makes apparent that the intersection of these invitations shaped not only her own spirituality but also her critical reflection on Christian spirituality and its relationship to biblical hermeneutics.

A key dimension of Schneiders's insight concerning Christian spirituality is that it involves living into an alternative, imaginative worldview. She reached this insight reflecting on the nature of ministerial religious life. She recalls that, on encountering the invitations of 1968, she "interiorly ran for cover" in the rules of her religious community.[7] But her community, like others, in agreement with Vatican II's mandate, did undertake renewal. Ministerial women religious read this mandate through the lens of *Gaudium et Spes,* particularly its call to live "in and with and for the world."[8] They deconstructed the walls separating religious from 1968's many invitations. Soon, ministerial religious took up new ministries, experimented with new forms of participatory governance, and moved away from the last vestiges of their previously mandated semi-cloistered life.[9]

For fifty years, Schneiders has reflected on the distinctive spirituality of ministerial religious life. In agreement with Vatican II, she maintains that a fundamental equality exists between religious and other Christians.[10] But, she argues, religious life is a non-superior form of life, distinguished by publicly professing vows of evangelical poverty, consecrated celibacy, and prophetic obedience. When read in light of *Gaudium et Spes*, these vows are not a summons to flee the world of God's creation but to die to one imaginative construction of the world and to live out of another. The vows empower religious to die to what she calls the Kingdom of Satan—the worldview marked by structures of domination built around the protection of material goods, the exploitation of human sexuality and relationships, and the oppressive maintenance and exercise of power. By living into their vows, religious simultaneously "create concretely, in the visible socio-historical context," and live into "a Gospel-based imaginative reality construction . . . devoted completely and exclusively to the project Jesus called 'the Reign of God.'"[11]

Intersecting with Schneiders's acceptance of the invitation to live into a renewal of ministerial religious life was accepting the invitation from liberation theologies, especially feminist theology, to read the Gospel anew. Mary Daly's *The Church and the Second Sex*, published in 1968, is generally considered the first major work of Catholic feminist theology.[12] Schneiders notes that her own feminist consciousness began to develop while studying for her doctorate in Rome. It "came into full bloom" only after returning to the United States in 1976 as she reflected on her experiences of gender- and sex-based oppression in the church and world in light of feminist theory and early works of feminist theology.[13] As she grew into her identity as a ministerial woman religious, she concluded that patriarchy, as "both the ideology and the system of social organization based on father-dominance," stands in radical opposition to the Reign of God.[14] Schneiders brought her growing feminist consciousness into dialogue with the Gospel and soon became a leading voice in feminist theology. Her critical, feminist theological engagement with scripture illustrates how feminism, which not only deconstructs all ideologies and structures of domination but also pursues a social order aimed at realizing "the full personhood of every human being and right relationships among all creatures, . . . must be espoused by Christians as a Gospel imperative."[15]

Schneiders's related insight that ministerial religious life involves living out of *and* into a feminist, Gospel-based imaginative construct of reality helped her answer how the Bible mediates a privileged encounter with God. Schneiders understands divine revelation as an invitation to share in a salvific communion of friendship, beginning here and now, with God and all of creation. The New Testament, in particular, serves as the normative witness to the fullness of God's self-revelation in Jesus and the Spirit because it mediates the paschal imagination. For Schneiders, the paschal imagination is the worldview into which a person is called to live as she comes to understand the meaning of the testimony that the fullness of God's self-revelation in the Spirit is made incarnate in Jesus of Nazareth.[16] A person reaches for salvation, then, by cooperating with the Spirit's initiative to transform creation toward a communion marked by the *shalom* that characterizes God's own life.[17] The proclamation that in Jesus one encounters the fullness of God's self-revelation affirms that he incarnates both God's salvific invitation and humans' affirmative response. It summons the disciple to share in the life of the risen Jesus by living into the worldview that both animated Jesus's cooperation with the Spirit in his mission to transform creation toward the Reign of God and is captured by the biblical witness to his life, death, and resurrection. Therefore, the life of Christian spirituality—the life of Christian discipleship—is the "life of faith, hope, and love within the community of the Church through which we put on the mind of Christ by participating sacramentally and existentially in his paschal mystery."[18] And to share in this life, as Schneiders argues, all disciples are called to appropriate the paschal imagination into their unique social and historical locations.[19]

Prophecy and Christian Spirituality

Schneiders does not explicitly describe her understanding of the most significant dimensions of the paschal imagination. But it is implicit in her work on both the Fourth Gospel and ministerial religious life. For her, the key to finding meaning in God's revelation in Jesus and the Spirit is the paschal mystery.[20] I maintain that her understanding of the paschal imagination flows out of her argument that the biblical witness to the first disciples' coming to Easter faith serves as a prototypical pattern that ought to characterize the Christian spirituality of all disciples.

Turning to the New Testament witness to the first disciples' experience, Schneiders argues that the meaning of the paschal mystery is not shaped by the events of Jesus's death, glorification, resurrection, and ascension alone. The first disciples' prior understanding as first-century Jews of God's self-revelation and their experience of Jesus's ministry saturated with meaning the events related to his death and resurrection.[21] Again turning to the biblical witness in her work on religious life, Schneiders argues that Jesus, with his disciples, took up a prophetic ministry in the pattern of the prophets of the Hebrew Bible, in response to the oppression that he witnessed in Roman-occupied first-century biblical Israel.[22] Taking up this prophetic ministry as a lay, itinerantly homeless, celibate man in a colonized land, Jesus chose to stand outside the clerical, economic, social, and political systems of oppression that marked his time.[23] He stood, instead, in solidarity with the victims of these systems. Heeding the Spirit's call to transform creation toward the Reign of God, which he heard most clearly in the laments of the oppressed, he invited all to share in the fullness of life. Through his very way-of-being-in-the-world, Jesus resisted the dominative structures that mar God's creation, and he cooperated with the salvific initiative of the Spirit. He, thus, built up a communion of *shalom* with his friends and disciples, who shared in his prophetic ministry.[24]

Schneiders's interpretation of the Johannine Resurrection Narrative (Jn 20) reflects this perspective. When Jesus's disciples encountered the fullness of divine love in the crucified, glorified, and risen Jesus, they recognized that love as the same love Jesus had manifested in his prophetic ministry inaugurating God's reign. Drawing on the immanent eschatology of the Fourth Gospel, Schneiders explains how this pericope affirms that in death a person shares in the fullness of the life which they manifested on earth. The disciples' encounter with the crucified and risen Jesus alive in the fullness of God's glory became the eschatological lens through which they discerned Jesus's life and ministry as the manifestation of the life of God in history. They came to believe that Jesus's prophetic ministry inaugurated the community of salvation through which all of creation would share in God's life. Through the indwelling Spirit of God, Jesus continues to share his life with his disciples so that they can live as the body of the crucified and risen prophet, Jesus of Nazareth, and cooperate with the Spirit to make manifest the *shalom* of God's reign in history.[25] Therefore, Schneiders concludes, there are no second-generation disciples. All disciples are called to encounter the risen Jesus in the life of the church and share in the life of his risen body by cooperating with the Spirit, through whom the risen Jesus continues to return to his disciples. In turn, through its cooperation with the Spirit, the church is empowered to incarnate his life and ministry in history.[26]

Schneiders offers no explicit argument for Christian spirituality, as a whole, being prophetic in nature. Yet her claim that Jesus's disciples live as his crucified, glorified, and risen body, thereby participating in the paschal mystery, by continuing and sharing in the prophetic life of Jesus implies that Christian spirituality must embody Jesus's prophetic life and mission. Jesus was crucified as a result of his prophetic life and ministry. Through his death, Jesus is glorified in the life of God, revealing that he both incarnates God's life in history and embodies what it means to share fully in God's salvific friendship as a human person. Returning to his disciples of every generation through the indwelling Spirit, the risen Jesus invites his disciples to participate in the paschal mystery and to continue the work of his ministry to transform creation toward God's reign through their cooperation with the Spirit's salvific initiative. As noted above, in her study of the foundations of religious life, Schneiders describes Jesus's ministry as unmistakably an embodiment of biblical prophecy. Taken together, these different dimensions of Schneiders's thought make evident that, for her, Christian spirituality is prophetic in nature. A disciple must strive to share in the life of Jesus by cooperating with the Spirit to embrace, in some way, the prophetic task. This work includes attending to the voice of the Spirit heard in the laments of the oppressed, standing in solidarity with them, resisting the structures of domination that mar creation, and striving to build up structures that reflect God's reign in history. Since Christian spirituality involves living as Christ's risen body within the church's communion, it is hardly a stretch of one's ecclesiological imagination to suggest that the church is called to a prophetic way of life as well.

Toward a Prophetic Ecclesial Spirituality

By highlighting the prophetic nature of Christian discipleship and spirituality, Schneiders's work develops Vatican II's understanding of the church's continuation of Christ's prophetic life. In *Lumen Gentium*, the council teaches that the baptized share in Christ's priestly, royal, and prophetic offices. Within the dogmatic constitution's framework, the church's teaching function fulfills its prophetic task.[27] Schneiders's work implies that prophecy is much more fundamental to the church's life. It suggests that the church is called to be prophetic in nature. Jesus's prophetic life and mission ought to shape the church's entire way-of-being-in-the-world, rather than just one dimension. Moreover, Schneiders's work illustrates that the church's prophetic nature is grounded in the paschal mystery—the mystery by which both Jesus and the Spirit continually birth the church into history. Every time that the church fails to live into a prophetic spirituality, it fails to live into its identity as the Risen Body of Christ and fails to attend to its communal life-project of participating in the paschal mystery. Understood in this way, Schneiders's work challenges the church to enact a prophetic ecclesial spirituality.

Building on Schneiders's interpretation of Jesus's prophetic ministry, the following concluding discussion identifies four dimensions of a prophetic ecclesial spirituality. First, and most obviously, the church is called to continue Jesus's prophetic mission: to lament and resist structures of domination with those victimized by them and to create alternate structures that embody the friendship and justice of God's reign. A prophet's mission always flows out of a fundamental prophetic way-of-being-in-the-world. As Schneiders notes, the prophet already has an intimate relationship with God that empowers her to share in God's work by embodying the vision of salvation she announced in her mission through both word and deed.[28] This embodiment of the salvific vision that the church announces constitutes the second dimension of a prophetic ecclesial spirituality. To live as the risen body of Jesus, the church must order its ways of living in communion to reflect and make manifest the self-giving love of God's life that all creation is invited to share—a life marked by friendship, *shalom*, and the absence of hierarchical domination.

Reflecting on the church's capacity to order its life in this way leads to the third dimension of a prophetic ecclesial spirituality—namely, recognizing and striving to correct failure. Prophets grow into their identity through fits and false starts. Even Jesus accepted correction from the Syrophoenician woman as he discerned the nature of his prophetic ministry (Mk 7:24–30; cf. Mt 15:21–28). Similarly, the New Testament captures not only the ideal of discipleship but also the limits of all disciples who inevitably fail along the way (e.g., Mk 10:35–45, Mk 14:66–72; Mt 19:13–15; Jn 18:15–27; 1 Cor 1:10–15:58). In the church's history, such failures have been institutionalized, causing the church to embody systemic evils like patriarchy, white supremacy, and clericalism. But failure is not the final word. The Spirit's salvific initiative calls the church to cooperate in making whole that which the community has corrupted or broken along the way. As Schneiders insists, a key dimension of any prophet's spirituality is her willingness to stand with persons marginalized and oppressed by structures of domination, to listen to their laments, and to discern with them how a community of *shalom* might be built.[29] The church must, first, admit that it can and does fail to live into its prophetic identity as the risen body of Jesus in history and then attend to the Spirit's voice heard in the cries of those persons victimized by its own institutional failings. Finally, it must discern how its institutional life might reflect more fully the non-dominative friendship of God's reign. This discernment requires building synodal channels into the church's polity to facilitate a collaborative exercise of ministry and church office that ensures that the marginalized voices within and at the borders of its communion are not only heard but also sought out in decision-making processes.

The church also needs to draw on tools of sociocritical analysis to assist in these processes. Here Schneiders's argument that discipleship is feminist in nature is helpful but needs to be expanded. Schneiders maintains that feminism is essential to discipleship since it is committed to the deconstruction of patriarchy, which she identifies as the root of all oppressive systems.[30] Theologians of color, however, have shown that in addition to the sexist and androcentric biases underlying patriarchy, many other biases have provided a foundation for the oppressive structures that mar the Christian tradition. These include white racist supremacy, settler colonialism, and supersessionism.[31] Their work illustrates the insufficiency of a single lens of sociocritical analysis. Rather, working to divest the church of its participation in such structures requires as many lenses as the victims who have suffered from the church's failure to live into its prophetic nature identify. Such tools can also assist the church in identifying the dynamics of domination beyond its own communion, throughout the rest of creation, so that it might fulfill its prophetic mission of resistance to oppression in the world.

Of course, naming and resisting structures of oppression involves a great deal of risk, which leads to the fourth dimension of a prophetic ecclesial spirituality. Schneiders notes that the ministry of every prophet is marked by strenuous, oftentimes violent, opposition from those seeking to maintain the privilege provided to them by the status quo. Jesus, like many prophets before and since, suffered a violent death at the hands of a hierarchical system of power. But as Schneiders argues, the vocation of the prophet is "not to survive within the system but to change it."[32] Thus, the church must resist the temptation merely to coexist in and live according to a world marked by hierarchical domination, even when it guarantees survival and privilege. This resistance requires taking an oppositional and, at times, confrontational position in relation to the world. But opposition need not mean isolation or withdrawal from the political, cultural, economic, or social realms of history. Rather, a prophetic ecclesial spirituality calls the church to engage in a patient and active resistance to the structures of sin at work in those realms of creation. It calls the church to name and root out the fear that feeds exploitative systems to facilitate their deconstruction. Thus, a prophetic ecclesial spirituality summons the church, even while facing the risk of harm, to live into the good news, revealed in Jesus's prophetic ministry and the paschal mystery, that in the fullness of time the life and justice of God's reign are victorious over the world's death-dealing powers.

Schneiders's Challenge to the Church

In 1968, Sandra Schneiders arrived in Paris with a piece of advice—"Never refuse an invitation"—a recommendation that she found terribly unsettling. Ultimately, however, she willingly accepted two life-transforming invitations. First, she accepted Vatican II's call to participate in the renewal of ministerial religious life. Second, she accepted feminist theology's challenge to read the Gospel anew. Her affirmative responses led her to become one of the most significant American Catholic theologians of the last fifty years. And through her theological vocation she continues to offer the church an invitation. Her work bids the church to divest itself of its practices and structures of domination and to adopt a prophetic ecclesial spirituality that embodies the prophetic life and mission of the crucified and risen Jesus in the world.

Notes

[1] Sandra M. Schneiders, *The Revelatory Text: Interpreting the New Testament as Sacred Scripture*, 2nd ed. (Collegeville, MN: Liturgical Press, 1999), 1.

[2] Ibid.

[3] Ibid., 2.

[4] Schneiders identifies ministerial religious life as a particular form of mobile or apostolic religious life emerging after the Second Vatican Council that seeks to embody "the absolute oneness of the great commandments of love of God and love of neighbor." Sandra M. Schneiders, "The Charism of Religious Life," *Religious Formation Conference National Congress: Proceedings* 12 (2001): 7-15.

[5] Sandra M. Schneiders, "Commencement Address" (Jesuit School of Theology, Santa Clara University, May 19, 2018), https://santaclarauniversity. hosted.panopto.com.

[6] Ibid.

[7] Ibid.

[8] Sandra M. Schneiders, "Women Religious in a Renewing Church: Development or Demise?" in *God Has Begun a Great Work in Us*, ed. Jason King and Shannon Schrein, The Annual Publication of the College Theology Society 60 (Maryknoll, NY: Orbis Books, 2015), 11; Sandra M. Schneiders, "A Contemporary Theology of the Vows," in *Journeying Resources* (Washington, DC: LCWR, 1977), 15; Sandra M. Schneiders, *New Wineskins: Re-Imagining Religious Life Today* (New York: Paulist Press, 1986), 96–97.

[9] Sandra M. Schneiders, *Prophets in Their Own Country: Women Religious*

Bearing Witness to the Gospel in a Troubled Church (Maryknoll, NY: Orbis Books, 2011), 56–62.

[10]Schneiders, *New Wineskins*, 44.

[11]Schneiders, "Women Religious in a Renewing Church," 24. See also Sandra M. Schneiders, *Buying the Field: Catholic Religious Life in Mission to the World* (Mahwah, NJ: Paulist Press, 2013), 53–68.

[12]Mary Daly, *The Church and the Second Sex* (San Francisco: Harper and Row, 1968).

[13]Schneiders, *The Revelatory Text*, 157–80; Sandra M. Schneiders, "The Bible and Feminism," in *Freeing Theology*, ed. Catherine Mowry LaCugna (New York: HarperCollins, 1993), 47–52.

[14]Sandra M. Schneiders, "Feminist Spirituality," in *The New Dictionary of Catholic Spirituality*, ed. Michael Downey (Collegeville, MN: Liturgical Press, 1993), 395.

[15]Sandra M. Schneiders, *With Oil in Their Lamps: Faith, Feminism, and the Future* (Mahwah, NJ: Paulist Press, 2000), 122.

[16]Schneiders, *The Revelatory Text*, 38, 101–10.

[17]Ibid., 34–39, 72–73, 80.

[18]Sandra M. Schneiders, "Religion vs. Spirituality: A Contemporary Conundrum," *Spiritus* 3 (2003): 168.

[19]Ibid., 157–80; Sandra M. Schneiders, "The Bible and Feminism," 47–52.

[20]Schneiders, *Buying the Field*, 55; Sandra M. Schneiders, "The Johannine Resurrection Narrative: An Exegetical and Theological Study of John 20 as a Synthesis of Johannine Spirituality," 2 vols. (STD dissertation, Pontifica Universitas Gregoriana, 1975), 1:634–46.

[21]Schneiders, *The Revelatory Text*, 38; Sandra M. Schneiders, *Jesus Risen in Our Midst: Essays on the Resurrection of Jesus in the Fourth Gospel* (Collegeville, MN: Liturgical Press, 2013), 38–41.

[22]Schneiders, *New Wineskins*, 277–81; Schneiders, *With Oil in Their Lamps*, 97–108; Schneiders, *Prophets in Their Own Country*, 87–90; Schneiders, *Buying the Field*, 465–84.

[23]Sandra M. Schneiders, "Evangelical Equality: Religious Consecration, Mission, and Witness—Part I—Friendship in God: The Biblical Basis of Christian Equality," *Spirituality Today* 38 (1986): 299–300; Schneiders, *New Wineskins*, 277–78; Schneiders, *With Oil in Their Lamps*, 104–8; Schneiders, *Buying the Field*, 179–88, 467–68, 473–77.

[24]Schneiders, *New Wineskins*, 277–84; Schneiders, *With Oil in Their Lamps*, 97–108; Schneiders, *Prophets in Their Own Country*, 80–97; Schneiders, *Buying the Field*, 465–84.

[25]Sandra M. Schneiders, "The Word in the World," *Pacifica* 23 (2010): 264; Sandra M. Schneiders, "The Raising of the New Temple: John 20.19–23 and Johannine Ecclesiology," *New Testament Studies* 52 (2006): 349–55; Sandra M. Schneiders, "The Lamb of God and the Forgiveness of Sin(s) in the Fourth Gospel," *Catholic Biblical Quarterly* 73 (2011): 15–29; Sandra M. Schneiders, "Touching the Risen Jesus: Mary Magdalene and Thomas the Twin in John 20," *Proceedings of the Catholic Theological Society of America* 60 (2005): 22–35.

[26]Schneiders, *Jesus Risen in Our Midst*, 53–60.

[27]See *Lumen Gentium*, paragraphs 11–14, 19–21, 25–27, 34–36, www.vatican.va.

[28]Schneiders, *Buying the Field*, 470–84.

[29]Sandra M. Schneiders, *Finding the Treasure: Locating Catholic Religious Life in a New Ecclesial and Cultural Context* (Mahwah, NJ: Paulist Press, 2000), 138–41, 318–33.

[30]Schneiders, *Buying the Field*, 428.

[31]For example, M. Shawn Copeland, "White Supremacy and Anti-Black Logics in the Making of US Catholicism," in *Anti-Blackness and Christian Ethics*, ed. Vincent W. Lloyd and Andrew Prevot (Maryknoll, NY: Orbis Books, 2017), 61–74; Nancy Pineda-Madrid, *Suffering and Salvation in Ciudad Juarez* (Minneapolis: Fortress, 2011); Willie James Jennings, *The Christian Imagination: Theology and the Origins of Race* (New Haven, CT: Yale University Press, 2011).

[32]Schneiders, *Finding the Treasure*, 144.

"A Desire for Encounter with the Absolute"

Néstor Paz and Revolutionary Mysticism

Glenn Young

My interest in this topic began when I read an essay by Latin American liberation theologian Segundo Galilea, in which a brief reference is made to Néstor Paz, a Christian who died in 1970 while participating in revolutionary political action in Bolivia. Galilea describes Paz as demonstrating "a high degree of Christian mysticism."[1] As a scholar of Christian mysticism and a person who values political engagement, I was intrigued by this reference to Paz.[2] In particular, I was interested in the possibility of a model that combined mysticism and militant activism.[3] In this essay, I consider how Néstor Paz's thought and practice offer an example of what I am calling a *revolutionary mysticism*, and how this mysticism might embody what it means to have, in Paz's words, "a desire for encounter with the Absolute."[4]

Néstor Paz was a former seminarian and university student who worked as a religious educator in Bolivia. At the age of twenty-five, in response to social inequality and military repression, Paz joined the National Liberation Army's Teoponte Campaign, a guerrilla movement that engaged in armed struggle against the Bolivian government. While participation in violent political action might be seen as controversial compared to the more widely accepted path of nonviolent resistance, some precedent did exist among Christians in Latin America. In 1968, a group of more than nine hundred priests issued a statement at the Second Conference of the Latin American Episcopate in Medellín, Colombia. Commenting on the struggle of persons to effect social change, the statement notes, "Because the privileged few use their power of repression to block this process of liberation, many see the use of force as the only solution open to the people. This same conclusion is being reached by many militant Christians whose own lives faithfully reflect the light of the gospel."[5] Further addressing this issue, the statement goes on to say, "We do not wish to draw an idyllic picture of violence. We simply want to give a new dimension to a recognized principle: the right of any unjustly oppressed community to react, even violently, against its unjust oppressor."[6]

An important influence in Néstor Paz's choice to use force in the struggle for justice was Camilo Torres, a priest who joined an armed revolutionary movement in Colombia, and who was killed in combat there in 1966. The message Paz wrote when he left to join the guerrillas in the Teoponte Campaign in Bolivia in 1970 begins with Camilo Torres's statement, "Every sincere revolutionary must realize that armed struggle is the only path that remains."[7] Paz goes on to quote Torres's claim that "in Catholicism the main thing is love for one's fellow men," and that "this is why the revolution is not only permissible but obligatory for those Christians who see it as the only effective and far-reaching way to make love for all people a reality."[8] In explaining his own decision to engage in armed revolutionary action, Paz declares: "I believe that taking up arms is the only effective way of protecting the poor against their present exploitation, the only effective way of generating a free man. I believe that the struggle for liberation is rooted in the prophetic line of Salvation History."[9] Although the extent to which Paz participated in combat during his time as a guerrilla is unclear, what is known is that on October 8, 1970, three months after joining the Teoponte Campaign and while involved in guerrilla maneuvers, Néstor Paz died of starvation.

Revolutionary Mysticism:
Preparation, Consciousness, and Effect

In this essay I consider the journal kept by Néstor Paz while he was a guerrilla as a modern mystical text. I view it through the lens of Bernard McGinn's conception of Christian mysticism. McGinn describes mysticism as "that part, or element, of Christian belief and practice that concerns the preparation for, the consciousness of, and the effect of . . . a direct and transformative presence of God."[10] Of particular note here is the suggestion of a process of preparation, consciousness, and effect. Elaborating on this, McGinn says that mysticism involves "an itinerary or journey to God," and therefore, "a proper grasp of mysticism requires an investigation of the ways by which mystics have prepared for God's intervention in their lives and the effect that divine action has had upon the mystic and those to whom he or she has communicated the message."[11] Although I employ this understanding of mysticism as an interpretive framework with which to consider Néstor Paz's journal, I also suggest that Paz's thought and practice offer the possibility of expanding on this conception of mysticism as a process.[12]

Beginning with the preparatory dimension in the process of mysticism, Paz's journal shows him engaging in two practices that are well established in Christian mystical traditions. The first is reading the Bible. Paz refers numerous times to reading scripture during his time as a guerrilla. For example, at one point Paz catalogs the items he carries with him. The list includes his pipe and tobacco, a spoon, canteen, his rifle and ammunition, and the Psalms and the New Testament.[13] In another journal entry, Paz describes how he is spending his time: "We're 'hibernating' in the campsite. Today I'll try to study the Gospels and the Psalms."[14]

Beyond these general references, Paz also reflects on particular scriptural themes and interprets them through the lens of his experience as a guerrilla fighter. One example is his reading of Jesus's statement in John 15:13: "Greater love no man has than to lay down his life for his friends." Referring to the verse, Paz says of himself and his comrades, "We will have fulfilled the commandment."[15] Similarly, Paz understands his revolutionary commitment in light of the apostles' mission in the church's early days, described in the New Testament: "Yesterday I read a little of the Apostles, their first steps, their hesitations, their discoveries, their cowardice, their confidence in the 'triumph.' It gave me courage and strengthened my desire to be in the vanguard, to be a prophet of a people on the march."[16] In statements such as these, we can see reading the Bible and the particular interpretation of it in terms of revolutionary action, as a practice by which one becomes aware of God's presence.

The scripture reading Paz describes also involves a shared practice of reflection carried out by Paz and the other guerrillas who accompany him: "Luis and some of our other 'ex-Christian' comrades have had long conversations with me and we read the Bible together. This is good, not for proselytism (which I can't stand), but for the deepening of all that is human and vital. It is a constant and profound enrichment."[17] Paz's journal thus shows individual reading and communal interpretation of scripture as ways of becoming conscious of God.

Asceticism is a second mystical practice to which Paz refers. This can be seen especially in his description of the hardships of guerrilla life. Paz sees his adjustment to this life as akin to religious training: "As the days go by we are little by little becoming better prepared. We know what we'll have to face in the days to come, and this is a perfect novitiate. We have already learned more or less how to adjust our bodies to this new world and to the tasks at hand."[18] Paz understands this asceticism as a purgative process. As with reading the Bible, this preparation is not only individual; it involves the guerrillas as a group. Reflecting on the fact that some persons have abandoned the fight, he says that "the column is being purified to a great extent."[19] Paz goes so far as to understand armed conflict itself as purgation. He writes of himself and his comrades, "We are being purified. Combat will purge us even more. Out of this experience that select group will be drawn which will bring the people to the happiness they so rightly deserve. This is a result of a long and constant faithfulness to the revolutionary ideal incarnated in the life of the guerrilla."[20]

Paz's explanation of why he has chosen to engage in armed struggle can also be seen in terms of ascetic practice. In the statement he wrote upon departing to join the Teoponte Campaign, Paz says that "conversion implies first an inner violence which is then followed by violence against the exploiter. May both men and the Lord together judge the rightness of our decision. At least no one can imply that we look for profit or comfort. These are not what we find in the struggle; they are what we leave behind."[21] Thus, asceticism's denial, which Paz understands as a type of violence directed toward the self, corresponds to the use of violence to effect social change.

Another reference to ascetical practices in Paz's journal concerns food, or more specifically the lack of food, as part of guerrilla life. As noted earlier, Paz died of starvation while participating in this campaign. His journal contains numerous references to hunger and the struggle to find food. For example, he writes, "We miss food a lot, and the most wretched morsel seems like a great delicacy."[22] A few days later, he refers to food again: "Yesterday we had a delicious meal and ate like mad. It's funny how every bite has an 'inexhaustible' worth. We're on to 'something' here."[23] Such statements connect clearly with the Christian ascetic practice of fasting. In this context, of course, forgoing food is a necessary aspect of guerrilla life, rather than a wholly voluntary practice. Yet Paz willingly makes this sacrifice in the interest of a greater social good. Paz's statements also suggest that what food he does eat is beyond measure in terms of its value; thus, the sense of deprivation carries with it a corresponding awareness of that which is infinite. In both his reading of the Bible and his understanding of guerrilla activity as a form of asceticism, we see the process of Christian mysticism at work, in that Paz is engaging in practices that are preparing him for an awareness of God.

I move now to the second dimension in the process of mysticism—consciousness of the direct presence of God. This consciousness is typically seen as the centerpiece of mysticism as a process, with preparation preceding it and effects following from it. Paz's writing exhibits a number of themes that are familiar in Christian mystical literature, though with the particular perspective of his revolutionary stance. Paz clearly encounters God in his specific sociopolitical conditions. Even in the midst of armed guerrilla activity, Paz says, "I keep trying to penetrate more into the reality of 'God, man, and history.' . . . God is here and I feel him."[24]

Because consciousness of God in the midst of historical circumstances is a key feature of the spirituality associated with Latin American liberation theology, we can see this particular theological perspective reflected in aspects of Paz's mysticism. For example, Segundo Galilea relates the Christian understanding of contemplation to social realities. He says that human beings possess "an innate vocation to contemplate God face to face."[25] While such a description is fairly traditional, Galilea suggests that this vocation is borne out in engagement with the world: "The contemplative today is the one who has an experience of God, who is capable of meeting God in history, in politics, in our brothers and sisters, and most fully through prayer."[26] This description of contemplation corresponds with the consciousness of God that Néstor Paz experiences as an inherent aspect of his revolutionary mysticism.

For Paz, the encounter with God is intimately connected to relationships with other persons. For example, in a pair of journal entries, Paz reflects on what he loves. On July 30, Paz addresses his wife, Cecy: "I'm taking advantage of this rest period to write you. We're doing fine. I think of nothing but you. I'm beginning to pray with a basis and a foundation, and this unites me with everything that is ours, besides providing me with the dimension of the Lord Jesus."[27] This union with both his wife and God takes on yet another layer of meaning in the journal entry for August 2, in which Paz, again addressing Cecy, writes, "Yesterday all of us who had not done it before swore an oath before a picture of Che Guevara. It will be a day of double memories for me—a double pledge of love for you and love for the revolution. Deep down they are the same thing."[28] For Paz, then, mystical consciousness takes the form of a union of love with God, as part of a seamless series of love relationships involving himself, his wife, his comrades with whom he struggles in revolutionary action, and God. In the introduction to the published edition of Paz's journal, Ed Garcia thus describes Paz as demonstrating "a profound integration of the loves in his life."[29]

Paz's description of mystical consciousness suggests the concept of *epektasis*, the eternal growth of a person toward God. Paz writes, "Personal conscious faith and the faith of all our comrades who, even if they don't believe, are 'on the road,' meet in the loving arms of the Lord. If it is a real encounter, even a mystical one because it is vital, it is becoming continuously more perfect."[30] The integrated relationships with God and other persons that Paz discusses take on the infinite quality of the Absolute; as such, they are capable of endless development into an ever-deepening experience of love.

Another familiar theme in Christian mystical literature seen in Paz's journal is desolation: the experience of an absence of the divine that in turn leads to a greater desire for and awareness of God. On September 12 (one of Paz's last entries before his death on October 8), Paz writes of his desire for God, but he also expresses a sense of desolation. Addressing himself to God, he says, "Today I really feel the need of you and your presence. Maybe it's because of the nearness of death or the relative failure of our struggle. You know I've always tried to be faithful to you in every way, consistent with the fulness of my being."[31] As he continues, however, Paz seems to anticipate a movement from feeling absence toward an eschatological experience culminating with mystical consciousness of God: "Ciao, Lord, perhaps until we meet in your heaven, that new land that we yearn for so much."[32]

The final dimension in the process of mysticism is the effect of God's presence. When this process is envisioned in a linear fashion, the effect is what happens as a result of the mystical consciousness one has experienced. The idea is that an encounter with the divine is transformative.[33] As Charlotte Radler explains, this transformation has implications for the way the mystic acts in the world: "For most Christian mystics, the experience of the presence of God not only alters their interior journey but also radically transforms their exterior life."[34] In the case of Paz's revolutionary mysticism, he clearly understands political engagement to be a manifestation of his Christian faith. One of Paz's possessions recovered after his death illustrates this. Inside the cover of his book of Che Guevara writings, Paz had written, "To be a revolutionary we have to discover Christ, and once we discover Christ we will be revolutionaries."[35]

Political Action as a Mystical Practice

Néstor Paz's journal entries certainly reflect the description of mysticism as a process that includes preparation, consciousness, and effect. Nevertheless, a consideration of Paz's thought and action can also expand on this description. Understanding political engagement as just an effect of the experience of God does not take the analysis of revolutionary mysticism quite far enough. Paz does not choose to participate in a guerrilla campaign only as a consequence of his awareness of God; rather, his involvement in revolutionary activity is itself a way in which he becomes increasingly aware of God's presence. Political action is thus an effect of, *but also a practice to prepare for*, mystical consciousness.

Paz say that he feels God in the midst of armed struggle, but he also suggests that participating in revolutionary activity is a means of actively working toward an awareness of God's presence. He says of himself and his comrades, "We're in the course of history, of truth. The Lord is showing his face, or rather, we are weaving it with the threads which reality gives us and we ourselves create."[36] It is not only that God is experienced in particular sociopolitical conditions; engaging those conditions is a practice through which the experience of God becomes a reality.

The way Paz talks about his development as both a mystic and a revolutionary implies such an experience. He writes, "I hope my ability to love continues to grow at the same rate as my ability as a guerrilla fighter. It is the only way of qualitatively improving the revolutionary spirit."[37] This statement could be understood as a straightforward expression of belief that spiritual commitment contributes to revolutionary action, so that it becomes substantively more than just a political movement.[38] Although this view certainly corresponds with Paz's words, the analysis can be pushed further. His emphasis on development in both love and ability as a guerrilla can also suggest that his actions lead to an experience of God. This is not a one-way process, wherein love for God results in political action. Political engagement itself may be a means by which mystical consciousness develops. Political struggle, understood in this way, is a mystical practice. Rather than being a linear process of preparation, consciousness, and effect, Paz's mysticism might better be envisioned as a dialectical spiral, in which consciousness of God leads to an effect, in this case revolutionary activity, which in turn leads back again to an ever-deepening consciousness of God.

The work of Latin American liberation theologians supports this suggestion of political action as a mystical practice. For example, Segundo Galilea says that "the Christian's commitment to liberation" must be "more than a chance to put into practice the demands of faith and to apply the postulates of charity"; rather, "the commitment to liberation in the Christian must be a place of encounter with God, and therefore a source of inspiration to his theological life and his contemplative life."[39] A similar claim is made by Leonardo Boff, who writes of the possibility of "being contemplative while working toward liberation," which "presupposes a new way of seeking sanctity and mystical union with God."[40] Boff goes on to describe this dynamic as "a question of living out a Christian practice that is simultaneously involved with prayer and commitment, so that commitment is born out of prayer, and prayer emerges from the midst of that commitment."[41]

These assertions from liberation theology clearly resonate with what is found in Néstor Paz's journal, in that Paz likewise suggests a dialectic between awareness of the divine and engagement in revolutionary activity. He writes that "this movement from love to faith and from faith to hope returning again to love becomes a concrete reality."[42] What Paz describes is an interaction that begins with love and faith, which can be understood as consciousness of God's presence. This love and faith in turn lead to hope, which can be interpreted as action, in the sense of a stance of readiness to act in the cause of realizing a just world. But the interaction does not stop there. This hope in turn leads to a new experience of love, that is, to a more profound consciousness of God. Paz's words thus suggest the possibility that, while mysticism is indeed a process, it is more complex than practice leading to consciousness leading to effect. Rather, it is a process in which practice, in this case political action, both follows from and leads to an awareness of God.

I began by asking about the possibility of a *revolutionary mysticism*. In considering the journal Néstor Paz kept during his time as a guerrilla, we can see the contours of such a mysticism. On the one hand, it has much in common with the conception of a linear process of preparation, consciousness, and effect. Paz engages in mystical practices of reading the Bible and asceticism, he describes his consciousness of the divine presence in terms of a union with God and other persons in the midst of sociopolitical conditions, and he understands his participation in armed struggle as an effect of this consciousness of God. On the other hand, Néstor Paz's revolutionary mysticism suggests something more. It suggests that political action need not be seen only as a consequence of the experience of God. It is more; it is a practice that actively prepares one for that experience. Paz himself expresses this when he quotes Psalm 130: "My soul waits for the Lord more than the watchman waits for the dawn." Reflecting on this biblical text, Paz describes his mysticism in this way: "It is a desire for encounter with the Absolute, for destroying everything that can separate us so that we can get at the heart of the 'matter,' where the ferment of the 'real,' of what 'is,' of the 'Absolute,' is in turmoil."[43] Néstor Paz's revolutionary mysticism shows an encounter with God that occurs in the midst of the turmoil of political action in the interest of social change; more than that, it shows that this action is itself one way to come to an ever-deepening consciousness of God's presence.

Notes

I thank those who participated in the Mysticism and Politics session at the 2018 CTS Annual Convention, where this essay was presented, and those who reviewed it for the CTS Annual Volume. Their questions and observations contributed much to the ideas being discussed here.

[1]Segundo Galilea, "Liberation as an Encounter with Politics and Contemplation," in *Understanding Mysticism*, ed. Richard Woods (Garden City, NY: Image Books, 1980), 532.

[2]In referring to my own experience relative to this topic, I am including in the discussion what Sandra M. Schneiders calls the "self-implicating character" of the study of spirituality. See "The Study of Christian Spirituality: Contours and Dynamics of a Discipline," in *Minding the Spirit: The Study of Christian Spirituality*, ed. Elizabeth A. Dreyer and Mark S. Burrows (Baltimore: Johns Hopkins University Press, 2005), 17.

[3]Leonardo Boff suggests the importance of this type of model in Christian spirituality. "The Need for Political Saints: From a Spirituality of Liberation to the Practice of Liberation," *Cross Currents* 30, no. 4 (Winter 1980–1981): 375–76.

[4]Néstor Paz, *My Life for My Friends: The Guerrilla Journal of Néstor Paz, Christian*, trans. and ed. Ed Garcia and John Eagleson (Maryknoll, NY: Orbis Books, 1975), 47.

[5]Second Conference of the Latin American Episcopate in Medellín, Colombia, "Latin America: A Continent of Violence," in *Between Honesty and Hope*, trans. John Drury (Maryknoll, NY: Maryknoll Publications, 1970), 83. See Ed Garcia, introduction to Paz, *My Life for My Friends*, 4–5.

[6]"Latin America: A Continent of Violence," 84.

[7]Camilo Torres, quoted by Paz, *My Life for My Friends*, 21. See Camilo Torres, *Revolutionary Priest: The Complete Writings and Messages of Camilo Torres*, ed. John Gerassi (New York: Vintage Books, 1971), 426.

[8]Torres, quoted by Paz, *My Life for My Friends*, 24. See Torres, *Revolutionary Priest*, 367–68.

[9]Paz, *My Life for My Friends*, 24.

[10]Bernard McGinn, introduction to *The Essential Writings of Christian Mysticism*, ed. Bernard McGinn (New York: Modern Library, 2006), xiv.

[11]Ibid., xiv–xv.

[12]It should be acknowledged that this consideration of mysticism as a process is based on the self-reported experience of one person as recorded in a journal. Although there are limits to the conclusions that can be drawn from such a source, this is inherent in almost any discussion of mysticism. As Bernard McGinn explains, "Experience as such is not a part of the historical record. The only thing directly available to the historian or historical theologian is the evidence, largely in the form of written records, left to us by the Christians of former ages." *The Foundations of Mysticism: Origins to the Fifth Century*, vol. 1 of *The Presence of God: A History of Western Christian Mysticism* (New York: Crossroad, 1991), xiv. Néstor Paz's journal represents the type of written record that has value for the study of Christian mysticism.

[13]Paz, *My Life for My Friends*, 54–55.

[14]Ibid., 46.

[15]Ibid.

[16]Ibid., 65.

[17]Ibid., 56.

[18]Ibid., 42.

[19]Ibid., 35.

[20]Ibid., 75.

[21]Ibid., 25.

[22]Ibid., 33.

[23]Ibid., 36.

[24]Ibid., 42.

[25]Segundo Galilea, *Following Jesus* (Maryknoll, NY: Orbis Books, 1981), 48.

[26]Ibid., 53.

[27]Paz, *My Life for My Friends*, 35.

[28]Ibid., 39.

[29]Garcia, introduction to Paz, *My Life for My Friends*, 12.

[30]Paz, *My Life for My Friends*, 47.

[31]Ibid., 87.

[32]Ibid.

[33]McGinn, introduction to *Essential Writings of Christian Mysticism*, xvii.

[34]Charlotte Radler, "*Actio et Contemplatio*/Action and Contemplation," in *The Cambridge Companion to Christian Mysticism*, ed. Amy Hollywood and Patricia Z. Beckman (Cambridge: Cambridge University Press, 2012), 211.

[35]Paz, *My Life for My Friends*, 100.

[36]Ibid., 46.

[37]Ibid., 34.

[38]This is a claim that is emphasized in Latin American liberation theol-

ogy, e.g., Galilea, "Liberation as an Encounter," 534, and Boff, "Need for Political Saints," 374.

[39]Galilea, "Liberation as an Encounter," 530.

[40]Boff, "Need for Political Saints," 370.

[41]Ibid., 372.

[42]Paz, *My Life for My Friends*, 48.

[43]Ibid., 47–48.

The Revolutionary Implications of Medellín and Pope Francis

John Sniegocki

The year 1968 was a watershed year for Catholic social teaching (CST). In that year the Latin American bishops met in Medellín, Colombia, and issued a series of powerful documents that profoundly influenced subsequent church teaching on issues of social justice. While affirming and reiterating the fundamental themes of CST, the Latin American bishops broke new ground in several crucial areas. Among these contributions were the introduction into CST of key terms from Latin American liberation theology, the development of a more systemic critique of capitalism, and emphasis on the centrality of grassroots movements and popular nonviolent social mobilization. These themes of Medellín, as we will see, are also central features of the social teachings of Pope Francis and have profound implications for the mission of the church in our times.

The Contributions of Medellín

The Medellín bishops' gathering was the first time the language of liberation and of preferential option for the poor entered official CST documents.[1] The bishops speak, for example, of giving "preference to the poorest and most needy" and highlight the crucial importance of "solidarity with the poor."[2] The bishops also strongly condemn the realities of structural injustice. "In many instances Latin America finds itself faced with a situation of injustice that can be called institutionalized violence."[3] The bishops enumerate especially the ways that capitalist neocolonialism has harmed Latin America, citing for example exploitative working conditions akin to "slavery,"[4] unjust distribution of land, inequitable terms of trade, capital flight, tax evasion and the repatriation of profits by foreign corporations, the impacts of foreign debt, and political and military intervention by outside powers.[5] In light of these injustices, the bishops emphasize the need for "all-embracing, courageous, urgent, and profoundly renovating transformations."[6]

To bring about more equitable distributions of economic and political power, the Latin American bishops stress the importance of active mobilization of the poor and marginalized. This is a crucial development in church teaching. Whereas CST had traditionally focused on forming the consciences of those with wealth and power to bring about change in a more top-down manner, at Medellín the agency of the poor becomes central. "The Church—the People of God—will lend its support to the downtrodden . . . so that they might come to know their rights and how to make use of them."[7] "Justice, and therefore peace," the bishops state, "conquer by means of a dynamic action of awakening [*concientización*] and organization of the popular sectors."[8]

Pope Francis and the Call to Structural Transformation

Like the bishops at Medellín, Pope Francis asserts the centrality of concern for and solidarity with the poor as being at the core of Christian faith. "Each individual Christian and every community," says Francis, "is called to be an instrument of God for the liberation and promotion of the poor."[9]

Among the central structures harmful to the poor that Francis critiques, like the bishops of Medellín, is the prevailing capitalist economic system. Pope Francis very powerfully articulates his critique of existing forms of capitalism in a talk to a worldwide gathering of grassroots social movements in Bolivia in 2015:

Do we realize that something is wrong in a world where there are so many farmworkers without land, so many families without a home, so many laborers without rights, so many

persons whose dignity is not respected? Do we realize that
something is wrong where so many senseless wars are being
fought and acts of fratricidal violence are taking place on
our very doorstep? Do we realize something is wrong when
the soil, water, air and living creatures of our world are under constant threat?. . . . These are not isolated issues. . . . I
wonder whether we can see that these destructive realities
are part of a system which has become global. . . . If such
is the case, I would insist, let us not be afraid to say it: we
want change, real change, structural change. This system
is by now intolerable.[10]

Francis offers at least eight significant criticisms of the prevailing economic order. The following sections briefly highlight
these critiques, as well as offer, in most cases, empirical evidence
that supports them.

Excessive Inequality

Francis strongly critiques the high levels of inequality that the
dominant economic order is generating and the free market and
deregulatory policies that facilitate this. "As long as the problems
of the poor are not radically resolved by rejecting the absolute
autonomy of markets and financial speculation and by attacking
the structural causes of inequality," says Francis, "no solution will
be found for the world's problems." "Inequality," he stresses, "is
the root of social ills."[11] This inequality, Francis suggests, derives
from an idolatrous pursuit of profit at the expense of all other
values: "We have created new idols. The worship of the ancient
golden calf has returned in a new and ruthless guise in the idolatry
of money and the dictatorship of an impersonal economy lacking
a truly human purpose."[12]

The evidence in support of Pope Francis's claims concerning
rising inequality is abundant. For example, recent estimates in
an Oxfam International report indicate that the forty-two richest
people in the world now possess as much wealth as the poorest 3.7
billion people (about half of the world's population) combined![13]
More broadly, it is estimated that seven out of ten people live in
countries where inequality has widened in the past thirty years.[14]

In the United States, inequality is at or near its highest levels since before the Great Depression.[15]

Creation of the "Excluded"

As part of the escalation of inequality, Francis argues that a permanent undercaste of the excluded is being created around the world. These are people who are permanently unemployed and marginalized, not needed by the economic system. "Masses of people," Francis says, "find themselves excluded and marginalized: without work, without possibilities, without any means of escape."[16] "The principal ethical dilemma of this capitalism," he declares, "is the creation of discarded people, then trying to hide them or make sure they are no longer seen."[17] In 2017, the number of unemployed persons globally rose to more than two hundred million, a new record high. In addition, 1.4 billion people experience employment that is classified by the International Labour Organization as highly "vulnerable," lacking the most basic employment security.[18]

Exploitation of Workers

Along with expressing concern for those who are excluded from employment, Francis also critiques the widespread violation of workers' rights in the existing global economic order. He laments the existence of "so many laborers without rights" and expresses his deep support for those who are fighting to obtain these rights.[19]

In the 2017 ITUC (International Trade Union Confederation) Global Rights Index, one of the major sources of data on violations of workers' rights, only twelve of the 139 countries investigated (mostly Western European/Scandinavian countries) were classified as experiencing no regular violations of workers' rights. The majority of the countries studied were placed in the worst two of five possible classifications—"no guarantee of rights" (forty-six countries) and "systematic violation of rights" (thirty-three countries, including the United States).[20] Throughout the world many workers are forced to work for less than a living wage. Half of the workers in South Asia and two-thirds of the workers in sub-Saharan Africa, for example, are classified as living in extreme or moderate poverty, according to the International Labour Organization.[21]

Conflict and War

Francis sees a strong connection between inequality, exclusion, and violence. "Until exclusion and inequality in society and between peoples are reversed," he states, "it will be impossible to end violence."[22] Moreover, Francis argues that major parties in our economic system in fact profit from violence and war:

> There are economic systems that must make war in order to survive. Accordingly, arms are manufactured and sold and, with that, the balance sheets of economies that sacrifice man at the feet of the idol of money are clearly rendered healthy. And no thought is given to hungry children in refugee camps; no thought is given to the forcibly displaced; no thought is given to destroyed homes; no thought is given, finally, to so many destroyed lives.[23]

Arms sales in 2016 by the top one hundred weapons producers totaled an estimated $375 billion, with US companies accounting for 58 percent of sales.[24] US government arms sales to foreign armed actors rose 25 percent in FY 2017.[25] These arms sales helped to fuel twenty-eight armed conflicts worldwide. Overall global military spending in 2016, the last year for which full data is currently available, totaled around $1.5 trillion.[26] To put this spending into perspective, this is over fifteen times the amount of funds that Oxfam International estimates is needed to end global extreme poverty.[27]

Consumerism and the "Globalization of Indifference"

Pope Francis also critiques the dominant capitalist economic system for fostering many harmful values such as consumerism, "rampant individualism," and a desire for instant gratification.[28] He suggests that these values are linked to a "throwaway culture," a decline in empathy (part of what is thrown away are people), and what he terms a "globalization of indifference."[29] We end up, he claims, "being incapable of feeling compassion at the outcry of the poor, weeping for other people's pain, and feeling a need to help them."[30]

Destruction of the Planet

At the core of Francis's critique of capitalism is the fact that it is destroying our planet, our "common home." "An economic system centered on the god of money," says Francis, "also needs to plunder nature to sustain the frenetic rhythm of consumption that is inherent in it. Climate change, the loss of bio-diversity, deforestation are already showing their devastating effects in the great cataclysms we witness."[31] Francis understands well the enormous depth of the problems and gives voice to a compelling sense of urgency: "Doomsday predictions can no longer be met with irony or disdain. We may well be leaving to coming generations debris, desolation and filth. The pace of consumption, waste and environmental change has so stretched the planet's capacity that our contemporary lifestyle, unsustainable as it is, can only precipitate catastrophes."[32] Speaking specifically of climate change, Francis states: "It is either now or never. . . . Every year the problems get worse. We are on the verge of suicide."[33]

Undermining of Democracy

Francis is highly critical of the ways that concentrated wealth translates into concentrated control of political systems, undermining authentic democracy. "The breach between the peoples and our current forms of democracy is growing ever greater," says Francis, "due to the enormous power of the financial and media sectors that would seem to dominate them." He speaks of the need for grassroots movements to "revitalize and recast the democracies, which are experiencing a genuine crisis."[34] Again, the data strongly support Francis's assertions. *The Economist*'s annual Democracy Index, for example, found that a majority of the 167 countries included in their rankings experienced a decline in democracy in 2017 and that the percentage of the world's population living in a democracy of any sort (they use

the language of "full democracies" and "flawed democracies")
fell to below 50 percent.[35]

The Promotion of a Culture of Fear and Scapegoating

As inequality widens and conditions for many become more
insecure, Francis warns that politicians may arise who will seek
to exploit this fear and try to scapegoat marginalized groups.
Sooner or later, he asserts, the problems of the current system
come to light.

> The wounds are there, they are a reality. The unemploy-
> ment is real, the violence is real, the corruption is real, the
> identity crisis is real, the gutting of democracies is real.
> The system's gangrene cannot be whitewashed forever
> because sooner or later the stench becomes too strong;
> and when it can no longer be denied, the same power that
> spawned this state of affairs sets about manipulating fear,
> insecurity, quarrels, and even people's justified indignation,
> in order to shift the responsibility for all these ills onto a
> "non-neighbor."[36]

Clearly, such scapegoating (against immigrants and ethnic and
religious minorities) is prevalent in many parts of the world today,
including the United States. Francis warns against seeking "the
false security of physical and social walls" and emphasizes instead
the need to "build bridges between peoples, bridges which enable
us to break down the walls of exclusion and exploitation."[37]

Catholic Social Teaching and Economic Democracy

The critique of capitalism that Pope Francis articulates, it
should be stressed, has deep roots in earlier Catholic social teaching. For example, in his encyclical *Populorum Progressio*, Pope
Paul VI states:

> It is unfortunate that . . . a system has been constructed which
> considers profit as the key motive for economic progress,
> competition as the supreme law of economics, and private

ownership of the means of production as an absolute right that has no limits and carries no corresponding social obligation. This unchecked liberalism leads to dictatorship rightly denounced by Pius XI as producing "the international imperialism of money." One cannot condemn such abuses too strongly.... [A] type of capitalism has been the source of excessive suffering, injustices, and fratricidal conflicts whose effects still persist.[38]

Similarly, Pope John Paul II expresses profound criticism of capitalism: "The Church, since Leo XIII's *Rerum Novarum*, has always distanced herself from capitalist ideology, holding it responsible for grave social injustices. I myself, after the historical failure of communism, did not hesitate to raise serious doubts on the validity of capitalism."[39]

Given that CST is highly critical of both Soviet-style communism and existing forms of capitalism, what is suggested as an alternative? The popes have emphasized that there is no single model that should be implemented, but rather that certain fundamental principles must be respected for any economic system to be judged morally acceptable. These principles include what CST terms a "universal destination of goods," which asserts that primacy must be given to meeting the basic needs of all over an unbridled right to accumulation for a few. Other principles include the importance of participation, respect for the dignity of workers, respect for creation, and the fostering of solidarity.

In broad terms, the principles of CST point toward a vision of what can be called "economic democracy." This entails a more equitable distribution of wealth, along with significantly increased worker and community participation in economic decision making and adequate governmental regulations to protect workers, consumers, and the environment.

In its most concentrated form, economic democracy can be seen in worker-owned cooperatives, member-owned credit unions, and similar enterprises. Pope John Paul II, for example, spoke of cooperatives as an integral part of efforts to "promote real economic democracy."[40] This support for cooperatives has been affirmed as well by Pope Francis. "The Church," Francis says, "has always recognized, encouraged, and appreciated cooperatives." The work of cooperatives, he adds, "is not only positive and vital, but also continues to be prophetic."[41]

The vision of economic democracy that CST sets forth recognizes the value of markets, as opposed to Soviet-style central planning, but stresses the need for extensive regulation of markets on behalf of the common good. "The market," Pope John Paul II argues, "[must] be appropriately controlled by the forces of society and by the state, so that the basic needs of the whole of society are satisfied."[42] Also, for markets to be effective in meeting true needs, wealth must be widely dispersed. "It is the task of nations, their leaders, their economic powers and all people of goodwill," John Paul II declares, "to seek every opportunity for a more equitable sharing of resources."[43] Similarly, criticizing what he terms "the scandal of glaring inequalities," Pope Benedict XVI highlights the crucial importance of "pursuing justice through redistribution."[44] He suggests that to protect the common good properly "the State's role seems destined to grow, as it regains many of its competences."[45] Thus, Popes John Paul II and Benedict XVI, like Pope Francis, are highly critical of libertarian free market policies. A key claim of CST from its inception is that the state has a vital role to play, especially in providing protection and support to those who are most vulnerable and marginalized in society.

As part of this overall vision of economic democracy, a few other specifics that are called for in Catholic social teaching include a critique of "free trade" and emphasis instead on well-regulated, fairer terms of trade,[46] debt relief for the world's poorer nations,[47] greater investment in areas such as health and education, significantly reduced levels of military spending,[48] land redistribution,[49] truly progressive systems of taxation,[50] and the use of tax and credit policy to provide preferential support to worker-owned businesses and smaller businesses and farms, with decreased subsidization and tax breaks for large corporations and the wealthy. These policy measures are to be complemented by fostering spiritualities of solidarity and ecological conversion, enabling us to hear both "the cry of the earth" and "the cry of the poor" and to find the commitment and courage needed to take constructive action in response to these cries.[51]

Implementing Alternatives

Although it is clear that alternatives are direly needed, the question remains as to how to create the far-reaching structural alternatives that Catholic social teaching envisions, especially in our context characterized by the immense concentration of economic and political power in the hands of a few. One of the most important contributions of Pope Francis to CST, I suggest, is his strong retrieval and further development of Medellín's emphasis on grassroots organizing and social movement-building as the primary mechanism for social change. Significantly, Francis calls the Catholic Church to enter actively into solidarity with grassroots movements, such as those which have played major roles in ending military dictatorships and challenging neoliberal capitalist economic policies in his home region of Latin America. He views this solidarity as a primary indicator of the church's faithfulness in our time. In my estimation, Francis's talks to the various global gatherings of grassroots popular movements, cited frequently throughout this essay, are some of the most powerful and significant documents in CST. Highlighting the crucial importance of grassroots mobilization in seeking the structural transformations that our world so desperately needs, Francis spoke to those gathered for the Second World Meeting of Social Movements:

> You, the lowly, the exploited, the poor and underprivileged, can do, and are doing, a lot. I would even say that the future of humanity is in great measure in your own hands . . . ; the future of humanity does not lie solely in the hands of great leaders, the great powers and the elites. It is fundamentally in the hands of peoples and in their ability to organize.[52]

The following year, at the Third World Meeting of Popular Movements, Pope Francis spoke again with these words of encouragement:

> You, the popular movements, are sowers of change, promoters of a process involving millions of actions, great and

small, creatively intertwined like words in a poem; that is why I wanted to call you "social poets." . . . I congratulate you, I accompany you and I ask you to continue to blaze trails and to keep fighting.[53]

The type of "fighting" that Francis calls for is firm commitment to active, nonviolent struggle. "Let us . . . make active nonviolence our way of life," Francis urges. "Jesus marked out the path of nonviolence. . . . To be true followers of Jesus today includes embracing his teaching about nonviolence."[54]

The Revolution of Pope Francis

In this essay, I have sought to highlight some of the central contributions of the 1968 Latin American bishops' meeting in Medellín, and to show how Pope Francis reiterates and deepens Medellín's themes in relation to our current global context. In particular, Pope Francis's reaffirmation of a preferential option for the poor (along with the addition of a preferential option for the earth), his systemic critique of capitalism, and his stress on nonviolent grassroots mobilization have profound, indeed revolutionary, implications for the mission of the church in our time.

Notes

[1]For discussion of "liberation," see the Medellín documents "Justice," 3, 4, 13, and "Poverty of the Church," 2. These documents, along with the Medellín document "Peace," can be found in Joseph Gremillion, ed., *The Gospel of Peace and Justice* (Maryknoll, NY: Orbis Books, 1976).

[2]"Poverty of the Church," 9–10.

[3]"Peace," 16.

[4]"Justice," 11.

[5]"Peace," 8–10.

[6]Ibid., 16.

[7]"Justice," 20. For discussion of the history of church teaching concerning mechanisms of social change, see John Sniegocki, "Implementing Catholic Social Teaching," in *Faith in Public Life*, College Theology Society Annual Volume 53, ed. William Collinge (Maryknoll, NY: Orbis Books, 2008), 39–61.

[8]"Peace," 18.

[9]Pope Francis, *Evangelii Gaudium* (2013), 187, w2.vatican.va.

[10]Pope Francis, Address to Second World Meeting of Popular Movements (July 12, 2015), w2.vatican.va.

[11]Pope Francis, *Evangelii Gaudium*, 202.

[12]Ibid., 55.

[13]Larry Elliott, "Inequality Gap Widens as 42 People Hold Same Wealth as 3.7bn Poorest" (January 21, 2018), www.theguardian.com.

[14]Oxfam International, "An Economy for the 99%" (January 2017), www.oxfam.org.

[15]"U.S. Income Inequality Highest since the Great Depression" (March 30, 2016), journalistsresource.org.

[16]Pope Francis, *Evangelii Gaudium*, 53.

[17]Pope Francis, Address to "Economy and Communion" Movement (February 4, 2017), w2.vatican.va.

[18]International Labour Organization, *World Employment and Social Outlook: Trends 2017*, 1–2, www.ilo.org.

[19]Pope Francis, Address to Second World Meeting of Popular Movements.

[20]International Trade Union Confederation, *2017 ITUC Global Rights Index: The World's Worst Countries for Workers*, www.ituc-csi.org.

[21]Ivana Kottasova, "Global Unemployment to Hit 200 Million as Wages Stagnate" (January 13, 2017), money.cnn.com.

[22]Pope Francis, *Evangelii Gaudium*, 59.

[23]Pope Francis, Address to World Meeting of Popular Movements (October 28, 2014), w2.vatican.va.

[24]Vera Kern, "SIPRI: Weapons Sales Up Again Worldwide" (December 11, 2017), www.dw.com.

[25]"US Arms Sales Jump 25% in FY 2017" (December 19, 2017), www.reuters.com.

[26]Project Ploughshares, "Armed Conflicts Report 2017," ploughshares.ca.

[27]Oxfam International, "Reward Work, Not Wealth" (January 2018), 10, www.oxfam.org.

[28]Pope Francis, *Laudato Si': On Care for Our Common Home* (2015), 162, w2.vatican.va.

[29]Ibid., 43; Pope Francis, *Evangelii Gaudium*, 54.

[30]Pope Francis, *Evangelii Gaudium*, 54.

[31]Pope Francis, Address to World Meeting of Popular Movements.

[32]Pope Francis, *Laudato Si'*, 161.

[33]Pope Francis, press conference (November 30, 2015), www.romereports.com. For a compilation of the latest news concerning climate change realities, see http://www.heatisonline.org.

[34]Pope Francis, Address to Third World Meeting of Popular Movements (November 5, 2016), w2.vatican.va.

[35]Scotty Hendricks, "New Report Shows Democracy Is in Decline Everywhere—Including the United States" (February 5, 2018), bigthink.com.

[36]Pope Francis, Message to Meeting of Popular Movements in California (February 17, 2017), www.usccb.org.

[37]Pope Francis, Address to Third World Meeting of Popular Movements.

[38]Pope Paul VI, *Populorum Progressio*, 26, w2.vatican.va.

[39]Pope John Paul II, "What Catholic Social Teaching Is and Is Not," *Origins* 23 (1993): 256–58. For extended discussion of John Paul II's views

on capitalism and related issues and the profound distortion of his thought by Catholic neoconservatives such as Michael Novak and George Weigel, see John Sniegocki, "The Social Ethics of Pope John Paul II: A Critique of Neoconservative Interpretations," *Horizons: The Journal of the College Theology Society* 33, no. 1 (Spring 2006): 7–32.

[40]Pope John Paul II, "Promote Real Economic Democracy," Address to the Central Institute of Cooperative Credit Banks of Italy (June 26, 1998), www.catholicculture.org.

[41]Pope Francis, "Address to Representatives of the Confederation of Italian Cooperatives" (February 28, 2015), zenit.org.

[42]Pope John Paul II, *Centesimus Annus* (1991), 35, w2.vatican.va.

[43]Pope John Paul II, "Message to the World Food Summit" (November 13, 1996), www.fao.org.

[44]Pope Benedict XVI, *Caritas in Veritate* (2009), 22, 36, w2.vatican.va.

[45]Ibid., 41.

[46]See, for example, Pope Paul VI, *Populorum Progressio*, 58–59.

[47]Pope John Paul II, *Centesimus Annus*, 35.

[48]Pope Paul VI, *Populorum Progressio*, 35, 51, 53, and many other CST statements.

[49]"I know that some of you are calling for agrarian reform in order to solve some of these problems, and let me tell you that in some countries—and here I cite the *Compendium of the Social Doctrine of the Church*—'agrarian reform is, besides a political necessity, a moral obligation.'" Pope Francis, Address to First World Meeting of Popular Movements. Also see Pope Paul VI, *Populorum Progressio*, 24; Second Vatican Council, *Gaudium et Spes*, 71, w2.vatican.va.

[50]See Pope John XXIII, *Mater et Magistra* (1961), 102, w2.vatican.va.

[51]See Pope Francis, *Laudato Si'*, 59, 216–21.

[52]Pope Francis, Address to Second World Meeting of Popular Movements.

[53]Pope Francis, Address to Third World Meeting of Popular Movements.

[54]Pope Francis, "Nonviolence: A Style of Politics for Peace," 2017 World Day of Peace Message, w2.vatican.va.

Epilogue

Beyond Land O'Lakes:
In the Year 2065
Will Catholic Theology Still Be Alive?

William L. Portier

On a July weekend in 1967, in Land O'Lakes, Wisconsin, the president of the University of Notre Dame, Fr. Theodore Hesburgh, gathered a group of Catholic educators to discuss "the nature and role of the contemporary Catholic University." Primarily from the United States and Canada, they met under the auspices of the International Federation of Catholic Universities. Received as a declaration of independence for Catholic universities, their brief statement, less than four full pages, assumed a significance far beyond its modest origins.

After half a century, the Land O'Lakes Statement shows its age. Consider the social identity of its twenty-six signatories: twenty-one clergy or bishops, including ten Jesuits, and only five laymen. Numerous religious women presidents led Catholic colleges in 1967; none were at Land O'Lakes. Among US Catholic universities, only Notre Dame, Georgetown, Boston College, St. Louis, Fordham, and Catholic University were represented.

Given the group's unrepresentative makeup, its statement has had a disproportionate impact. Recently assimilated descendants of Catholic immigrants were surely looking for legitimacy, but the statement's impact is due in good measure to another factor: the charisma of Fr. Ted Hesburgh, whose likeness recently graced a US postage stamp. In 1967, distinguished priests and religious played key roles in shaping Catholic universities. We might call this the Hesburgh effect. One would be hard-pressed today to find comparable figures.

This essay reflects on how a diminishing Hesburgh effect and a growing politicization of knowledge increasingly marginalize Catholic theologians in both church and academy. Its brief conclusion urges contemporary theologians to embrace Pope Francis's pastoral revolution and make academic theology more ecclesial.

A Diminishing Hesburgh Effect

The Land O'Lakes Statement highlights theology's role in Catholic universities. However, the post–Vatican II conditions that made Catholic theology a university discipline are changing fast. Fifty years from now, will Catholic theology still exist as an academic discipline in Catholic universities? In responding to Massimo Faggioli's "A Wake-Up Call to Liberal Catholic Theologians," Michael Hollerich writes, "Our work never depended on the marketplace but always on patronage of some kind. It remains to be seen where future patronage will come from—and what those patrons will expect in return."[1]

Of the Land O'Lakes Statement's ten numbered sections, the first four deal with theology explicitly. Thanks to theology, Catholic universities can add "to the basic idea of a modern university distinctive characteristics which round out and fulfill that idea."[2] Land O'Lakes hopes for "interdisciplinary dialogue" in which "theology confronts all the rest of modern culture and all the areas of intellectual study which it includes."[3] With the increasing specialization and religious diversification of the past fifty years, however, the accompanying strong warning against "theological or philosophical imperialism" might strike many contemporary faculty as hollow.

Even more jarring is the section on the Catholic university as "the critical reflective intelligence of the church."[4] Jarring because Land O'Lakes claims, at the same time, "a true autonomy and academic freedom" for Catholic universities "in the face of authority of whatever kind, lay or clerical, external to the academic community itself."[5] That claim's reception history plays havoc with the statement's vision of theology's ecclesial role.[6] As Faggioli puts it, subsequent events not only "emancipated theology from ecclesiastical control, but . . . also emancipated the Catholic Church from academic theology."[7] From the perspective of conservative commentators, Land O'Lakes was simply a disastrous "suicide pact."[8]

The distinguished career of the Roman-trained David Tracy is instructive. His involuntary 1969 migration from Catholic University to the University of Chicago Divinity School prefigures Catholic theology's late twentieth-century pilgrimage to academic legitimacy and ecclesial marginalization. Nearly forty years ago, Tracy enshrined this new situation in his sociological portrait of the theologian's three publics: society, academy, and church. He left little doubt that the theologian's primary public was the academy.[9] In retirement, Tracy remains a priest of the Diocese of Bridgeport. Most of his students, however, were lay people.

My first academic job, in 1979 at Mount St. Mary's College, found me as the theology department's only lay member. By the mid-1990s, the department had lost to death or retirement the four diocesan priests who had been my colleagues. Lay people replaced them. As department chair, I found myself in the once but no longer strange position of looking for at least one priest for a theology department. In 1997, the Catholic Theological Society of America held its fiftieth anniversary meeting. Here's how Hollerich remembers it:

> Down in front for a plenary session were Richard McBrien, Richard McCormick, and Charles Curran. . . . Those guys still spoke with authority to the hierarchy, even when they made bishops angry. They were perceived as players, even if disloyal players, because they were priests and subject ultimately to clerical command and control. The same does not apply to us layfolk, who are mostly irrelevant to the closed world of the celibate clergy.[10]

This describes the Hesburgh effect perfectly. And it's not just that those three men were priests. With many others of their generation—Ladislas Orsy and Avery Dulles also come to mind—their learning and character made them impressive figures. Many of these giants of old belonged to the religious congregations that sponsor Catholic universities. Along with some diocesan bishops, they have been theology's patrons. My own theological labors are possible only because of the patronage of the Society of Mary. When I first came to the University of Dayton in 1999, more than forty Marianists worked at the university. Now there are only about twenty. What will happen in increasingly corporate universities with fewer and fewer members of sponsoring religious congregations?

The Politics of Knowledge

Faggioli asks, "Who really threatens the 'true autonomy and academic freedom' of Catholic higher education today?" Corporatization and adjunctification pose bigger threats than "the dreaded intrusions of the magisterium." "If there is to be an update of the Land O'Lakes Statement," he concludes, "the real starting point would be to learn where leaders in American Catholic higher education really stand on increasing marketization and politicization of knowledge."[11]

Long a part of the history of philanthropy in the United States, the politicization of knowledge began to intensify after 1968 and the fracture of the postwar consensus with its promise of the end of ideology. By the early 1970s, political conservatives felt excluded from government decision making at all levels and began to form "advocacy funding" organizations such as the Heritage Foundation (1973), the Koch Foundation (1979), and the Charles Koch Foundation (1980), the latter with special interest in university business and economics departments. "Advocacy funding" involves strategically targeted giving designed to influence economic policy and laws regulating the market. As the recent interdisciplinary work *The Business Turn in American Religious History* makes clear, religious institutions, including Catholic higher education, have not been untouched by "advocacy funding."[12]

The phrase "advocacy funding" comes from chapter 10 of journalist Bill Bishop's 2008 *The Big Sort: Why the Clustering of Like-Minded America Is Tearing Us Apart*.[13] Bishop may have written the most important ecclesiology text of the early twenty-first century in the United States. The largely white immigrant Catholic Church in which I grew up participated in the postwar consensus. It was the time of the melting pot and racial integration. Everyone shared three national TV networks. The diverse ethnicities of the last names on a class roster made it easy to imagine the church as a big Catholic tent. The demographic, political, and cultural dynamics of the "big sort" help make sense of the ecclesial fissures now running through parishes, and even the episcopate itself, of a very different and deeply riven Catholic Church.

The early 1970s saw the postwar consensus break down and the midcentury immigrant Catholic subculture demographically collapse. As like-minded Catholics clustered, the church reflected subsequent cultural divisions. New kinds of "passionately Catholic" universities appeared. In 1974, Fr. Michael Scanlan, T.O.R., assumed the presidency of the struggling Steubenville College in what was once a thriving Ohio steel town. With the help of the Catholic charismatic renewal, Scanlan revitalized the school's Catholic heritage and, by 1980, it became Franciscan University of Steubenville.[14] The phrase "passionately Catholic" is from their website. In 1977, historian Warren Carroll, rejecting the spirit of the Land O'Lakes Statement, founded Christendom College in Front Royal, Virginia.

Anne Hendershott teaches at Franciscan. Her 2017 reflection on the fiftieth anniversary of Land O'Lakes laments that most Catholic colleges and universities have abandoned their religious identities. She lists, along with Steubenville and Christendom, Ave Maria University, the University of Dallas, Wyoming Catholic College, John Paul the Great Catholic University in California, St. Thomas More College in New Hampshire, and Thomas Aquinas College in California as examples of the "flourishing of Catholic colleges" at a time when most have "lost their way."[15]

To view such new and relatively small schools as marginal and irrelevant would be a tremendous mistake. Over ten years from 2006 to 2016, Franciscan sent out a total of 2,312 graduates into a church workforce whose hiring agents are no longer Vatican II–era pastors.[16] These graduates and like-minded contemporaries are reshaping the networks that once hired the graduates of mainstream Catholic universities, such as the ones that signed the Land O'Lakes Statement, and fed graduate students to their programs. "Liberal Catholic theologians" find themselves outflanked at every level of the grassroots Catholic Church from archdiocesan structures and programs to Catholic high schools, parish youth ministry, and campus ministry. Members of the Catholic Theological Society of America and the College Theology Society may wake up one day in the near future to find that their ecclesial public has vanished.

Most Catholic universities founded since the 1970s are small, niche institutions. The Catholic University of America is older, larger, and more comprehensive. Founded in 1887 as a research university by the US Catholic bishops, it has a long history as a leader in American Catholic intellectual life. In 1967, the president's representative signed the Land O'Lakes Statement. Once home to Fr. Charles Curran and an epicenter of conflict between theologians and the magisterium, the university recently undertook a campaign to re-brand itself as more authentically Catholic. At least for the present, the market would not bear such re-branding on the scale of an institution as large as Catholic University with more than six thousand students. Enrollment and budget shortfalls resulted.[17]

The case of Catholic University involves advocacy funding from high intensity politically conservative philanthropic groups promoting libertarian economics. It offers a cautionary tale about "the business turn in American religious history," and, specifically, about where the new patronage for Catholic higher education is coming from and how it might affect the "academic integrity" so prized by the authors of the Land O'Lakes Statement. In response to their budgetary situation, the administration issued a "Proposal for Academic Renewal," to restructure and cut full-time faculty positions by 9 percent. Just prior to the university's June 2018 board meeting an "unofficial group of faculty" conducted an on-line vote of no confidence in President John Garvey and Provost Andrew Abela. Though the vote had no formal standing and a university spokesperson disputed the eligibility of some voters, 78 percent of 225 respondents voted no confidence in President Garvey and 76 percent voted no confidence in Provost Abela. However one interprets this vote, it shows considerable unrest at Catholic University.

A few days later, the university's governing board reasserted "great confidence" in President Garvey. At the same time, Garvey announced a $2 million gift from the Koch Foundation "to help open a branch campus in Tucson in 2019." Garvey described the Tucson branch as a project that "serves the needs of poor and underserved Catholic populations" and insisted that the university would retain control of faculty hiring decisions for the Tucson branch. That a university president had to offer such assurance about faculty hiring is deeply disturbing. The Koch Foundation's $2 million gift is in addition to the $10 million it gave Catholic University in 2016.[18]

In that same year, Catholic University renamed its business school for Tim and Steph Busch who gave a $15 million gift. Tim Busch is the co-founder of the Napa Institute, a conservative organization of lay Catholics founded in response to Archbishop Charles Chaput's challenge in his 2010 article "Catholics and the Next America."[19] Archbishop Chaput serves as Napa Institute's "ecclesiastical advisor."[20] Despite the infusion of libertarian money into the university, Provost Abela dismisses "claims that we are moving right or somehow moving more conservative" as "just an attempt to make a caricature of what we're doing." Abela is firm: "We, in general, recognize that libertarianism and the Catholic faith are inconsistent, because the libertarian position has a view of the human person that is atomistic, that is completely at odds with Christianity."[21]

Consistent with Abela's claims, the university has, in response to Pope Francis's call for "ecological conversion" in *Laudato Si'*, established the Institute for Human Ecology under the direction of moral theologian Joseph Capizzi. This is an intriguing development about which there has been little publicity. Despite the provost's assurances, however, many remain unconvinced. In a poignant essay on the situation at her alma mater and present employer, historian Julia Young expresses both her devotion to Catholic University and her genuine concern for what is happening there. "At times," Young writes, "it seems that the administration's interpretation of Catholicism—and of who belongs in the Catholic Church—has narrowed considerably since I was an undergraduate."[22] "While Catholic social teaching is still present on campus," she told a reporter, "there's a growing emphasis on libertarian economic policies. It feels like the tent has gotten smaller."[23]

On the increasing marketization and politicization of knowledge, Catholic University's administration is trying to walk a fine line, which, given the university's historic preeminence in Catholic higher education, has much significance for the future of Catholic universities in general, and for theology in particular. As Jesuits and other religious sponsors of Catholic universities age out and look to apostolic works other than education to better serve the poor, new patrons such as the Koch foundations and the Busch Family Foundation are emerging. Despite appeals to the principle of subsidiarity, libertarian economic approaches remain difficult to square with the common good.

The Fellowship of Catholic University Students, commonly known as FOCUS, offers another example of the "business turn" in American religion and the involvement of politically conservative advocacy funding in educating young Catholics. FOCUS sends missionary volunteers, usually partly self-funded recent graduates, to work on college campuses. Over the past ten years, their presence has grown from just 29 campuses to 130 today. One of its founders is Franciscan graduate Curtis Martin. Thomas S. Monaghan's Legatus, an organization of Catholic CEOs, funds FOCUS's annual budget of $57 million.[24] Monaghan founded and continues to provide funding for Ave Maria University. A recent *America* article described the "feeling" of a Chicago FOCUS conference as "a traditionalist ethos infused with a mega-church aesthetic."[25]

It is time, I fear, for an agonizing reappraisal of what I have written about "evangelical Catholics" over the past twenty years. It is not that evangelical Catholics haven't continued to grow and assume leadership roles in the church. I interpreted them, however, from the perspective of the postwar consensus, big tent church of my youth. In hindsight, that was naïve. The argument is no longer that Eucharistic adoration and praise music be included to enrich the church. Rather, as last summer's "Convocation of Catholic Leaders: The Joy of the Gospel in America" in Orlando illustrated, these practices are becoming increasingly normative.[26] I hoped for evangelical Catholics as a Spirit-filled leaven to help renew both the church and academic theology. "Here Come the Evangelical Catholics," upbeat and even exhortatory, appeared in 2004.[27] Four years later, Bishop published *The Big Sort*. That "the clustering of like-minded America," un-catholic as it may be, has come to the Catholic Church and to its theologians is undeniable. Empirically, if not theologically, events have outrun my "here comes everybody" Catholicism.

A decade after Bishop's book, evangelical Catholics, rather than a leaven, appear more often to have grown into just another information silo in battles of the Catholic brands, each brand with its own news outlets and websites. The evangelical Catholic silo now often combines the least fortunate aspects of both Tridentine piety and American evangelical ethos. In theology's ebb and flow, the rationalistic lack of feeling for traditional devotion and its spaces that too often accompanied implementation of Vatican II must bear some blame for this. Faggioli's "liberal Catholic theologians" also often appear as just another tribe, one more information silo with confirmation biases of its own. The church's sheer largeness as Christ's mystical body in place, history, and culture keeps fading further from view. Only the rules and beliefs remain, their lifeless notional clarity frozen in seeming timelessness. Such constriction means a narrower Catholic Church, more "nones," and more ex-Catholics.

Bringing Pope Francis's Pastoral Revolution to Theology

A "field hospital" from which we go forth! This image captures *Evangelii Gaudium*'s vision for a pastorally renewed church.[28] A field hospital church is the antithesis of the siloed church in which we now live, a church where the ideal whole is more and more narrowly imagined and conceived theologically. How can theology reclaim its ecclesial role and contribute to Pope Francis's pastoral revolution?

Catholic theology has, over the past four decades, achieved academic legitimacy. Land O'Lakes, however, also envisioned an ecclesial role to go along with academic integrity. That half of the vision has not worked out so well. In 1967, Fr. Hesburgh and his colleagues could not have imagined that, within a generation or two, the thick immigrant Catholic subculture from which they came would be no more. We, their successors, no longer have a Catholic culture. In a voluntary religious culture, it is not enough to proceed as if Catholic theology were simply an academic discipline addressed primarily to an academy which is now anything but "the critical and reflective intelligence of the church" they hoped for.

In our new context, only the kind of nonjudgmental, accompanying, evangelical ethos Francis describes in *Evangelii Gaudium* can hope to navigate the tribal boundaries that mark out a church of Catholic silos. History challenges us to transpose Francis's evangelical ethos into academic theology, to fashion theology programs that somehow, without sacrificing the academic integrity Land O'Lakes dreamed of, bear witness to the faith in Jesus and his body the church that drew us to theology in the first place. Not confined to one silo or another, our theology must be full-bodied.

We do not readily know how to do this.[29] We need models, and Pope Francis gives us one. His pastoral revolution is based on reimagining the relations between the doctrinal and the pastoral in ways akin to St. Ignatius Loyola's *Spiritual Exercises* and analogous to Newman's distinction between the "notional" and the "real," or "theology" and "devotion."[30] Go first to the heart! Appeal to the imagination and affections, the mind will follow. Adorn systematics with biography and history.

With wisdom, prudence, and sheer political savvy, Pope Francis goes about his daily work, dealing with bureaucracies both inside and outside the church, without bitterness, trying to reflect the joy of the Gospel. He doesn't always get what he wants. From an evangelical point of view, the fact that he arouses opposition might be a hopeful sign. So did Jesus. If we do succeed in bringing Francis's pastoral revolution into theology, meeting the politicization of knowledge by teaching theologies that witness to the joy of the Gospel, we shall have fulfilled the trust bequeathed to us by Hesburgh and his generation, and we shall have good reason to hope that fifty years from now Catholic universities will still have robust academic theology.

Notes

The subtitle alludes to "In the Year 2525," a dystopian hit song released by Zager and Evans in 1968. The next year it topped the charts in both England and the United States.

[1]Michael Hollerich, "The Future of Academic Theology: An Exchange," *Commonweal*, May 18, 2018, 11. In addition to these two articles, see

also Massimo Faggioli's earlier piece "Showing Its Age? The Land O'Lakes Statement Could Use an Update," *Commonweal*, October 31, 2017, www.commonwealmagazine.org. I am grateful to Hollerich for an enjoyable discussion of these issues last June in St. Paul. My thanks as well to the two anonymous annual volume reviewers.

[2]"The Idea of the Catholic University," Statement on the Nature of the Contemporary Catholic University, paragraph 1, www.archives.nd.edu.

[3]Ibid, paragraph 4.

[4]Ibid, paragraph 5.

[5]Ibid, paragraph 1.

[6]Ibid, paragraph 5.

[7]Massimo Faggioli, "The Future of Academic Theology: An Exchange," *Commonweal*, May 18, 2018, 7.

[8]See Anne Hendershott, "Taking the Catholic Out of Catholic Universities," *City Journal*, Autumn 2017, www.city-journal.org.

[9]David Tracy, *The Analogical Imagination: Christian Theology and the Culture of Pluralism* (New York: Crossroad, 1981), chap. 1.

[10]Hollerich, "The Future of Academic Theology: An Exchange," 11.

[11]For a chilling look at the future of US higher education, in terms of corporatization and adjunctification, see Frank Donoghue, *The Last Professors: The Corporate University and the Fate of the Humanities* (New York: Fordham University Press, 2008). A decade ago, Donoghue wrote from a large state university describing conditions that have now overtaken tuition-driven Catholic institutions.

[12]See Amanda Porterfield, John Corrigan, and Darren E. Germ, eds., *The Business Turn in American Religious History* (New York: Oxford University Press, 2017); Ruth Perry and Yarden Katz, "Higher Ed, Inc.: How the University Became a Profit-Generating Cog in the Corporate Machine," *Chronicle of Higher Education*, October 7, 2018, www.chronicle.com.

[13]Bill Bishop with Robert G. Cushing, *The Big Sort: Why the Clustering of Like-Minded America Is Tearing Us Apart* (Boston/New York: Mariner Books, 2009).

[14]Jeffrey D. Warren, "Creating a 'Normal Catholic University': Franciscan University of Steubenville and the Catholic Charismatic Renewal, 1974–1992." MA thesis, University of Dayton, 2004.

[15]Hendershott, "Taking the Catholic Out of Catholic Universities."

[16]Based on information from Franciscan's 2016 *Fact Book*, 47–48, they have had 476 BA graduates in catechetics, 1,281 theology BA graduates, and 555 MA graduates in theology and Christian ministry. I am grateful to my colleague William Johnston for this information and for his extensive comments on an earlier draft.

[17]Jack Stripling, "Is Catholic U.'s Chaste Brand Scaring Off Students?" *Chronicle of Higher Education*, April 16, 2018, www.chronicle.com. See also Nick Anderson, "Catholic University Plans to Cut Full-Time Faculty by 9 Percent," *Washington Post*, April 30, 2018, www.washingtonpost.com.

[18]Nick Anderson, "Board Endorses Catholic U's Leaders," *Washington Post*, June 6, 2018, B4.

[19]September 17, 2010, www.firstthings.com. See also the Napa Institute website, www.napa-institute.org.

[20]On the Napa Institute, see Paula M. Kane, "St. Homobonus Leads the CEOs: Doing Good versus Doing (Really) Well," in *The Business Turn in American Religious History*, ed. Porterfield, Corrigan, and Germ, 209–13.

[21]The quotation from Abela appears in Jack Jenkins, "A Battle over 'Catholic Identity' at Catholic University of America," June 21, 2018, www. religionnews.com.

[22]Julia G. Young, "Saving the Catholic University of America" *Commonweal*, May 9, 2018, www.commonwealmagazine.org.

[23]The second quotation from Young is in Jenkins, "A Battle over 'Catholic Identity' at Catholic University of America." See also John Gehring, "Business Class: A High-Priced Conference at Catholic University," *Commonweal*, October 4, 2018, www.commonwealmagazine.org.

[24]On Legatus and FOCUS, see Kane, "St. Homobonus Leads the CEOs: Doing Good versus Doing (Really) Well," 202. See also the three-part series on FOCUS by Heidi Schlumpf, published at www.ncronline.org on March 20, 21, and 22, 2018. "FOCUS Campus Ministry Has Big Money, Conservative Connections" is the second article in the series.

[25]Michael J. O'Loughlin, "With an Eye toward Tradition, Young Adult Catholics Gather with FOCUS to Talk Evangelization," *America*, January 12, 2018. www.americamagazine.org.

[26]On the "Convocation of Catholic Leaders: The Joy of the Gospel in America," see www.usccb.org.

[27]William L. Portier, "Here Come the Evangelical Catholics," *Communio, International Catholic Review* 31, no. 1 (2004): 35–66; "Rising to the Evangelical Moment," *Current Issues in Catholic Higher Education* 26, no. 1 (Winter 2007): 49–58.

[28]For the text of *Evangelii Gaudium*, see w2.vatican.va.

[29]See Matthew Lewis Sutton and William L. Portier, eds., *Handing on the Faith*, The Annual Publication of the College Theology Society 59 (Maryknoll, NY: Orbis Books, 2013), especially the contributions by Sandra Yocum and Aurelie A. Hagstrom.

[30]For reflection on how Newman's distinctions might translate into contemporary theology classrooms, see William L. Portier, "Newman, Millennials, and Teaching Comparative Theology," in *Comparative Theology in the Millennial Classroom: Hybrid Identities, Negotiated Boundaries*, ed. Mara Brecht and Reid B. Locklin (New York: Routledge, 2016), 36–49.

Contributors

Susie Paulik Babka is an associate professor of theology and religious studies at the University of San Diego. She has published several articles exploring the relationship between visual art and theology, between popular culture and theology, and between Buddhism and Christianity. *Through the Dark Field: the Incarnation through an Aesthetics of Vulnerability*, was published by Liturgical Press in 2017; her newest work in progress is tentatively titled, *Imagining Resilience: Religion, Aesthetics and Encounter*, which will explore the religious role of art in community resilience.

B. Kevin Brown is an adjunct instructor of religious studies at Gonzaga University. He is currently developing a monograph that explores Sandra Schneiders's contribution to the development of a theology of the church's prophetic mission and builds on her work to propose a critical prophetic ecclesiology. His research focuses on ecclesiology, Christology, liberation and praxis-based theologies, and Christian spirituality and discipleship. He earned his PhD in systematic theology from Boston College in 2018.

William J. Collinge is a professor emeritus of theology and philosophy at Mount St. Mary's University, Emmitsburg, Maryland. He is the author of *Historical Dictionary of Catholicism* (Scarecrow, 2nd ed., 2012) and numerous articles, including two on Catholic Worker farming.

Stephanie C. Edwards is a doctoral candidate in theological ethics at Boston College. Her research interests include interdisciplinary trauma studies, feminist and womanist theology, race and whiteness, and liberation theologies. Her dissertation is in the area of Christian bioethics and titled "Pharmaceutical Memory Modification and Christianity's 'Dangerous' Memory." In addition, she is a practicing social worker and community advocate in Biddeford, Maine.

Willie James Jennings is an associate professor of systematic theology and Africana Studies at Yale University. He is the author of *The Christian Imagination: Theology and the Origins of Race* (Yale, 2010) and fifty-five peer-reviewed essays and review essays. His book *Acts: A Commentary, The Revolution of the Intimate* is forthcoming from Westminster/John Knox.

Erin Kidd is an assistant professor in the Department of Theology and Religious Studies at St. John's University (Queens, NY), where she teaches courses in systematic theology and gender studies. She is the co-editor of *Putting God on the Map: Theology and Conceptual Mapping* (Lexington Books/Fortress Academic, 2018) and is currently writing a book titled *Doing Theology from the Gut: Body, Method, and God* (forthcoming with Lexington Books/Fortress Academic).

Doris M. Kieser is an associate professor of theology at St. Joseph's College at the University of Alberta. She is the author of *Catholic Sexual Theology and Adolescent Girls: Embodied Flourishing* (Wilfrid Laurier University Press, 2015) and a former president of the Canadian Theological Society.

Oswald John Nira has been teaching at Our Lady of the Lake University in San Antonio, Texas, since 2001 and is currently head of the Theology and Spiritual Action program. He earned his graduate degrees at the Catholic University of America in Washington, DC, specializing in faith and culture. His dissertation focused on Mexican American lay leadership in the Diocese of Austin, Texas.

William L. Portier is Mary Ann Spearin Chair of Catholic Theology in the Religious Studies Department at the University of Dayton, where he also serves as PhD Program Director. His most recent book is *Every Catholic an Apostle: A Life of Thomas A. Judge, CM, 1868–1933* (Catholic University of America Press, 2017).

Christopher Pramuk is University Chair of Ignatian Thought and Imagination and Associate Professor of Theology at Regis University in Denver, CO. He is the author of dozens of articles and six books, including *Hope Sings, So Beautiful: Graced Encounters across the Color Line* and two award-winning studies of Thomas Merton. His latest book, *The Artist Alive: Explora-*

tions in Music, Art and Theology, will be published by Anselm Academic in May 2019.

Elena Procario-Foley is the Br. John G. Driscoll Professor of Jewish-Catholic Studies at Iona College. She is the co-editor of *Righting Relations after the Holocaust and Vatican II* (Paulist Press) and *Frontiers in Catholic Feminist Theology: Shoulder to Shoulder* (Fortress Press). Recent articles include "The Refugee Status: Political Ethics and Moral Politics," in *CrossCurrents* and "Fulfillment and Complementarity: Reflections on Relationship in 'Gifts and Calling,'" in *Studies in Christian-Jewish Relations.*

Daniel A. Rober is an assistant lecturer in Catholic Studies at Sacred Heart University. He holds a PhD in systematic theology from Fordham University. His first book, *Recognizing the Gift: Toward a Renewed Theology of Nature and Grace*, was published by Fortress Press in 2016.

Julie Hanlon Rubio is a professor of Christian Social Ethics at the Jesuit School of Theology of Santa Clara University. Prior to her current appointment, Rubio taught for nineteen years at Saint Louis University in the areas of Christian ethics and women's and gender studies. Her most recent book is *Reading, Praying, Living: Pope Francis's The Joy of Love* (Liturgical Press, 2017). She publishes frequently in journals such as *Theological Studies* and the *Journal of the Society of Christian Ethics* as well as in more popular periodicals such as *America, US Catholic,* and the *Washington Post.*

John Sniegocki is an associate professor of religious ethics and director of the Peace and Justice Studies minor at Xavier University in Cincinnati, Ohio. He is the author of *Catholic Social Teaching and Economic Globalization: The Quest for Alternatives* (Marquette University Press, 2009), as well as numerous journal articles and book chapters on Catholic social teaching, economic justice, food ethics, ecology, the Catholic Worker movement, and Buddhist-Christian dialogue.

Donna Teevan is an associate professor and chair of the Theology and Religious Studies Department at Seattle University. She is the author of *Lonergan, Hermeneutics, and Theological Method* (Marquette University Press, 2005). Her articles have appeared in *Theological Studies, Zygon, Catholic Education: A Journal* *of Inquiry and Practice*, and *Teaching Theology and Religion* as well as in *Theology and the New Histories* (College Theology Society Annual 44, 1998).

Tracy Sayuki Tiemeier is an associate professor of theological studies at Loyola Marymount University in Los Angeles, CA. She is the author of numerous articles and essays in Hindu-Christian studies, Asian and Asian American theology, comparative theology, feminist theology, and interreligious dialogue. She is co-editor of *Interreligious Friendship after* Nostra Aetate (Palgrave Macmillan, 2015). She is also the Catholic co-chair of the Los Angeles Hindu-Catholic Dialogue.

David von Schlichten is an associate professor of religious studies at Seton Hill University in Greensburg, PA, where he is also the coordinator of the Gender and Women's Studies Program.

Sandra Yocum is University Professor of Faith and Culture and associate professor of religious studies at the University of Dayton. She has served as president of both the College Theology Society and the Association of Graduate Programs in Ministry. In addition to publishing in venues such as *Theological Studies*, *Horizons*, *Church History*, and *U.S. Catholic Historian*, she is the author of *Joining the Revolution in Theology: The College Theology Society 1954-2004* (Sheed and Ward, 2007) and co-editor of *American Catholic Traditions: Resources for Renewal*, College Theology Society 42, 1996.

Glenn Young is an associate professor of theology and religious studies at Rockhurst University in Kansas City, MO. His research focuses on Christian mysticism and comparative religion. His recent publications include "Meister Eckhart and Fred Craddock: Preaching as Mystical Practice," in *Homiletic*, and "Practice and the Comparative Study of Mysticism: The *Yoga Sūtra* and *The Cloud of Unknowing*," in *Journal of Hindu-Christian Studies*.